A VARIETY OF
CATHOLIC MODERNISTS

*The Sarum Lectures in the University of Oxford
for the year 1968–1969*

To
Malcolm and Kitty Muggeridge

A VARIETY OF CATHOLIC MODERNISTS

BY

ALEC R. VIDLER

Not chaos-like together crushed and bruised,
But, as the world, harmoniously confused:
Where order in variety we see,
And where, though all things differ, all agree.
Alexander Pope, *Windsor Forest*

CAMBRIDGE
AT THE UNIVERSITY PRESS
1970

Published by the Syndics of the Cambridge University Press
Bentley House, 200 Euston Road, London N.W.1
American Branch: 32 East 57th Street, New York, N.Y. 10022

© Cambridge University Press 1970

Library of Congress Catalogue Card Number: 70-93712
Standard Book Number: 521 07649 8

Printed in Great Britain by
Alden & Mowbray Ltd
at the Alden Press, Oxford

ACKNOWLEDGMENTS

I wish to thank the electors to the Sarum Lectureship for inviting me to give these lectures. While as published they contain more than was actually spoken, I have not tried to remove all traces of the lecture form.

I also wish to thank all who have given me access to, and have allowed me to use, unpublished sources.

I am grateful for various kinds of help to Dr Nigel Abercrombie, Mr A. W. Campbell, Mr Nigel Hancock, Miss Barbara Lilley, The Rev. Dom Mark Pontifex, o.s.b., M. Emile Poulat and M. Raymond de Boyer de Sainte Suzanne.

A.R.V.

ABBREVIATIONS

(For full titles, etc., see bibliography, p. 221 below.)

Bedoyere	M. de la Bedoyere, *The Life of Baron von Hügel*
BLE	*Bulletin de littérature ecclésiastique*
BM	British Museum
BN	Bibliothèque Nationale
BP	Papers of Edmund Bishop
Caron	Jeanne Caron, *Le Sillon*
Corr. phil.	Blondel–Laberthonnière, *Correspondance philosophique*
Entretiens	Dagens and Nédoncelle, *Entretiens sur Henri Bremond*
Frémont	A. Siegfried, *L'Abbé Frémont*
Heaney	J. T. Heaney, *The Modernist Crisis: von Hügel*
LP	Papers of A. L. Lilley
Mém.	A. Loisy, *Mémoires*
MMRC	A. R. Vidler, *The Modernist Movement in the Roman Church*
n.a.f.	nouvelles acquisitions françaises
Rivière	J. Rivière, *Le modernisme dans l'Eglise*
Selected Letters	F. von Hügel, *Selected Letters*
Tyrrell et Bremond	A. Loisy, *George Tyrrell et Henri Bremond*
VHSA	Papers of F. von Hügel at St Andrews
Vie de Loisy	A. Houtin and F. Sartiaux, *Alfred Loisy: sa vie, son œuvre*
YP	Papers of G. W. Young

AUTOBIOGRAPHICAL INTRODUCTION

My excuse for this egotistic introduction is that I could think of no better way of explaining the reasons for my choice of subject; my qualifications, such as they are, for handling it; the limits within which I propose to do so; and the sources of information that have been at my disposal.

I should state at the outset that, while the term must be allowed to have many other meanings, by 'modernists' I shall mean those who were in one way or another implicated in the movement in the Roman Catholic Church that is called by that name—the movement which originated about 1890, was condemned by Pope Pius X in 1907, and was snuffed out to all intents and purposes in 1910.

My interest in the modernists dates from my undergraduate days. As a schoolboy during the first world war I had come to embrace the anglo-catholic creed and cultus. When after the war I went up to Cambridge and embarked on the study of theology, the question soon struck me how I was to combine my enthusiasm for anglo-catholicism with that historical criticism of the Bible and of Christian origins which very soon I was embracing with an equal enthusiasm. That being so, I pricked up my ears when my tutor—S. C. Carpenter[1]—talked about Alfred Loisy and George Tyrrell. Carpenter had been one of the group of young Cambridge divines who in November 1907 had sent a letter of gratitude and sympathy to Father Tyrrell.[2]

The fact that the modernists were reputed to be extreme or radical in their critical views and theological reconstructions, so far from repelling, was calculated to attract me, since I do not think that I was for long inclined to rest in the position of Charles

---

[1] (1877–1959) Fellow and Tutor of Selwyn College, Cambridge; afterwards Master of the Temple and Dean of Exeter; author of *A Large Room: a plea for a more inclusive Christianity* (1923), etc.

[2] See M. D. Petre, *Autobiography and Life of George Tyrrell* (1912), ii, 371.

Gore (1853–1932) and the anglo-catholic establishment, with which at first I had been more or less satisfied. I find, for instance, that in April 1922, after reading a book by N. P. Williams,[1] I commented in my journal: 'His critical views are curiously conservative.' The writings of A. E. J. Rawlinson[2] and W. L. Knox[3] appealed to me much more, since they appeared to be pointing in a direction that was concordant with what had been the aims of the modernists in the Roman Church.

Anyhow, during the 1920s I began to collect the works of Loisy and Tyrrell. In those days I used to keep a record of all the books I read, and I see that from 1926 onwards I was steadily reading books by the modernists—not only Loisy and Tyrrell, but Miss Petre, von Hügel, Houtin, and Buonaiuti. I remember that when Prebendary J. F. Briscoe,[4] a leading anglo-catholic, stayed with me in Birmingham about 1930, how surprised and pleased I was to discover that he shared my zest for Loisy's *Evangiles synoptiques*. He was attending a meeting of the Council of the Federation of Catholic Priests, a body that I supposed to be as antipathetic to modernists as to protestants.

Thus when I returned to Cambridge in October 1931 and could look forward to having more time for study and research, I was already considering the possibility of writing a book about the modernists. In fact, during my summer holiday in September 1931 I paid my first visit to M. Loisy. As I shall have a good deal to say about him in these lectures, I will give a fairly detailed account of this occasion, which will serve to introduce him. I had written the following letter to him beforehand (on 6 August 1931):

I am a young Anglican priest (aged 31). Ever since I began the study of theology at Cambridge, your name has been for me an honoured one. I have read several of your books and have been much influenced by them. I have also studied the history of Catholic modernism. It seems to me that in England—at least among the members of the younger generation who should be interested in such matters—that

---

[1] (1883–1943) The book in question was *The First Easter Morning* (1920).
[2] (1884–1960) Author of *Dogma, Fact and Experience* (1915), etc.
[3] (1886–1950) Author of *The Catholic Movement in the Church of England* (1923), etc.
[4] (1878–1939) Rector of Bagborough, Somerset.

history is little known and its significance still less appreciated. At the same time—and perhaps in consequence of this—very poor justice is done to yourself by English students of religion. You are known to them chiefly from references in the writings of Inge and von Hügel, and in neither case is the resulting impression of your work and thought likely to be entirely fair or favourable.

I have just finished reading your *Mémoires*, and from beginning to end I have found them of absorbing interest. I have also seen Miss Petre's review in the *Hibbert Journal*. I feel there is more to be said than she says; and perhaps an Anglican is more able in *some* respects to appreciate your position than a Roman Catholic. For what in my judgment differentiates Anglicanism from Roman Catholicism is the former's rejection of that papal absolutism which was the rock on which modernism inevitably foundered. It seems to me (but perhaps the wish is father to the thought) that the Anglican Church, because of its width and comprehensiveness, may be of some special importance in the evolution of that religion of the future which is so much needed in the world.

What is now called 'Anglican Modernism' does not promise much in this direction, for it is hardly distinguishable from Liberal protestantism, and it is often more protestant than liberal. English criticism of the New Testament remains for the most part incurably conservative, and this again creates a prejudice against yourself.

I am at present engaged in parochial ministry, but shall shortly be returning to Cambridge when I hope to do some research and writing. Among other things I hope further to study the history of Catholic modernism and to suggest the significance it may have for Anglicans, and also to try to give a just account of your own life and work for English readers. This sounds ambitious, and perhaps impertinent, and I do not know whether it will ever be realized...

All the foregoing remarks will, I think, tell you how great an honour and privilege I should regard it to meet and converse with you, if only for a short time. And I am writing to you now because I hope to be in France on holiday from Septr 5th to 15th, and I wonder if you would be so kind as to allow me to call on you at Ceffonds on any day during that period.

On 9 August M. Loisy replied to me as follows:[1]

---

[1] Quotations from French I shall normally translate when they come in the text, and leave untranslated in footnotes.

I have been much interested and indeed touched by your letter which tells me nothing I did not know about my extremely restricted influence in England but which also shows me that I can find very real sympathizers in your country. If I had been able to visit England in the past, I fancy I should have more friends there now. Today, age as well as infirmity prevents me from travelling. My great annual journey is that from Ceffonds to Paris in October, and from Paris to Ceffonds in April.

If you persevere in your intention of coming to see me in September, I shall be happy to converse with you...

And he proceeded to tell me how to get to Ceffonds (which is in the department of Haute-Marne).

Needless to say, I did persevere in my intention, and called on M. Loisy on 9 September. Immediately afterwards I made a memorandum of what transpired which I will reproduce since it forwards the purpose of this introduction:

at 2 p.m. I called on M. Loisy. His house is at Ceffonds—only a few minutes from the station at Montier-en-Der (the two places adjoin). He had walked towards the station to meet me (supposing I was just arriving by train, but I had in fact arrived the day before) and was in his garden when I arrived. He greeted me very kindly, and took me to a room indoors where we sat and conversed for over two hours. He is short of stature: and though not robust, he looks well-preserved and in good health for his years. He wears a beard—grown white—and neatly trimmed; the top of his head is bald. His eyes are clear blue and sparkling; his manner is charming and his laugh infectious.

He allowed me freely to ask him questions, and he talked at length when given a cue. I listened, understanding most but not all of what he said. What he said was (as he put it) *'tout à fait entre nous'.*

I told him I hoped to study further the history of modernism and suggested the possibility that what failed in the Church of Rome might succeed in the Church of England. He explained how the Church of Rome was becoming more and more strictly papal—this is illustrated by the latest revision of the Canon Law—so that the bishops and clergy had no real independence left. The method of training etc. prevented the intrusion of new elements. He agreed that the Anglican modernists (so-called) are no more than liberal protestant.

He spoke much about the criticism of the N. T. and his own

conclusions—the summary of which is 'the more you know the less you know'. Before Irenaeus we have not history but pre-history, sacred legend. Still the origin of Christianity was a momentous event, and Christianity will continue in some form or other. He agreed that religion must have a cultus. The alienation of the people from the Church in 'Catholic' countries is a very serious thing from the point of view of morality; but the Church itself is chiefly responsible. Anti-clericalism is the result of clericalism. While he would say nothing definite, he seemed to favour the idea that a truly modernist movement might succeed in the Church of England.

He told me the detailed history of *l'affaire Turmel*.[1]

His comment on Bethune-Baker's review of his *Mémoires*[2] was that he knew Duchesne and Batiffol a great deal better than Bethune-Baker did![3] He had in fact defended Duchesne against the imputation that he was a pure sceptic and Batiffol against the imputation that he was a delator of the modernists.

Loisy said that if he had been able to travel with '*la bonne parole*' the modernist affair might have had a much greater success.

I asked him whether a life of Mgr Mignot had been or would be published.[4] He answered that although an abbé had his papers and was charged with the writing of it, it would never be allowed to appear. In his time Mgr Mignot was a bishop of unique quality in the episcopate; there is no possibility of such a bishop being appointed now.

Rivière's book on modernism[5] is an attempt to glorify the school of Batiffol, whose pupil Rivière was; it alters the whole perspective of the truth. Rivière is far less intelligent than Batiffol. Lagrange[6] is not primarily a theologian: he was a lawyer before ordination and that remains.

M. Loisy said I might certainly visit him again.

This will be his last course of lectures at the Collège de France, as he will have reached the retiring age. He is uncertain as yet whether he will settle permanently at Ceffonds or in Paris; the one suits his health in summer, the other in winter.

---

[1] See pp. 56–62 below.   [2] See *Journal of Theological Studies*, July 1931, p. 443.
[3] Louis Duchesne (1843–1922), the ecclesiastical historian. Pierre Batiffol (1861–1929): see J. Rivière, *Monseigneur Batiffol* (1929).
[4] *Monseigneur Mignot* by Louis de Lacger, which is only a brief memoir, was not published till 1933.
[5] J. Rivière, *Le modernisme dans l'Eglise* (1929).
[6] M. J. Lagrange (1855–1938), the biblical scholar: see *Le Père Lagrange au service de la Bible: souvenirs personnels* (1967).

I remarked that the people in the hotel still speak of him as M. l'abbé—and he said not only so, but some of them still call him M. le Curé, as 50 years ago he was curé of a village about 20 kilometres away! I called his attention to the book *The Riddle of the New Testament*[1] which was causing a considerable *éclat* in England. He asked if Bishop Gore was still alive; Gore visited him at Neuilly years ago. Loisy remembered that Gore was Bishop of Birmingham and Oxford and was connected with the revival of religious communities in the Church of England. Loisy had never heard of Dr Barnes![2]

Houtin's history of modernism[3] is a correct chronicle of the facts (not more than that)—though even that with certain exceptions, e.g. the idea of a meeting at which the plot was hatched is an illusion; the supposed meeting was no more than a '*bon déjeuner*'!

Loisy said that the story of Turmel (who has written under 14 pseudonyms including Delafosse and Louis Coulange) is very sad. Turmel still says mass *chez lui*, although degraded by the Church. He is mentally abnormal.

Buonaiuti is very changeable. Loisy thinks that, although ex-communicated at present, he is probably negotiating with the Vatican again—and also with Mussolini, whose ambitions are similar to those of the pope!

M. Loisy's house—by an odd coincidence—is practically opposite the house in which (according to a tablet affixed to the wall) Jacques d'Arc, Jeanne's father, was born...

When, shortly after this visit, I did return to Cambridge it was with a firmer intention of doing something about the modernists. I was not however in the least expecting an announcement which appeared in May 1932 that the subject for the Norrisian Prize Essay at Cambridge in 1933 was 'The origins and outcome of the modernist movement condemned by the encyclical *Pascendi gregis*.' This naturally clinched the matter. Only later did I surmise (what I believe to have been the case) that the setting of this subject was due to the then Vice-Chancellor, Mr Will Spens (1882–1962), who had always been keenly interested in the modernists and had also been one of the signatories of the letter

---

[1] E. C. Hoskyns and N. Davey, *The Riddle of the New Testament* (1931).
[2] E. W. Barnes (1874–1953), Bishop of Birmingham, at that time a prominent and controversial figure in the Church of England.
[3] A. Houtin, *Histoire du modernisme catholique* (1913).

from Cambridge to Father Tyrrell which I have already mentioned.

Accordingly I got to work and produced an essay in time which to my great satisfaction was awarded the prize and which, owing to the good offices of one of the examiners, Professor J. M. Creed, was published as it stood by the Cambridge University Press.[1] The book had a mixed reception. Roman Catholic reviewers were disposed to regret that the first history of the modernist movement to appear in English was so sympathetic to the modernists and so unappreciative of the acts of Pius X.[2] The *Catholic Times* opened its review with this sentence: 'About thirty years ago there ended a movement within the Church which would never have started had the chief participators not succumbed to the temptation of intellectual pride'; and ended succinctly thus: 'The encyclical "Pascendi" brought the Modernist Movement to an end. It is dead, let it lie buried. This attempt at exhumation, even on a plea of history, is not worth the attention of Catholics.'[3] Other reviewers, to whose opinion I attached importance, notably A. L. Lilley,[4] were more favourable. M. Loisy wrote approvingly about it to our mutual friend, John Collins, and said that in the chapters concerning himself he had noticed only one trivial inexactitude.

I was particularly gratified by a review by Dr Joseph Needham, the present Master of Gonville and Caius College, Cambridge, who said that my book's 'real lack of bias' became 'all the more strikingly exhibited the more carefully' it was read, and that it would 'be extremely difficult to discover the theological allegiance and the prejudices of the author, if they were not already known'.[5] I was also told on good authority that the examiners of my Norrisian essay, who, until they decided on their award, had only a motto to signify who the author was, had been uncertain whether, when his identity was revealed, he would turn out to be a Roman Catholic, an Anglican or an infidel.

---

[1] *The Modernist Movement in the Roman Church: its origin and outcome* (1934).
[2] See *Catholic Book Notes*, December 1934. Cf. *The Tablet*, 24 November 1934.
[3] *Catholic Times*, 19 October 1934.
[4] See *Theology*, November 1934, pp. 306–10.
[5] *Cambridge Review*, 8 March 1935.

Ever since that time I have gone on collecting literature about the modernist movement, and I had in mind that I might one day have more to say about it. Moreover, various occurrences and developments that I am now going to say something about in chronological order made it increasingly likely that I should return to the subject if an opportunity offered.

First, when I was conducting a university mission in St Mary's Church, Oxford, during the Hilary term 1938, a man came up to me one day—in the church, if I remember rightly—and said he believed that I was interested in the modernist movement. He proceeded to ask me whether I would care to have a lot of the modernists' letters and also a collection of some rare modernist pamphlets and other papers which he possessed. Naturally, I accepted his offer with warm gratitude, and I told him that, though I had no immediate prospect of doing further work on the modernists, I hoped to do so eventually.

This surprising and benevolent donor was the son of a Mr G. W. Young. I have often reproached myself that I did not at the time find out all I could about him. I should be glad to hear from anyone who remembers him or who can tell me how I can get into touch with his descendants. He was, as I have since learned, a member of the Queen's College, who matriculated in 1883 and died in 1932. He lived at 30 Holywell Street where his son was also living in 1938.

From the letters that he gave me it is evident that he held some appointment in the university but I do not know what. Though not a Roman Catholic he had been in close rapport with the modernists and had taken an ardent interest in their fortunes and misfortunes. Baron von Hügel, who in 1904 had advised Young to 'wait and make no effect to be received',[1] in 1909 described Young as 'an outsider moving in the right direction'.[2] Young had

---

[1] Von Hügel to Young, 3–4 June 1904: YP 'The very Priests who would be most ready to minimize or liberalise with and for you, whilst you were outside and to get you in, would be probably the very ones who, once you were inside, would, in all conscientiousness, worry and work at you, in the other direction... But you can show yourself, on occasion, to certain of our officials: it is good for them to know that such men as you exist.'
[2] Von Hügel to Lilley, 18 April 1909: LP.

acted as the unofficial representative or liaison officer in Oxford of the modernists. Von Hügel, who, as I shall later have occasion to observe, was the principal organizer of the movement, kept Young well-informed about what was going on behind the scenes. He also got him to make arrangements for continental modernists when they were visiting Oxford. For example, in June 1904 he wrote to Young—in characteristic style:

I heard some 4 days ago from Mgr Mignot, Archbishop of Albi, Abbé Loisy's courageous and most cultured supporter, that he will come and stay with us, in this our house, *from July 15th or 16th to the 23rd, possibly 26th*. Now *you* will be one of people [*sic*] I shall want him to see. But I am also anxious, if at all possible, to secure, say, 2 or 3 Oxford scholars to be in Oxford during a couple of those days...who wd be able and willing to help me show him the University. He is a thorough and keen Biblical scholar, and has read all the best English work of that kind; but he does not speak English, and understands it most imperfectly when spoken.[1]

Young also acted as a kind of agent for the dissemination in Oxford of modernist publications. For instance, von Hügel, when writing to A. L. Lilley in 1905 about securing subscribers for the new modernist periodical *Demain*, said: 'That little brick of a Young has gone and got 15 first-rate ones at Oxford: Caird, Cheyne, Bigg, Sanday, Strong, Rashdall, Allen, etc.—really an impressive list.'[2] During these lectures I shall make further use of the letters that Young's son gave me.

In the Easter vacation that followed the university mission at Oxford I had already arranged to pay a second visit to M. Loisy at Ceffonds, this time in company with John Collins who knew him better than I did and had previously visited him more than once. In his autobiography Collins explains how he conceives himself to have been influenced by Loisy.[3] My recollection is that we called on him on two successive afternoons and had long conversations with him. I am fairly confident that I made my own

---

[1] Von Hügel to Young, 21 June 1904: YP.
[2] Von Hügel to Lilley, 27 January 1905: LP.
[3] See L. J. Collins, *Faith under Fire* (1966), pp. 51–7.

record of these conversations, but if so it has disappeared or been mislaid, to my acute vexation. One point I remember perfectly clearly and vividly. I had asked M. Loisy to comment on the allegations that were constantly made by von Hügel that he did not believe in the transcendent or that he was a pure immanentist. M. Loisy raised his arms and declared, with great deliberation and solemnity, that of course he believed in 'le Grand Mystère'. This was for me a numinous moment which conveyed to me a sense of the ineffability of the Divine as few other moments have. It should be noted that this was in 1938, that is, in the last period of his life when Loisy affirmed the theistic and even Christian character of his faith in a way that he had not done during his middle period when von Hügel had been so worried about him.[1]

Collins and I realized that Loisy, who was now over 81 and had never been robust, was not likely to live much longer, and we made a pact that we would go together to his funeral whenever it should take place. However, this proved to be impossible, for he died on 1 June 1940 at the time of the fall of France.

I have a letter about Loisy's last days from which I will quote a passage at this point. It was written to Miss Maude Petre on 19 June 1940 by Madame Bounot who had been nursing him:

Forgive me for not sending you sooner than this details about the last moments of our dear M. Loisy whom we miss so much. We were kept so busy caring for him; night and day we looked after him for six weeks. You will believe that we were very tired. At last he went without too much suffering, as tranquil as he always was.[2] He was unconscious during the last two days, but some days before he had given us all his instructions and had made us promise not to leave him till his last breath. His death was very distressing for us, since for seven years we had been greatly attached to him. In the end we sadly took him back to Ambrières [his birthplace] with Mlle Royer, his niece.

[1] See Loisy, *Un mythe apologétique* (1939), *passim*; R. de Boyer de Sainte Suzanne, *Alfred Loisy* (1968), pp. 145–9; Houtin and Sartiaux, *Vie de Loisy* (1960), pp. 252 f.

[2] J. Bonsirven, in his article on Loisy in *Supplément au Dictionnaire de la Bible* (1957), V. 543, writes: 'On assure que peu avant sa fin (1er juin 1940) il disait: "Je meurs en paix avec Dieu" ', but he cites no authority for this statement.

The letter went on to tell how the writer and her family had shortly afterwards to leave their home and were now refugees.

The next event I will mention is a visit that I paid to Miss Petre on 5 November 1941, a little over a year before her death. I had corresponded with her before, but had never met her. I do not seem to have made any written record of our conversation, but three things stick in my memory. First, she repeated what she had said to me in a letter some years previously, that modernism was still at work in the Church though not under that name, and she now instanced the writings of Père Teilhard de Chardin.[1] Secondly, I remember saying in comment on something she said about her own beliefs: 'But that surely is pantheism'; and she answered: 'Yes, I think it may be, but I do not regard that as a decisive objection', or words to that effect.[2] Thirdly, Miss Petre told me that she had some years before attended a conference at Pontigny at which Loisy also was present. He could not go into the Abbey church for the solemn mass on Sunday since he was *vitandus*, but he was discovered outside with tears in his eyes.[3]

But I can give more information about this conversation because I now have a letter about it that Miss Petre wrote to A. L. Lilley on the same day:

I must tell you [she wrote] of an interesting talk I had this morning with Fr Vidler. He came *a-propos* of my Loisy study[4] which he introduced, through Mr [Ashley] Sampson, to Centenary Press, which has not accepted.

Now his criticism, as regards the practical finding of a publisher, is 1. Loisy is not known, and where known is not liked, in England. 2. He says that there should be an attempt to bring it into relation (or I suppose into contradiction) with the late school of English theology. Now this interested me, but I do not know how far he is right in

---

[1] Cf. M. D. Petre, *Alfred Loisy* (1944), pp. 97, 106 f.
[2] Cf. M. D. Petre, *My Way of Faith*, pp. 196 f.
[3] This incident is also mentioned by Miss Petre, *Loisy*, p. 56. On 4 November 1917 Loisy wrote to R. de Boyer de Sainte Suzanne (see his *Alfred Loisy*, p. 184): 'S'il n'était pas interdit de célébrer en ma présence aucune cérémonie catholique, il y a de ces cérémonies auxquelles j'assisterais volontiers, et en spectateur édifié.'
[4] I.e. the book *Alfred Loisy: his religious significance*, which was eventually published in 1944 by the Cambridge University Press.

such a criticism, and whether there is any sound reason to attempt this connection. He says 'orthodoxy' has taken on a new meaning—but surely the old one remains. The whole question bristles with problems —chief of which is 'will this new orthodoxy survive?' Of course I felt how far apart we were—how much further I have gone into the wilderness in my search for the promised land, and, of course, Loisy too...

Vidler had a real friendship with Loisy—he visited him with Collins, which I did not know. And what is curious is that it is precisely, almost if not quite, exclusively the critical work for which he values him.

It is to me a great problem this hearty acceptance of critical results with no corresponding effect on faith. I think faith can survive, but at the cost of a tragic farewell to much use and wont.

Now my work sought to show what Loisy had found after the tragic separation—and it seems to me that what he found was something that has got to be found by all, though the finding is by no means final —certainly not his. I am giving you a very inadequate account of our talk, and of my reaction to it—but I think it may help me to do some work on my book...[1]

Perhaps I should remark that in 1941 my flirtation with, or seduction by, what was called 'neo-orthodoxy' was probably at its height.

From 1941 till well into the 1950s I was fully occupied with work on Gladstone, F. D. Maurice and Lamennais, and the modernists had to be kept in the background of my mind. But in the later 1950s two or three things happened that strengthened my resolve to take up the subject again, though my employments in Cambridge did not leave me time for what I wanted to do.

In April 1957 Mrs J. M. Creed, the daughter of A. L. Lilley, kindly gave me her father's numerous letters from Tyrrell, von Hügel, Miss Petre and others on the understanding that I would in due course make use of them, before depositing them in a library. This was an important accession to my sources of information, and after Mrs Creed's death her son was good enough to

---

[1] She introduced some references to *On to Orthodoxy* by D. R. Davies, which doubtless I had mentioned to her.

Autobiographical Introduction

hand over to me further personal papers and letters, etc., of Archdeacon Lilley's.

Then in 1958 I had the great advantage of becoming acquainted with M. Emile Poulat. We have corresponded and interchanged visits ever since and have become close friends. M. Poulat is an inexhaustible mine of information, especially about the French modernists, as is shown of course by what he has published.[1]

Finally, as Roger Aubert observed (writing in 1966), 'recently ...there has been a sudden and general revival of interest in the subject [the modernist movement], and a point which is of special importance to the historian is that documents long unavailable are now beginning to make their appearance'.[2] The modernists, I may say, were indefatigable letter writers and also—with the exception of Father Tyrrell—preservers of letters. While much of their correspondence has now been published, there is still much more that is unpublished. Their correspondence is of great importance to students of the subject since, for obvious reasons, they expressed themselves much more freely in their private letters than they could do in their published writings.

Undoubtedly the revival of interest in the modernists has been stimulated and heightened by the developments in the Roman Catholic Church since John XXIII became pope. It is not however my intention to institute a comparison between what so-called progressive, radical or avant-garde Roman Catholic theologians have been saying in recent years and what the modernists said during the first decade of the century. *Prima facie* there is plenty of scope for such a comparison, but in my view it is too soon for the question to be dealt with historically. Nevertheless, I would say that one reason why further work on the modernists may serve a good purpose is that it may prevent sweeping, over-confident or premature statements from being made about resemblances or differences between what happened then and what is happening now.

[1] *Histoire, dogme et critique dans la crise moderniste* (1962); *Alfred Loisy, sa vie, son œuvre* by A. Houtin and F. Sartiaux, ed. by E. Poulat (1960).
[2] See *Concilium*, September 1966, p. 47.

13

What I have said so far will explain why I had decided that, after my retirement in September 1967, I would take up this subject again. I could not have foreseen that earlier in that year I should receive the honour of being invited to deliver the Sarum Lectures nor that the electors would approve my choosing the modernist movement as my subject and so give me the beneficent incentive to industry that I required and a time limit for the accomplishment of my task.

As regards the question of publication, for some time I was not sure whether the outcome would be a much expanded new edition of my earlier book or a sequel to that. In the event I found that I had so much fresh matter that the outcome would be an altogether new book with hardly any repetition of what I had previously published.

I never intended to use the same title as before, namely *The Modernist Movement in the Roman Church: its origins and outcome*. That title, which I used because of the Norrisian essay subject, is now unsuitable on more than one account. I am concerned with the movement itself, or with those who took part in it, rather than with its origins or outcome. Then, I am not trying to produce such a definitive or comprehensive history of the movement as my previous title might suggest. A definitive history will not be possible until the Vatican Archives are accessible, and the preparation of a comprehensive history would not only take a very long time but would require the use of sources that are located in many different places and some of them in languages which it would be painful for me to have to read.

One of the reasons, moreover, why I looked forward to retirement was that I should be able to remain fairly stationary in one of the most agreeable spots in England and make as sure as possible that I shall die in the house in which I was born. But I can also plead as an excuse for not having been exceedingly peripatetic the consideration that I have over the years collected a large amount of the literature of the modernist movement, certainly as much as I can satisfactorily digest, and that this together with the unpublished letters in my possession and some other readily accessible archives in Britain and France have provided me with more than enough material for what I want to do. I have in fact had much more source-material at my disposal than I anticipated, for when I went to work in the Bibliothèque Nationale I made the exciting discovery that many volumes of M. Loisy's private papers, which were not to have been opened for inspection till 1971, had been opened three years earlier.

There are at least two distinct and legitimate ways of studying the modernist movement. One is to start from the papal acts which defined and condemned modernism, especially the encyclical *Pascendi*. In that case the system of ideas which the pope called 'modernism' would have to be expounded and examined, and the pedigree and profession of those ideas would, so far as possible, have to be observed. This would be a schematic study in the history of Christian doctrine or heresy. The other way is, without presuppositions concerning orthodoxy or heresy, to look at the various persons or some of them who were involved in the movement that provoked the papacy to define and condemn the system which it called 'modernism', with a view to ascertaining what they conceived themselves to be doing, whether individually or collectively. While I acknowledge the legitimacy of the former way of studying the modernist movement, my own decided preference is for the latter, and for more than one reason.

First, what has always engaged my interest is not modernism, but modernists, not the alleged 'synthesis of all heresies'[1] but the persons who were presumed to be responsible for all the trouble.

Secondly, modernism as described by the pope was regarded by nearly all the modernists as a misleading misrepresentation of what they had been about. That is to say, it gave the impression that they were a coordinated group of people with a coherent body of ideas whereas, apart from a few manifestations of group-modernism chiefly in Italy,[2] they were in fact a highly diversified collection of individuals with inchoate and inconsistent ideas. What, according to their own testimony, they had in common was

---

[1] See the English translation of *Pascendi* in P. Sabatier, *Modernism* (1908), p. 309.
[2] See Pietro Scoppola, *Crisi modernista e rinnovamento cattolico in Italia* (1961), ch. 4–6.

not the system defined in the *Pascendi* or any system of the sort, but a desire in one way or another to promote the adaptation of Catholicism, of the Church and its teaching, to new conditions. That this was so would now be generally granted, even by those who accept the authority of the *Pascendi* and admire it. As M. Poulat has said:

What is modernism? Certainly there is the theological definition of it given by the encyclical *Pascendi*, but all historians today agree in recognizing that, whatever its value and interest may be, it cannot be for them either an iron collar or even, on the level on which they work, a sufficient norm: at most it is an element of the problem that has to be elucidated.[1]

Those who wish to do so may still claim that, even if no body of people or no individual in the Church actually or consciously subscribed to the system condemned in the *Pascendi*, yet the encyclical was an extremely skilful articulation of the logical implications and outcome of ideas that were being canvassed and disseminated in the Church at the time, of ideas that were in the air though not necessarily crystallized in any single person's consciousness. This justification of the *Pascendi* is quite consistent with an admission that much of the official reaction in the Church to modernism was regrettable and even panic-stricken.

Since the manner in which the encyclical was composed has some bearing on this matter, and since information that is now available about the genesis of the *Pascendi* has not, so far as I know, been hitherto publicized in English, I will say something about it. M. Jean Rivière, before his death in 1946, was able to make some interesting revelations, of which he had not been aware when he wrote his book *Le modernisme dans l'Eglise*, concerning the manner in which, and by whom, the encyclical was composed.

There had naturally from the outset been conjectures by journalists and others about who had actually drafted the encyclical, for no one supposed that Pius X had written it him-

---

[1] See *Entretiens sur Henri Bremond* (1967), ed. Dagens and Nédoncelle, p. 70. Cf. *ibid.* p. 90; and C. Guignebert in *Revue historique* (1933), pp. 103 f.

self. While several names were canvassed, the most favoured was that of the Jesuit theologian, Louis Billot (1846–1931).[1] Of course the whole truth will not be known until the Vatican Archives are opened, but it can now be said with confidence that the principal author of the encyclical, i.e. of the doctrinal part, was Father Joseph Lemius (1860–1923), an Oblate of Mary Immaculate, an able theologian who held various posts in the Curia at Rome.

I cannot mention all the evidences that have come to light and that justify this conclusion. One of the most striking is a letter written to M. Rivière in 1939 by a priest (Abbé Castagnet) who had been a student at the Gregorian University from 1904 to 1906. I will translate his letter to Rivière which, as you will see, bears on the character, as well as the authorship, of the *Pascendi*:

When the encyclical *Pascendi* appeared, I was quite sure that the Rev. Fr Joseph Lemius had collaborated in drafting it. For this reason:

In 1906, while I was working for my doctorate at Rome, I submitted to Fr Lemius some difficulties to do with M. Loisy and his associates. Fr Billot, who was then a professor at the Gregorian University, had given me a cold reception when, with the utmost simplicity, I had submitted the same difficulties to him, and his replies had been as much lacking in clarity as in serenity. Fr Lemius was much amused when I told him of my misadventure.

Then he said to me that, in order to reply successfully to MM. Loisy, Laberthonnière and all the rest, we should be careful not to follow them into the area of particular difficulties, since as soon as one was resolved it was easy to put up another. The thing to do, he said, was to attack their doctrinal system and overthrow it. He added that for years he had devoted himself to this task of reconstruction and demolition. He had made it his business to note all the doctrinal assertions in the books and articles of these gentlemen, especially those that served as the basis of some argument. So, step by step and not without much effort—for these gentlemen avoided as far as possible making statements of this kind—he had managed to construct the synthesis of 'modernism'. And, before my astonished eyes, he unfolded this synthesis, from the agnosticism in which it began to the prag-

---

[1] E.g. see A. L. Lilley, *Modernism* (1908), p. 259; Frémont, ii. 505. F. Sartiaux in *Joseph Turmel*, p. 125, describes Billot as 'auteur de l'encyclique *Pascendi*'.

matism in which it ended. That done, he demolished the whole system with some good philosophical and theological arguments...

When I read the encyclical, you can imagine my surprise as I recognized practically word for word the exposition of modernism which Fr Lemius had given me. For my part, I was at once convinced that the work had been done or had been very closely inspired by him.[1]

Fr Lemius himself never acknowledged the part he had played in this famous affair, but there are other testimonies now available from men who were acquainted with the facts. From these it emerges that several theologians had produced drafts of the desired encyclical for submission to the pope, but he had been dissatisfied with them all. It was then that Cardinal Merry del Val, his Secretary of State, heard of Fr Lemius and turned to him with a somewhat embarrassed urgency. Fr Lemius had in his head or at his finger tips all that he wanted to say, so he shut himself up in his room for four days and produced his draft with which Pius X was delighted.

I do not suppose that this information is likely to alter anyone's opinion of the encyclical, but it confirms its schematic or abstract character and also helps to explain what many have accounted its uncanny perception of what was implicit, though not explicit, in modernist writings.

When the time comes for a definitive history of the modernist movement to be written, the *Pascendi's* construction and demolition of the synthesis of all heresies will have to be thoroughly considered. But in my view what is most needed at this stage, now that the subject can be treated in a less controversial atmosphere than used to be the case, is more light on what the modernists were really like, and wherein they resembled and differed from one another. This then is my third reason for choosing to inspect modernists rather than modernism.

Whenever a movement or a collection of people with apparently similar ideas comes to be called an 'ism', there is an inevitable tendency on the part of everyone to exaggerate the extent to which they agreed with one another and so to distort the move-

---

[1] See BLE, April to September 1946, pp. 153 f. Cf. *Corr. phil.*, pp. 197 f.

ment's character. It is always easier to handle a movement that has been verbally unified in this manner. This temptation has been peculiarly powerful in the case of the modernist movement.

Thus I am going to look more or less closely at a number of those who, in France and England, were, or have been, regarded as modernists in order to show in each case in what their modernism consisted, for no two of them were quite alike. Some were mainly marked by a determination to accept what seemed to them the consequences of the critical and historical study of the Bible; others by an aversion to philosophical and theological scholasticism and by the quest for an alternative; others again by a revulsion from papal authoritarianism as currently exercized; or finally, in the case of Marc Sangnier and the sociological modernists, by the will to achieve a break away from the conservative political and social doctrines and affiliations that had been traditional in the Church and which Lamennais and others had vainly tried to change in the previous century. It was perfectly possible to be modernist or modernistic in one or more of these respects and not in the others, so that generalizations in this field of study should be looked upon even more suspiciously than in others.

2

THE ENIGMA OF ABBÉ LOISY

I have explained why I am going to consider some of the modern-*ists* rather than modern*ism*. I must needs be selective and I shall run less risk of being slight and superficial if I confine my attention to French and English modernists. My reason for attending to the English is more than patriotic. On the one hand, information about them is most readily accessible to me, and, on the other hand, some of the most interesting figures in the movement were located in England. I put it in that way so as to avoid saying that they were English by birth.

As regards France, in so far as the modernist movement had a centre, its centre was there. Pius X used to call modernism the *mal francese* of the Church, which was the amiable name the Italians had for venereal disease.[1] While I cannot persuade myself that this was an edifying thing for a pope to say, he was certainly justified in using the epithet *francese*. I cannot improve on M. Emile Poulat's demonstration that the modernist movement was centred in France:

It is in France, unquestionably, that modernism was on its home-ground. There it had its eponymous personality, Loisy,—its precursor, Duchesne,—its philosophers, Hébert and, above all, Edouard Le Roy, —its erudite scholars among whom Turmel stands out,—its moderator, Mgr Mignot, archbishop of Albi,—its publicist and historiographer, Houtin,—its reporters and its propagandists,—its publisher, Emile Nourry; its journals and periodicals...its adepts and sympathizers, its third order, with Paul Sabatier and Paul Desjardins, the one a liberal protestant and the other an 'ultra-Christian'; and even its self-styled bishop, Mgr Lacroix, who resigned his see of Tarentaise when he had promulgated the *Pascendi* in his diocese.'[2]

I begin then with the French, and therein with Alfred Loisy who, with some plausibility, has been called 'the Father of Catholic

---

[1] See Count Carlo Sforza, *Makers of Modern Europe* (1930), p. 125; also Shakespeare, *Henry V*, v. i. 80.   [2] Poulat, *Histoire, dogme et critique*, p. 19.

The Enigma of Abbé Loisy

Modernism',[1] though he himself disclaimed the title.[2] I am not going to repeat, or even to recapitulate, the detailed account of Loisy's career in the Church which I gave in my book *The Modernist Movement in the Roman Church*. So far as it goes, I am still satisfied with it. That it met with M. Loisy's approval[3] is not, I suppose, surprising, for I had depended closely on his own record of his career in the three volumes of his *Mémoires*. They had been published only a year or two before I wrote. They were not only extremely full and precise, but they had seemed to me remarkably candid. I remember reading them for a second time while I was suffering from an acute attack of lumbago and finding them more absorbing and diverting than any of the lighter literature that was within reach.

A good deal has happened since then to make further reflection on Loisy's career as a modernist necessary. Moreover, I am no longer content to have concluded my previous portrait of him abruptly with his excommunication. For that reason alone, I should welcome an opportunity to supplement what I said before. But, apart from that, I feel impelled on more than one count to re-examine Loisy's character as a modernist.

In the first place, I am much less confident than I used to be of my capacity to understand other people. It is said that, when Max Beerbohm in his later years read somewhere that 'posterity will be puzzled what to think of Sir Edmund Gosse', he noted in the margin: 'posterity, I hope, will be puzzled what to think about anybody. How baffling and contradictory are our most intimate and contemporary friends! And how many of us can gauge even himself?'[4] I feel the force of those remarks.

---

[1] F. Heiler, *Der Vater des katholischen Modernismus: Alfred Loisy, 1857–1940* (1947). Cf. Lagrange, *M. Loisy et le modernisme* (1932), p. 136.
[2] See *Mém.*, iii. 430.
[3] On 21 April 1938 he wrote to John Collins: 'J'ai bien reçu *The Modernist Movement* ...et je l'ai déjà lu d'un bout à l'autre avec beaucoup d'interêt. C'est une œuvre très soignée et bien documentée. J'y ai appris beaucoup de choses sur le modernisme dans votre Eglise et dans votre pays. En ce qui me concerne, j'y ai noté seulement une légère inexactitude p. 92. n. 1.' The last point concerns the editorship of the *Revue d'histoire et de littérature religieuses*; Paul Lejay, not Loisy, was its editor at the time in question.
[4] See David Cecil, *Max Beerbohm* (1964), p. 3.

All the same, some persons are more puzzling or enigmatic than others, and I must confess that Alfred Loisy is much more of a puzzle than I realized thirty or forty years ago. Although *prima facie* his *Mémoires* constituted an unusually complete self-revelation, the *Vie de Loisy* by Albert Houtin and Félix Sartiaux, which was not published till 1960, purports to put a very different complexion on the whole story. Then again, Loisy's own publications, subsequent to the *Mémoires*,[1] have to be taken into account, as also have collections of his letters that have appeared since then,[2] and not least M. Poulat's invaluable display of source material in *Histoire, dogme et critique dans la crise moderniste* (1962). In addition, there are now the many volumes of Loisy's papers that are accessible in the Bibliothèque Nationale.

Loisy was always a contentious figure who excited ardent feelings of one kind or another, but that is not the same thing as being exceptionally puzzling. Originally, most of those who admired or sympathized with him supposed that they understood him, as did also most of those who disapproved of him. To the latter he was a fairly straightforward heretic or apostate. At least this was so until he published his first autobiographical work, *Choses passées*, in 1912–13 though of course many who had at first followed him had already tended to retract as the successive *petits livres rouges* had appeared. *Choses passées* more than anything else disconcerted his friends, who felt that they had been deceived, and caused his enemies to proclaim that he had at last disclosed the enormity of his infidelity.

Against this background, the *Mémoires*, published in 1930–1, had the character of an elaborate apologia or essay in self-justification. I have acknowledged that I myself found them convincing, but for some readers they only deepened the unfavourable impression made by *Choses passées*. Here is the view of one who was evidently unconvinced. Père Jean Levie, s.j., in a study of Loisy composed in 1944, wrote as follows:

---

[1] Especially, *George Tyrrell et Henri Bremond* (1936); *La crise morale du temps présent et l'éducation humaine* (1937); and *Un mythe apologétique* (1939).

[2] See M. D. Petre, *Alfred Loisy* (1944); Maria dell' Isola, *Alfred Loisy* (1957); R. Marlé, s.j., *Au cœur de la crise moderniste* (1960); BLE, 1966 and 1968 (letters to Mignot); and R. de Boyer de Sainte Suzanne, *Alfred Loisy* (1968).

The Enigma of Abbé Loisy

Without anyone's knowledge, not even that of his most intimate friends, without his having given up any of the outward marks of the priestly life, or his daily mass... he had in fact since 1886 completely lost his faith, as he let it be known in 1911 [*sic*]; he went on living for twenty-two years, from 1886 to 1908, this double life, outwardly christian, inwardly an infidel, until his final revolt in 1908.[1]

The Houtin-Sartiaux *Vie de Loisy*, published in 1960, confirmed and strengthened this opinion in those who already held it, and at the same time it was a serious challenge to any who like myself were still disposed to accept M. Loisy's apologia in his *Mémoires*. I will explain the doubts that it raised in my mind, and whether or how far they have survived investigation. It will be an involved inquiry, since profound theological issues arise as well as curious, though comparatively manageable, questions such as an historian is accustomed to handling. The present chapter may seem to consist of somewhat irksome prolegomena: one has to go a long way round to get at the truth about Loisy.

I may add that my previous view of his character was further shaken when I found that so judicious and liberal-minded a Roman Catholic historian as M. Roger Aubert had apparently swallowed Houtin-Sartiaux more or less whole. This is what he said of their *Vie de Loisy*:

Houtin and Sartiaux's combined testimony, despite its bias as being the work of two disappointed admirers, sheds new light on Loisy's personality. What appears most clearly is the touchiness, short temper, vindictiveness and pitiless egocentricity of this desk-bound intellectual, not to mention his vanity over honours in the intellectual sphere, his taste for extremely flexible formulas of compromise and above all his special capacity for assimilation and adaptation rather than creation.[2]

Since Albert Houtin's testimony can have such devastating results, I must say something about him, before considering his relations with Loisy. His dates are 1867 to 1926. M. Poulat's description of him as the historiographer of the modernist move-

---

[1] Levie, *Sous les yeux de l'incroyant*[2] (1946), p. 192.
[2] See *Concilium*, September 1966, p. 47.

ment was apt for three reasons: first, because he published in
1912 the first history of the movement;[1] secondly, many of
Houtin's other publications had to do with the modernist movement, notably his two books on *La question biblique* and his
biography of Marcel Hébert; thirdly, Houtin was better described
as an historiographer than as an historian: he was a diligent collector of facts, a reporter of details and a retailer of documents, a
lucid, astringent and ironical character.

Houtin was of humble, rural parentage and had a pious
upbringing. He received his early education from a village
priest, and was himself as a boy set on becoming a priest. His
course of training at the diocesan seminary at Angers was
interrupted for a year while he tested his vocation at the Benedictine abbey of Solesmes. For some years he was attracted to the
monastic life, partly because of the opportunity it afforded for
study. After his ordination in 1891 he joined the staff of the
diocesan school where he had himself been a pupil, and eventually he was in charge of the history teaching. He remained there
till 1901. He was never a parish priest or charged with pastoral
responsibilities and never in his life occupied a Catholic pulpit.
The extravagant eulogy of Houtin by Sir J. G. Frazer, prefixed
to the English translation of his *Une vie de prêtre*, is somewhat at
sea when it speaks of him as a shepherd who 'had sought to guide
the lost sheep and to carry the strayed lambs of Christ's
flock'.[2]

At Angers Houtin devoted his leisure time to investigating and
writing about local ecclesiastical history. Through reading the
works of Duchesne and others he had learned how to study and
write history from a critical point of view, which was still a novel
and provocative thing to do in the Church of France. Duchesne
had already had trouble as a result of his exposure of the legendary
character of the traditions about the apostolic foundation of

[1] *Histoire du modernisme catholique* (1913; but it was published in November 1912:
see Houtin, *Ma vie laïque* (1928), p. 426). Alfred Fawkes had been intending to
write a history of the movement, but gave up the idea when he saw Houtin's book:
see Houtin, *Une vie de prêtre* (1928), pp. 432 f.
[2] Houtin, *The Life of a Priest* (1927), p. v. This eulogy had appeared in *The Times*,
4 August 1926.

French sees.[1] Houtin ran into graver trouble for the same reason. In giving an account of the controversy about the apostolicity of French sees, he denied the historicity of St Renatus, or St René, the most popular of the bishops of Angers, who, according to legend, had as a child been restored to life after having been dead for seven years.[2] The consequence was that Houtin had to resign his post at Angers in April 1901, and he then went to live with his parents in Paris.

The bishop of Angers continued to let him have a *celebret* for the time being. But Houtin now devoted his attention to the even more explosive controversy about the Bible. The outcome was his book *La question biblique chez les catholiques de France au XIXe siècle*, published in March 1902. This book caused a sensation, which was naturally increased when later in the year Loisy's *L'Evangile et l'Eglise* appeared. In December 1903 they were to be put on the Index together. Houtin could not get his *celebret* renewed after March 1903. Thereafter he was without any ecclesiastical status or appointment, though he continued to wear the soutane till 1912—apparently because his mother, to whom he was devoted, wished him to do so, though in his autobiography he gives a different reason.[3]

He entered into relations with Loisy in the summer of 1901 when he asked his advice about his projected book on *La question biblique*. Loisy, while encouraging him, had warned him that it was a perilous subject to take up.

Houtin was ten years younger than Loisy, and approached him as a disciple approaches a master.[4] Their experience of the Church had so far been similar. Both had been brought up in the tenets and atmosphere of an assured traditional orthodoxy and both had entered the priesthood with a certain youthful idealism. Both had experienced disillusion and had come to regard the Church's teaching, in the form in which it had been presented to, and accepted by, them as incredible—Loisy primarily in conse-

---

[1] See Houtin, *La controverse de l'apostolicité des églises de France au XIXᵉ siècle*[3] (1903), ch. xii.
[2] Houtin, *Les origines de l'église d'Angers: La légende de Saint René* (1901).
[3] See *Une vie de prêtre*, pp. 436 f.; *Ma vie laïque*, p. 372; *Mém.*, iii. 257.
[4] See Houtin, *Ma vie laïque*, p. 155.

quence of his study of the Bible; Houtin in consequence of his discovery that his idealized picture of the Church did not correspond with reality and that stories of the saints that had been transmitted to him as historical were in fact legendary (it was only afterwards that he made a similar discovery about the Bible). Loisy and Houtin, however, were both still dedicated to the service of the Church and—so at least it seemed when they first met—to a radical reinterpretation of the Catholic faith which they could commend to contemporary intelligence—a reinterpretation inspired by evolutionary ideas which both conceived themselves to have been encouraged to adopt by the writings of Cardinal Newman.

Anyhow, they became close, though not perhaps intimate, friends, and their friendship was not disturbed—so far as Loisy was aware[1]—until Houtin's death in 1926. During twenty-five years they helped one another in various ways, and Loisy had so much confidence in Houtin that early in 1907, when his state of health seemed to be precarious, he charged Houtin with the task of seeing his *Evangiles synoptiques* through the press and further asked him to prepare a biography for publication in the event of his death. For this purpose he let him have the use of confidential papers.[2] When Loisy published his autobiographical work, *Choses passées*, in 1912–13, he says that he presumed Houtin realized that he was no longer expected to produce a biography,[3] though there seems to be no evidence in writing that he made this clear to Houtin.[4]

It was only after Houtin's death that Loisy came to know that his supposed friend had been treating him—in private, and particularly to Félix Sartiaux, Houtin's executor—in a way that seemed to Loisy entirely inconsistent with their continued friendship.[5] Félix Sartiaux, I should explain, whose dates are 1876–1944, was by profession a railway director, but he was also

---

[1] Loisy was disappointed by, and critical of, Houtin's *Histoire du modernisme catholique*, but looked upon it as a sign of bad judgment, not of unfriendliness.

[2] Houtin provided a former pupil of his with information for the production of a short biography of Loisy which was published in 1909: Alfred Détrez, *L'Abbé Loisy*. See *Vie de Loisy*, p. 159; *Mém.*, iii. 89.

[3] See *Mém.*, iii. 251. [4] See *Vie de Loisy*, pp. 245 f.

[5] See *Mém.*, iii. 503.

a highly educated[1] intellectual with philosophical, artistic and historical interests. He had had a number of modernist contacts and had attended Loisy's lectures at the Collège de France, but he shared Houtin's scepticism and his penchant for priests who had lost their faith, such as Joseph Turmel, whose biography he wrote.[2] Loisy learned from Sartiaux that among Houtin's papers there was an important *Vie de Loisy avec plusieurs annexes*, concerning the existence of which he had been kept in the dark and which Sartiaux did not offer to let him see. However, he soon had reason to suspect that it would have a malicious character,[3] and when two years later (1928) the second part of Houtin's autobiography (*Ma vie laïque*) was published it was apparent that this suspicion was likely to be more than justified. For among the numerous 'documents and souvenirs' which Sartiaux, in accordance with Houtin's instructions,[4] published along with *Ma vie laïque* were a dozen 'silhouettes of ecclesiastics': one of these was headed '*Chez un tacticien*'.

Though Loisy's name was not given, it was in fact an extract from the *Vie de Loisy* which Houtin had prepared, and it was manifestly intended to portray Loisy at the time when Houtin first came to know him and started to visit him frequently. It was the time when Loisy was living at Bellevue. After mentioning his first visit, Houtin proceeds to describe Loisy's appearance, his bearing and style of conversation, the furnishings of his apartment, etc., in such a way as to convey the impression that he was hypocritically acting the part of a devout priest. I will translate one specimen passage:

Whenever you entered the apartment you were at once struck by the idea that the master of the house was a pious priest who, notwithstanding his daring opinions, observed all the rules of the Church and indeed was a faithful disciple of its greatest thinkers. Splendid engravings of Newman and Fénelon as well as a large photograph of Mgr

---

[1] He had been educated at the Ecole Fénelon under Marcel Hébert (see p. 65 below) and at the Ecole polytechnique. See also *Revue archéologique* (1952), xxxix. 98 ff.

[2] *Joseph Turmel, prêtre, historien des dogmes* (1931); cf. p. 56 below.

[3] See *Mém.*, iii. 507; *Ma vie laïque*, p. 381.

[4] See *Vie de Loisy*, p. 93; *Ma vie laïque*, pp. 155–61.

Mignot—not to mention an altar—adorned the drawing room. In the dining room a breviary was placed in a conspicuous position. Over his desk there was a crucifix with which he had had himself photographed.

In order to drive home the impression these things were calculated to create, he was careful in the course of conversation to mention that, since his deplorable health prevented him from going to the parish church, he said mass daily at home, thanks to an indult which he had procured. Soon afterwards he found occasion to add that he hardly ever went to Paris except once a fortnight to make his confession...

And so on for several pages.

This 'silhouette', together with much similar matter about himself and other people which appeared in the same posthumous volume, not only took Loisy by surprise but warned him of what Houtin's *Vie de Loisy* would probably be like. One of his motives, if not his principal motive, for starting in 1927 to write his *Mémoires* was the desire to forestall what he now anticipated would be the malicious biography that Houtin had prepared and that Sartiaux would withhold from publication till Loisy was dead. In thus deferring its publication Sartiaux would be following Houtin's own intention,[1] for being ten years younger than Loisy, and until his final illness more robust in health, he had naturally expected to survive him. Loisy had plenty of other good reasons for writing a full autobiography,[2] but this reason was decisive and lent urgency to the undertaking.

It seemed to Loisy that Houtin, in his last years and perhaps previously, had been beset by a pathological venom[3] that caused him not only to see no good whatever in the Church—he had for long been fond of saying that it was 'the organization of pious falsehood'[4]—but also to blacken the characters of nearly everyone that he had known. In his *Mémoires* Loisy was at pains to give his

---

[1] See *Vie de Loisy*, p. 189.
[2] See *avant-propos* to *Mém.*, i. 5 ff.
[3] See *Mém.*, III. 503–6. Cf. Loisy's letters of this period to F. Cumont; BN, n.a.f. 15644.
[4] In his 'second inventory' (1904), published in *Une vie de prêtre*, pp. 315 f., Houtin wrote: 'Dès 1901, mon expérience se résumait en ce que j'avais constaté et que je constatais "l'organisation du pieux mensonge", partout et toujours, dans le présent comme dans le passé, dans l'histoire ancienne de l'Eglise comme dans son histoire contemporaine.'

own interpretation of those incidents that Houtin seemed likely to have used in presenting his full portrait of '*un tacticien*'.

Until Houtin's *Vie de Loisy* was at last published in 1960 (together with Sartiaux's notes and a long essay by him on '*l'œuvre d'Alfred Loisy*', written from the same standpoint as Houtin's), it was impossible to say how far Loisy's anticipations would prove to have been justified. When it was published it was seen to be a work of thorough denigration, and Sartiaux had of course been in a position to extend the process of denigration to Loisy's *Mémoires*.

By the use of this language I do not wish to prejudge the question of how much substance there is in the Houtin–Sartiaux case against Loisy. What is their case? I would distinguish between their general view of Loisy's character on the one hand, and on the other hand their particular charge that during the modernist movement he was a sceptic and/or atheist in disguise. I am principally concerned with the latter charge, but I will say something first about the more general question.

They allege that Loisy, despite his obvious talents and powers of attraction, was an extreme egotist, absorbed in his own interests and uninterested in other people, ambitious, suspicious, jealous, self-opinionated and resentful of criticism and contradiction, a master of equivocation, using the work of others without due acknowledgement, without aesthetic, artistic or literary appreciation. Houtin and Sartiaux find evidences of these faults, failings and deficiencies throughout Loisy's career and work. I have carefully studied all that they say in comparison with what Loisy said on his own behalf and along with other relevant evidence. I can give here only my broad conclusions, since it would be inordinately tedious to discuss the matter in exhaustive detail.

Some of the charges against Loisy, even if true, are hardly to be regarded as morally culpable or as a grave blot on his character. He does seem to have had little appreciation of the beauties of nature or of art except in the case of literary style. His experience, and maybe his sympathies, were limited by the circumstance that he never travelled abroad nor indeed scarcely ever off his own beaten track in France. He can fairly be described as a bookworm or as a desk-bound intellectual, though he was by no means desiccated. The hold that his rustic origins had upon him and his life-long addiction to horticulture and poultry-keeping should be remembered. When towards the end of his life someone spoke to him of 'his school' or his disciples, he was content with a rueful smile to point to his hens.[1]

I should say that he was a natural pastor and director of souls. He told Mgr Mignot in 1902 that he wanted to exercise a pastoral and teaching ministry in the Church and that he had not become a priest in order to pursue an academic career.[2] By all accounts he was an admirable chaplain to the Dominican nuns at Neuilly. Von Hügel used to tell 'how on one occasion Pope Pius X, impressed by the distinguished gravity and dignity of a certain *religieuse* whom he was receiving in audience, inquired who had trained her, and was not a little taken aback when she told him that it was Loisy'.[3]

Moreover, it should also be remembered that, in addition to his extraordinary concentration on his work as a savant, Loisy took a keen interest in all questions of religion and morality and was also a shrewd spectator of the political scene and of international relations. It remains true, however, that there were areas of human culture and activity that were to him more or less a closed book. But surely many eminent scholars have had limitations of this kind, witness the case of Charles Darwin which in some respects resembles that of Loisy.[4] His intellectual industry did not prevent him from having many warm friendships, more than would be inferred from his *Mémoires*, for he was careful not to embarrass anyone who might be discredited in the eyes of the establishment by association with him.

[1] See Bonsirven, *Supplément au Dictionnaire de la Bible*, v. 544.
[2] See Loisy to Mignot, 21 October 1902: BLE, July to September 1966, p. 172.
[3] C. C. J. Webb, *Journal of Theological Studies*, April 1952, p. 145. See also Loisy's letters of advice to Raymond de Boyer de Sainte Suzanne in his *Alfred Loisy*, pp. 181–91.
[4] See Gertrude Himmelfarb, *Darwin and the Darwinian Revolution* (1959), ch. vi, 'Portrait of the Scientist'.

As regards the moral defects which Houtin and Sartiaux ascribe to Loisy, they are defects, to which many men, and not least intellectuals, are prone. No one has claimed that Loisy was a saint. He was certainly not exempt from the egotism that is native to man, but I see no warrant for saying that he was exceptionally egotistic. Henri Bremond, after reading *Choses passées*, wrote to Loisy: 'What touches me most, in your case as in Tyrrell's, is to see how the ego does not engross your auto-biographies, as it does engross, deplorably in my view, Newman's *Apologia*. *Myself and my Creator* is one of the most dreadful sayings that has ever been written.'[1]

Nevertheless, it must be allowed that Houtin and Sartiaux, in searching everywhere for signs of Loisy's moral turpitude, do put their finger on some weaknesses in his character of which he himself was not aware or which, perhaps unconsciously, he sought to conceal. For example, they show that, when in 1902 he was being considered as a candidate for the episcopate,[2] he was less indifferent to the outcome and less inactive in seeking to promote his candidature than he allowed to appear in his auto-biographical works. Unless it is always culpable to seek the office of a bishop, Loisy's ambition was in itself excusable since the modernist enterprise as well as his personal prospects stood to gain in the event of a favourable outcome. Loisy in fact had good reasons for wanting to be a bishop,[3] and Miss Petre recalled that Louis Canet 'who knew him better than anyone knew him and who was also too independent minded to form anything but his own judgment' once told her that 'he believed that Loisy would have become a great and noted bishop'.[4] So all that he can be blamed for in this matter is a lack of candour in having subse-quently sought to draw a veil over his ambition;[5] I fancy that

---

[1] Bremond to Loisy, 15 June 1913: BLE, July to September 1968, pp. 174 f.
[2] On this matter, see *Choses passées*, pp. 232–40; *Mém.*, ii. ch. xxv; *Vie de Loisy*, ch. xvi.
[3] Cf. his letter to Mignot, 21 October 1902: BLE, 1966, p. 172.
[4] M. D. Petre, *Alfred Loisy*, p. 13. On Canet, see *Revue d'histoire diplomatique*, 1968, pp. 134–80.
[5] For Loisy's own view of the part that ambition had in his nature see the entry in his journal of 14 July 1892: *Mém.*, i. 211.

many candidates for the episcopate, both successful and unsuccessful, have done the same.

The faults that Houtin and Sartiaux found in Loisy's character were not altogether imaginary, but they so grossly exaggerated them and were so determined to look for wickedness where often there was nothing but innocence that the total effect of their portraiture brings much more discredit on them than on him. It is important to notice that Loisy was far from being the only person whom they treated in this way, or whom Houtin treated thus with Sartiaux's connivance or acquiescence. In Houtin's autobiographical works there are other characterizations that are equally scurrilous if more summary. For instance, he says that John Ireland, archbishop of St Paul, and John Spalding, bishop of Peoria, were *'purs rationalistes'*.[1] A. L. Lilley was *'complètement positiviste'*.[2] George Tyrrell was *'un pur sceptique'*.[3] When Henri Bremond read this last statement, he wrote to Loisy: 'Nothing surprises me from this poor Houtin. Once again, he has entirely failed to understand'.[4]

Indeed, these sweeping assertions, and others that could be mentioned, would not bear examination. They illustrate Houtin's fondness for alleging that clerics were more or less infidels in disguise; and before he finished, it was not only clerics that Houtin treated in this way. Towards the end of his life he wrote:

Personal interest dictates to most men what they dare to call their 'convictions' not only in matters of religion but in every sphere of thought. Just as some people acquire honours and wealth by zealously but insincerely defending the religions in which they were born, so other people exploit to their profit the ideas of the State and of the Fatherland, about which they are as sceptical as ecclesiastics are about religious institutions.[5]

It would not be far from the truth to say that Houtin was dedicated to debunking. Already in 1912, when he was preparing

[1] *Une vie de prêtre*, p. 318. Cf. *Mém.*, i. 547.
[2] *Ma vie laïque*, p. 423.
[3] *Ibid.* p. 255. See also Loisy, *Tyrrell et Bremond*, pp. 41–6, where the reactions of Bremond and Miss Petre to Houtin's assertion are reported.
[4] Bremond to Loisy, 11 November 1926: BN, n.a.f. 15650.
[5] *Ma vie laïque*, pp. 79 f.

his *Histoire du modernisme catholique* which was a debunking of the modernists, Paul Desjardins had written to Loisy:

I know his frame of mind. He is set on becoming more and more virulent. I do not say that he is wrong in the main, and anyhow I have confidence in his integrity as an historian. But together with serenity he has lost the sense of what is fitting...He has an assurance in negation which goes far beyond the degree of assurance that history allows us. He is a dogmatic nihilist.[1]

Charles Guignebert, when reviewing Loisy's *Mémoires* in 1933, said of Houtin that he was 'a great collector of letters and of bits of paper, a shrewd journalist, but an annalist who welcomed tittle-tattle, quick to adopt risky interpretations and malicious conclusions, a lively mind, but embittered and disparaging rather than truly critical; for the rest, a sombre and unbalanced character'.[2] But we cannot yet dismiss Houtin.

The most formidable charge that he, and Sartiaux with him, laid against Loisy has still to be investigated. This was that from 1886 onwards he was really an atheist and a sceptic, and therefore during the modernist movement was only pretending to be a Catholic. On the first page of his foreword to the *Vie de Loisy* Sartiaux speaks of him as 'this atheistic priest' as though there were no question about it, but actually a whole complex of

---

[1] See *Mém.*, iii. 243. On Houtin as an historian, see also Poulat, *Histoire, dogme et critique*, pp. 334 f., 340 f.

[2] See *Revue historique*, 1933, p. 91; cf. *ibid.* p. 114: 'Houtin ... qui, ulcéré par l'erreur fondamentale de sa vie, révolté par ses déceptions, usé par ses pénibles difficultés matérielles, a fini par gâter des qualités d'esprit et de coeur incontestables assez pour devenir un égocentriste outrecuidant, soupçonneux, jaloux, méchant, et perdre, par ses propos d'outre tombe, l'estime que ne lui refusait pas, de son vivant, l'illusion de bien des honnêtes gens.' Alfred Fawkes, who had known Houtin well, in an obituary article in the *Modern Churchman* (December 1926, p. 549) wrote that his 'mind was detached; it moved like a machine, looking neither right nor left, but automatically, as it were; and there were some temperaments and outlooks which he seemed constitutionally unable to understand'. Later, when he had read *Ma vie laïque*, Fawkes wrote to Loisy: 'I hope Houtin's unfortunate book has had little effect. It can injure no one but the writer. His animus against yourself, Duchesne and others is so unaccountable that one almost thinks that his illness must have affected his mind.' Fawkes to Loisy, 12 February 1929: BN, n.a.f. 15653.

questions has to be considered in this connexion which will occupy us in the next chapter as well as in this.

The hinge of Houtin's case is a confession that he alleges Loisy made to him at Garnay in March 1907.[1] The crucial passage is in the *Vie de Loisy*,[2] where Houtin tells how, when Loisy had been seriously ill and wanted to take precautions in case of his death, he revealed to Houtin his fundamental beliefs or rather unbeliefs.

I knew [writes Houtin] that he was no longer a Christian, though he always claimed to be something of a Catholic, but I believed that he was like me[3] a spiritualist and a deist. He told me that twenty years ago he had ceased to believe in the soul, in free will, in the future life, in the existence of a personal God. These confidences gave me no pleasure. He had been expressly deceiving me ever since we had got to know one another. He had never regarded me as a friend, but only as an ally, as an instrument, indeed as a dupe, for he had often, and even at the beginning of 1905, advised me to submit to the Index, a piece of dishonesty which I did not commit.[4]

Houtin does not profess to report Loisy's exact words, and there are aspects of this alleged confession which, while they need not lead one to suppose that Houtin's story was entirely without foundation, do nevertheless throw a cloak of uncertainty round it.

First, if, as Houtin says, he was profoundly shocked by Loisy's confession, and considered that his supposed friend had practised an intolerable and irretrievable deception on him, it is strange that he never apprised Loisy of the effect his confession had had, but on the contrary continued outwardly to maintain his friendship as though nothing had happened. His explanation

---

[1] 4 March was the exact date: see *Ma vie laïque*, p. 248.

[2] *Op. cit.* pp. 137 f.

[3] It is not easy to say what Houtin's religious beliefs really were at this time. In the preface to his *Histoire du modernisme catholique* (1913) he gives the impression that from 1903 onwards he was entirely detached and, in particular, was no adherent of the modernist movement. But elsewhere he speaks differently. See *Une vie de prêtre*, pp. 316, 322 f., 406, 420, and in particular pp. 433 f.: 'En 1904, je m'étais trouvé "théiste chrétien" ou "théiste catholicisant". Dans les années suivantes, l'intransigeance de la papauté m'avait convaincu que la religion de l'avenir ne sortirait pas du catholicisme par une évolution naturelle, mais par mutation brusque, par rupture, par cassure. Je m'étais ainsi peu à peu détaché du catholicisme.' [4] *Vie de Loisy*, p. 138; see also *ibid.* p. 157.

seems very weak, except in so far as it justifies his willingness to
see *Les Evangiles synoptiques* through the press if Loisy himself
were unable to do so. Can it justify his having, for the rest of his
life, concealed from Loisy his real sentiments towards him? This
is what he says:

I was filled with indignation by the revelation of his thought which
[Loisy] had made to me, and I was tempted to break with him. I was
mollified somewhat when I reflected that he had duped a number of
other people more intelligent than I. He was relying on me to see to the
publication of his manuscript in which, he told me, he had said everything he had to say about the origins of Christianity... I thought the
publication of this work would be a service not so much to M. Loisy
as to innumerable adherents of Christianity. So I promised to do all he
wanted...[1]

Secondly, when Houtin returned from Garnay, he told Père
Hyacinthe Loyson, whose biography he was writing, about his
visit to Loisy. Loyson entered an account of it in his journal, but
subsequently cut the page out.[2] Why he did so is a mystery and
Houtin, who reports the fact, suggests no reason. It might have
provided contemporary evidence of what transpired during the
visit to Garnay.

Thirdly, as I have said, in writing his *Mémoires*, Loisy was at
pains to give his own interpretation of those incidents in his life
which Houtin in his *Vie de Loisy* seemed likely to have used in
order to present him as '*un tacticien*'. Now, in the *Mémoires*[3]
Loisy mentions that Houtin visited him early in March 1907 and
undertook, if necessary, to correct the proofs of *Les Evangiles
synoptiques*, and also, in the event of his death, to write a bio-
graphical notice for which purpose he lent him some of his
private journals. But he says nothing about having made the kind
of revelation or confession that Houtin alleges nor does he betray
any awareness that Houtin might make such an allegation. If the
episode had had the character and importance that Houtin
attributes to it, Loisy would surely have remembered it and have
given his own version of it.

[1] *Vie de Loisy*, p. 158.   [2] *Ma vie laïque*, p. 248.   [3] ii. 512.

However, the question about what Loisy said or did not say to Houtin on 4 March 1907, while it obviously has an important bearing on their personal relations, is not so important, as at first it may appear to be, in its bearing on Loisy's state of mind before and during the modernist movement. He provided sufficient data elsewhere (especially in his autobiographical writings) to raise in an acute form the question of his faith and of the sincerity of his profession of Catholicism during that period.

He left the readers of *Choses passées* and of the *Mémoires* in no manner of doubt that he experienced a crisis and a loss of faith in the years preceding 1886. His doubts about the system of traditional scholastic orthodoxy arose partly from its inconsistency with what his own study of the Bible brought home to him and partly from his discovery of the gap between his ideal of the Church and the reality. An event which particularly impressed upon him the extent of his departure from what he was expected to believe was the fate of the doctoral thesis on the inspiration of the Bible which he finished in 1884 and which then had to be shelved. The Rector of the Institut Catholique, Mgr d'Hulst, asked to see it before it was submitted to examiners. The Rector praised the thesis, but advised Loisy to pigeon-hole it since, if it were presented and published, it would cause a furore among the theologians and compromise still further the theological faculty of the Institut which had already been compromised enough by Duchesne.[1]

In November 1886 Loisy wrote in his journal:

For several months past I have experienced no religious feeling. Since my second year in the seminary my feelings of piety have always been crossed by the fear of illusion. Perhaps this fear was pathological; anyhow it no longer exists at present, being without any object.

I have practically nothing to look forward to. I am determined to work and to serve the Church which has been and is responsible for the education of humanity. Without disowning its tradition, and provided it holds to its spirit rather than its letter, it is still a necessary institution and the most divine thing on earth. It has capitalized the subtleties of the theologians, but it has also stored up the principles of

[1] See *Mém.*, i. 130 ff.

order, devotion and virtue which guarantee the welfare of the family and the peace of society. To wish today to reconstitute the moral order apart from Christ and the Church would be a utopian project. That there are elements in ecclesiastical discipline that are superannuated,—that our forms of worship are not altogether in accord with the needs of the present time,—that the literal sense of the theological formulas becomes every day less tenable,—I believe I see with increasing clarity the more I know the past history of religion and of humanity. I may be mistaken, and I am entirely willing to admit the contrary of what I think, if the contrary can be shown to be true. The interior conflict which I have been through during the last eight years and which has come to an end only a few months ago has tired me out. I ask myself whether I shall ever recover my youthful resilience. Probably not. If I can still muster some vigour I shall reckon myself happy.[1]

This disillusioned and melancholy piece of self-examination dates from a time several years before anything like a reforming movement in the Church was envisaged. Various circumstances subsequently gave Loisy a new zest for the service of the Church as the moral educator of humanity and a sense of obligation to work for an adaptation of Catholic teaching to contemporary conditions and needs.

In the first place, when he became responsible for the teaching of Holy Scripture at the Institut Catholique, he had to consider the effect on his pupils of his teaching which would of course be given from a critical point of view. He could not conscientiously leave them in a state of bewilderment; he had to help them to see how the critical approach and conclusions could be reconciled with the Catholic tradition. This entailed his thinking the matter out for himself.[2]

Then again, after his destitution from the Institut Catholique in 1893, his work as chaplain to the convent school at Neuilly impelled him to look for a way of giving Catholic teaching to children which was consistent with his integrity as an historical critic, and at the same time strengthened what was now his settled

---

[1] See *Choses passées*, pp. 76 f.; *Mém.*, i. 150–3; *Vie de Loisy*, p. 43. In *Mém.* he says that 'eight years' must have been a mistake for 'ten years'. For an alternative English translation, see *My Duel with the Vatican*, p. 101.
[2] See *Mém.*, i. 179.

37

view that it was the moral rather than the metaphysical elements in Catholicism that were vitally and permanently important. He found that the speculative doctrines that agitated the minds of theologians meant very little to the Dominican nuns to whom he was ministering and still less to the girls in their school. As he wrote in his *Mémoires*:

The poor old mysteries over which the doctors of past ages sweated blood and water do not arouse the slightest interest or curiosity in the minds of the young. They are no more affected by the mystery of one God in three persons than they would be if they learned that in the arithmetic of heaven two and two equal five. What counts is the sense of what is good, the sense of duty, Jesus understood as the exemplar of self-sacrifice and moral perfection. But if the abstract dogmas are of no consequence, religious practices do have salutary emotional effects. The Christian ideal lives and works in the ceremonies of the cultus.[1]

The apologetic for Catholicism which issued in *L'Evangile et l'Eglise* germinated in Loisy's mind during his ministry at Neuilly. By this time also he had acquired the friendship of Baron von Hügel and of Mgr Mignot who warmly encouraged him in this enterprise.

In the course of a letter to von Hügel written when he was preparing *Choses passées*, Loisy summed up his changes of mind during these years:

There will be things in it [i.e. in *Choses passées*] of which the Catholics will take advantage against me. My journal shows that, during the winter of 1885–1886, I became definitely aware that I could no longer uphold the orthodox position, or rather I realized that I had abandoned it altogether. I went through a gloomy period, since I judged that a transformation of Catholicism was impossible. It was my time of teaching [at the Institut Catholique] from 1889 to 1893 which, for the sake of my pupils, made me hope afresh and attempt a reconciliation; and it was my ministry [at the convent school at Neuilly] from 1894 to 1899 which confirmed me in this hope and purpose.[2]

The enigma of Abbé Loisy, about which I shall have a good deal more to say in the next chapter, centres in the question

---

[1] *Mém.*, i. 364 f.
[2] Loisy to von Hügel, 7 June 1912: *Mém.*, iii. 246.

whether, his state of mind or his faith being what it was at the time, he was justified in engaging in the modernist movement. Today I would remark in conclusion that the case of M. Loisy, admittedly in an extreme form, exemplifies, on the one hand, the dilemma which can confront any member of a church who determines to work for its transformation from inside and, on the other hand, the problem of the degree of reforming or revolutionary thinking and agitation which a church can be expected to tolerate in its members.

3

THE ENIGMA RESOLVED?

Alfred Loisy is an extraordinarily elusive character.[1] The particular enigma on which I am now going to try to throw some further light is the question whether his profession of Catholicism, at the time when he stood out as a prominent modernist, had sufficient substance or sufficient honesty to justify his having done so. We have seen that on his own confession, but in a sense that has yet to be determined, he lost his faith around 1886. Houtin and Sartiaux maintain that from then onwards he was a sceptic and an atheist so that as a modernist he was a deceiver and not true. Loisy himself however, as we have also seen, says that his confidence in, and hopes for, the future of Catholicism revived in the 1890s in such a way as to justify his part in the modernist movement. Although in the end he came to see that the movement had been based on an illusion—on an illusory hope about what the Church as it was then constituted might tolerate or about what services it might be disposed to accept—yet at the time, particularly in 1902 when he published *L'Evangile et l'Eglise*, which was the watershed of his career as a modernist, he was sincerely Catholic.

This was not to say that in *L'Evangile et l'Eglise* he unfolded all that was in his mind. His refutation of Harnack's liberal protestantism was entirely sincere, but the primary object of the book was to utilize material which he already had available in a much larger manuscript[2] and which was calculated to show that a more radical criticism of the New Testament sources than Harnack's could issue in the thesis that the essence of the Gospel, in so far as it had an essence, was really perpetuated in Catholic Christianity.[3] It was implied rather than emphasized that this thesis involved the abandonment of many tenets of the scholastic

---

[1] Cf. E. Poulat in *Entretiens*, p. 92: 'Loisy est un homme insaissable. Il y a des choses extraordinaires . . .'
[2] See *Mém.*, i. ch. xvi, 'Le livre inédit'.   [3] *Ibid.* ii. 167.

theology concerning the instruction of the Church and Sacraments, the immutability of dogma, and the nature of ecclesiastical authority.[1] Loisy's thesis was propounded with discretion and a certain prudent reserve, but was that inconsistent with sincerity and honesty? If there is a proper 'reserve in communicating religious knowledge', there is also a proper reserve that may be exercised in seeking to win toleration for the reformation of a received theology. While it is true, as the present bishop of Durham has said, that 'sometimes what is in fact theological advance may seem at the beginning to be very negative, even theological erosion',[2] a wise theological reformer, especially under such conditions as prevailed in the Roman Catholic Church at the beginning of this century, will endeavour to cushion the negative or erosive effects of his theses at their first onset. It may be said that Loisy did no more than this, and that therefore there is no reason to challenge his sincerity.

On the other hand, although Léonce de Grandmaison was quite unjustified in saying that Loisy before this time had already, in several pseudonymous writings, 'denied the Christian faith and all positive religion',[3] yet we know now—and Loisy himself knew at the time—that his faith had undergone a sea-change many years before, and the question must be put whether he had privately retained or recovered enough faith to warrant his publicly adopting the stance of an apologist for Catholicism.

In seeking an answer to this question, I have derived most help from a little book that appears to be very little known. I bought a copy when it was published in 1931 and read it with interest, but I had never heard of the author who was evidently a warm, though not altogether uncritical, admirer of M. Loisy, and I did not assign to it the value that I do now. It was entitled *Un clerc qui n'a pas trahi*, which I translate *A Clerk who has not played*

---

[1] See *ibid*. i. 168.
[2] Sermon in Great St Mary's Church, Cambridge, 12 November 1967.
[3] See *La vie catholique dans la France contemporaine* (1918), p. 275. In *Mém.* (ii. 110) Loisy says that he had not at this time thought out fundamentally the 'problème de Dieu', but he preferred von Hügel's belief in a personal God to Marcel Hébert's doctrine of the impersonality of God.

false—a title suggested of course by that of Julien Benda's well-known book.[1] There was a sub-title, *Alfred Loisy d'après ses Mémoires.*
The author's name was Sylvain Leblanc. I had no suspicion at the time that this was the pseudonym of a famous writer and member of the Académie française. It is only in recent years[2] that Henri Bremond[3] has been revealed as the real author. The manuscript is now in the Bibliothèque Nationale.[4] Perhaps I might have guessed at least thirty years ago that Bremond was the author not only from the style of the book,[5] but from the fact that Loisy in his book *George Tyrrell et Henri Bremond*, which was published in 1936, while he tells at length what Bremond thought about his other books, had practically nothing to say when he comes to Bremond's reaction to the *Mémoires* which presumably would have interested him intensely.[6] They had indeed interested him so much that he had written a book about them. Loisy could not allude to this because he was bound not to reveal the authorship. The book was noticed after its publication by Jean Rivière[7] who supposed the author to be a layman, and by Maurice Goguel[8] who evidently had no idea who the author was. A reviewer in the *Revue d'histoire ecclésiastique*[9] did, however, realize that 'Sylvain Leblanc' was a pseudonym.

[1] *La trahison des clercs* (1927).
[2] See the 'index bio-bibliographique' in *Vie de Loisy*, p. 372, where Sylvain Leblanc is said to be the 'pseudonyme d'un prêtre dont l'amitié fut à Loisy "infiniment bienfaisante et précieuse" ',which is precisely what Loisy says of Bremond in his *Tyrrell et Bremond*, p. 195. See also Poulat,*Histoire, dogme et critique*, pp. 655, 685.
[3] (1865-1933) I was for long puzzled by the fact that some authors always put an accent on the 'e' in Bremond's name, whereas those whom I regarded as more likely to be correct did not. And what was the correct pronunciation of the name? Since reading *Entretiens* (p. 18), I know that it is correct to spell the name without an accent on the 'e' but to pronounce it as if it did have an accent. This usage is common in the Midi of France, and Bremond was a provençal.
[4] See BN, n.a.f. 15667.
[5] As André Blanchet has said: 'Écrivain de race, Bremond avait son style bien à lui, reconnaissable entre tous.'*Histoire d'une mise à l'index*, p. 227.
[6] See *Tyrrell et Bremond*, p. 176. It was also relevant that Bremond was in close relations with Emile Nourry who published *Un clerc qui n'a pas trahi*, though he was not Bremond's regular publisher: see *ibid.* p. 194.
[7] *Revue des sciences religieuses* (1932), xii. 156 f.
[8] *Revue d'histoire et de philosophie religieuses* (1932), p. 90.
[9] (1932) xxviii. 212.

The Enigma Resolved?

The book is important not only because one would like to know anyhow what Bremond's considered view was of Loisy and of the modernist movement but also because his view is singularly sharp and penetrating. Bremond himself, I should say, is an even more enigmatic figure than Loisy, but I must not now be diverted into exploring that enigma. I may, however, just remind you of the flavour of the man by quoting an unpublished post-card that he wrote to A. L. Lilley on 8 August 1909, that is, when he had been condemned for what he had done at Father Tyrrell's deathbed and funeral.[1]

30 Rue Pierre, Neuilly   8 August 1909 (postcard)
Dear Lilley, Tis done—Merry del Val, *nomine sanctae sedis* suspends me *a divinis* (i.e. prohibits my saying mass)—It is not known yet. As soon as the papers will give it, they give too my answer to the Arch of Aix (through whom the news came)—a very calm, half-fenelonian, half voltairian answer—I accept humbly the *chastisement* and briefly sum up the case, with a sort of *perfide ingénuité*. Now, of course, they want to go further on. But the letter will puzzle them very much. I need not tell you I do not give up anything. I simply accept the sentence, just as a soldier, and I imply that *je reste sur mes positions*. If they now want new conditions, we shall see and then only will be time to say the *non possumus*. Do not write before it is known. But it will be kind to say then something. Of course the chief point is that they condemn me, without having even asked one word of me—without having read the *mémoire* I sent to my bishop. This is simply monstrous. My only accuser is Amigo and what can Amigo say of the state in which Tyrrell was (Remember their first [?idea] was against my absolution. They give it up, little by little, but we must try *tenir là dessus*. Then, it is the first time, a priest is punished for what he has done by a death bed.   Yours

In the event, Bremond did not say *non possumus* when they wanted new conditions, but a few months later made a submission of which von Hügel[2] disapproved, but which Loisy[3] and Miss

---

[1] See Loisy, *Tyrrell et Bremond*, pp. 18–39.
[2] See *Tyrrell et Bremond*, p. 40. On 20 November 1909 von Hügel wrote to Lilley that Bremond's submission was 'painful and unlovely', and concluded: 'Alas, alas,—no hope of true love for Rome by discerning minds, no spontaneous, proud admiration for the acts entailed,—as long as this system lasts; and when will it end?' LP.   [3] See *Tyrrell et Bremond*, pp. 37 f.

Petre[1] defended. Bremond may not have been a modernist, but he was a non-combatant participator in the movement. Loisy said of him: 'Bremond was not intimately involved in the modernist struggle. But he enlisted in the service of the Red Cross. He brought in the dead and tended the wounded.'[2]

There are two perceptions in Bremond's view of Loisy on which I wish to remark. First, Bremond holds that Loisy was, both by vocation and by disposition, a 'clerk' in two senses. He writes of 'les deux cléricatures de M. Loisy: le critique et le prêtre'.[3]

On the one hand, he was a priest, dedicated to the service of religion. As long as he was allowed to do so he exercised his priesthood within the Church. After his excommunication he continued to be a priest, in the religious though not in the ecclesiastical sense: he was still constantly concerned with the religious well-being of mankind, and not only with the historical study of religions, and also he exercised a pastoral ministry. Support for this view of Loisy's continuing priesthood could later have been found in the inscription that he directed to be put on his tombstone:

Alfred Loisy
Prêtre
Retiré du ministère et de l'enseignement
Professeur au Collège de France
Tuam in votis tenuit voluntatem.[4]

The last words are characteristically enigmatic.[5]

On the other hand, Bremond says, Loisy was equally a clerk

---

[1] See M. D. Petre, *My Way of Faith*, pp. 267 ff.; also Miss Petre to Lilley, 10 December 1909: LP.

[2] See A. Blanchet, *Histoire d'une mise à l'index*, pp. 37 f.; BLE, January to March 1968, p. 7. An article on 'Henri Bremond et le modernisme' in *La Revue de l'Université de Laval* (April 1966), by Clément Moisan, minimizes Bremond's involvement in the movement.

[3] *Un clerc qui n'a pas trahi*, p. vii.

[4] On this inscription, see *Entretiens*, p. 92.

[5] They are misquoted by R. Rouquette in *Études*, June 1956, p. 321, who is also mistaken in saying that Loisy's tomb is at 'Montiers-en-Der' (*sic*): see p. 10 above. John Ratté, in *Three Modernists* (1968), p. 136, purporting to follow Rouquette, introduces a further misquotation.

in that he was dedicated to the service of science—of historical criticism. He was a savant. Neither as a priest nor as a savant did he betray his vocation. He did not allow either vocation to lead him to play false to the other. The critic did not strangle the priest, nor the priest the critic. He neither preferred nor subordinated one of his missions to the other. He carried them out as though they were on parallel lines, convinced that they were not opposed to one another.[1]

The other striking feature of Bremond's interpretation of Loisy's career is the distinction he draws between different types of Christian faith, in particular between dogmatic faith and mystical faith. Dogmatic faith is acceptance of revealed dogmas which are guaranteed by the Church to be infallibly and immutably true. Mystical faith is allegiance to the Church as the witness to, and guardian of, the spiritual and moral order and the educator of humanity. Bremond was not so simple as to suppose that loss of faith is a sudden, clear-cut occurrence or that a man switched overnight from one kind of faith to another. In the modification or changing of faith, as in the process of conversion, there could be many oscillations, many swingings to and fro, many hesitations, before a firm conclusion was reached and the outcome was unmistakable.[2]

Loisy's dogmatic faith had been sapped by 1886, but until 1904 he retained a sincere mystical faith. In 1904, Bremond says, Loisy

had no longer faith, if one means by faith adherence of the mind to revealed dogmas. But he still has faith, if one means by that a profound, suprarational, in a word mystical, adherence of the whole being to the invisible realities of which he still believes the Catholic Church is the

---

[1] See *Un clerc qui n'a pas trahi*, pp. ix, 62.
[2] See *ibid.* p. 48. Cf. E. Amann in *Revue des sciences religieuses*, 1930, p. 684: 'L'expression "foi traditionnelle" est susceptible de multiples interprétations. Le rejet plus ou moins complet, plus ou moins explicite de la "foi traditionnelle" pouvait se concilier avec la croyance à des réalités supérieures et mystérieuses, dont les formules dogmatiques seraient alors considérées comme des symboles, fort inadéquats, sans doute, et dès lors revisable et provisoires, utiles néanmoins et partant dignes d'être conservés.' From a critical review of Rivière's *Le modernisme dans l'Eglise*. See also Bremond's letter of 26 July (1931) to M. D. Petre: BM, Add. MSS, 52380.

principal and the indispensable guardian. He loves the Church. There is no love which does not imply faith, and how much more real and living a faith than that which the theologians define... From the confused block of his original beliefs, all the dogmatic element has disappeared; all the mystical element remains, though it is being more and more shaken.[1]

This seems to be broadly true. There is room for doubt whether when he wrote *L'Evangile et l'Eglise* Loisy did not still have more dogmatic faith left in him than he would afterwards recognize.[2] Maude Petre said that she had 'witnessed in others than Loisy an almost mischievous pleasure in condemning past work which no longer represented their mental attitude.'[3] The testimony of Abbé Félix Klein (1862–1953), who was in close touch with Loisy in those days and who used to accompany him on his walks at Bellevue, should not be disregarded. In his autobiography Klein says that he had no doubt that Loisy retained at that juncture what was essential in the Catholic faith, and that in *Choses passées* and in the *Mémoires* he tended too much to project into the past his subsequent lack of dogmatic faith.[4] This testimony, though less discriminating, is not inconsistent with the distinction that Bremond draws.

A small but noteworthy sign of the sincerity of Loisy's faith at the time of the publication of *L'Evangile et l'Eglise* may be seen in a (surely unpremeditated) remark that he made in the margin of a periodical which is among the books from his library that are now in the Sorbonne. The article in question was by Louis de Lacger who wrote: 'While M. Loisy's Catholic friends regarded him as a defender both of the Gospel and of the Church against the anaemic evangelicalism of liberal protestantism, the author in

---

[1] *Un clerc qui n'a pas trahi*, p. 45.
[2] Cf. J. Lebreton, *Léonce de Grandmaison*, p. 159.
[3] M. D. Petre, *Alfred Loisy*, p. 110.
[4] See F. Klein, *La route du petit Morvandiau: VI. Au début du siècle* (1950), p. 13. Cf. Bonsirven in *Supplément au Dictionnaire de la Bible*, v. 530 f.: 'Gardons-nous ... de prendre au pied de la lettre les jugements que Loisy portait, après vingt et trente ans, sur ses propres attitudes de naguère: ils contredisent des écrits et des affirmations de ces époques et, pourtant, nous ne pouvons l'accuser de duplicité; par ailleurs, les quelques amis et confidents de ces temps lointains, qui demeurent, affirment qu'il a raidi et durci le portait qu'il trace de lui-même après des années de distance, projetant dans le passé les sentiments de l'heure où il écrit.'

his heart of hearts had long ago rejected the Gospel.' Against these words, Loisy noted 'Ah! c'est faux.'[1] Some significance may also be seen perhaps in the fact that in January 1903, i.e. during the commotion that followed the publication of *L'Evangile et l'Eglise*, Loisy ordered a new soutane.[2]

But from 1904 onwards Loisy's Catholic faith, whether dogmatic or mystical, received a series of blows that finally killed it.[3] The most decisive of these blows was struck in March 1904 when in a letter to Pope Pius X he had not only made an act of submission to the condemnation of his books but had offered to give up his lectureship at the Ecole des Hautes Etudes and to suspend the scientific publications that he had in hand. His letter to the pope had begun with the words: 'Most Holy Father, I well know your Holiness's goodness of heart and it is to your heart that I now address myself.' On 12 March he was summoned by Cardinal Richard to hear the pope's reply.

'I have received a letter from the Rev. Abbé Loisy', wrote Pius X, 'in which he appeals to my heart, but this letter was not written from the heart[4]...', and the pope went on to demand an unqualified submission and to urge Loisy to burn what he had adored and to adore what he had burned.[5] In *Choses passées* Loisy described the effect that this letter had upon him.

Something gave way within me when I heard the opening words. The head of this Church to which I had given my life, for which I had worked so hard for thirty years past, which I had loved and could not help loving still, outside of which I had no hopes nor ambitions, could find nothing else to say, when I had responded to absurd demands by a supreme sacrifice, than the harsh words: 'That letter addressed to my heart was not written from the heart.' All the same, it was written from the heart. Pressed into it was the last drop of feeling left in my Catholic soul... And because I asked to be allowed to die peaceably in this

---

[1] See Poulat, *Histoire, dogme et critique*, p. 452.

[2] See Loisy to Mignot, 23 January 1903: BLE, 1966, p. 183.

[3] I.e. except in so far as it revived, or became articulate again, in the last period of his life.

[4] This appears to be how the original Italian words should be understood despite a suggestion to the contrary by Père Lagrange (see his *M. Loisy et le modernisme*, p. 150). Cf. Poulat, *Histoire, dogme et critique*, pp. 253 f.

[5] *Mém.*, ii. 360 f.

Church of my baptism, without being made to lie in order to remain in it, I was treated contemptuously as a false martyr...[1]

Bremond says that he could think of no passage so moving or so crushing as this in either the *Affaires de Rome* of Lamennais or the *Paroles d'un croyant*.[2]

This communication from the pope, more than anything else, snapped the mystical bond that still held Loisy to the Church. A series of further blows hammered the lesson home: the pope's high-handed and stupid mismanagement of the separation of church and state in France, the gross misrepresentation (as it seemed to Loisy) in the papal documents condemning modernism of what the modernists had attempted, the ruthless and disreputable campaign against every form of liberality conducted by the integrists with papal support. Amid these blatant manifestations of what the papacy stood for, Loisy's excommunication in March 1908 and the declaration that he was *vitandus* were a comparatively minor incident which did little more than register a *fait accompli*. Finally, he found Pius X's brutal condemnation of the Sillon in 1910, though it did not affect him personally, even more repulsive than any of the pope's other actions;[3] it put the possibility of any eventual reconciliation with the church entirely out of court.

Bremond brings all this out forcibly and movingly. His readers are left in no manner of doubt about his opinion of what on another occasion he called *Pie-dixisme*.[4] In fact, we already knew what he thought of the régime of Pius X. In his speech at his reception into the Académie française in 1924 he had said: 'I have lived under four pontiffs: Pius IX, Leo XIII, Benedict XV and Pius XI', implying that the reign of Pius X had been so deadly as to be best left unmentioned.[5]

---

[1] *Choses passées*, pp. 295 f.
[2] *Un clerc qui n'a pas trahi*, pp. 49 f.
[3] See Loisy, *L'Eglise et la France*, pp. 94 f. Cf. what Bremond said of himself: 'Pour moi, si j'avais été capable de me révolter contre l'Église, c'était alors que je l'aurais fait, bein que je n'aie jamais été sillonniste'; see M. Martin du Gard, *Henri Bremond* (1927), p. 102. On the condemnation of the Sillon, see pp. 215–18 below.
[4] See Loisy, *Tyrrell et Bremond*, p. 71.
[5] See C. Falconi, *The Popes in the Twentieth Century*, p. 37.

The Enigma Resolved?

Perhaps I should say something about how the *affaire Loisy* was affected by the circumstance that Pius X was pope during its last phase. Since I first wrote on the subject, he has been canonized. He has been the subject of much hagiography. His undoubted piety has been praised. As regards his handling of the modernist movement and analogous policies, Roman Catholics, until recently, have mostly praised that too or, if unable to praise, have held their peace. Nowadays critical studies of Pius X are able to appear,[1] and these are in line with the earlier judgment expressed by Count Carlo Sforza in his book, *Makers of Modern Europe* (1930). That shrewd statesman remarked that it is all very well to admire peasants who get to the top of the ladder, but too often they are tied and bound 'within the narrow confines of their conceptions and traditions'. Whereas 'the prejudices of the aristocrat are often counterbalanced by his scepticism, always by his laziness...those of the peasant have no counterpoise'.[2] Characters of this type, he said, are 'hard on the noblest minds whose doubts and misgivings they do not understand' and 'very often put their whole trust in fanatics who please them with certainties'.[3]

It is clear enough now that Pius X was a peasant pope of this type, just as John XXIII was sensationally different. It is also clear that Pius X was directly responsible for his policies.[4] He is not to be excused as though he were the innocent dupe of Cardinal Merry del Val and his other advisers. Another pope like Leo XIII would surely have dealt with the modernist movement with more diplomatic finesse, but it can hardly be questioned that—in the then condition not only of the curia at Rome but of the Church as a whole and not least of its theological climate—all but the most tepid and unenterprising modernists would sooner or later have been suppressed or reduced to silence. Under Pius X the dénouement came more swiftly and ferociously than it might otherwise have done and, in particular, the 'black terror'

[1] E.g., 'Intransigent Pontificates', by E. E. Y. Hales in *The Tablet*, 9 March 1968, pp. 223 f.   [2] *Op. cit.* p. 122.   [3] *Ibid.* pp. 123 f.
[4] See Falconi, *op. cit.*, p. 53. In particular, the evidence adduced in Poulat's *Intégrisme et catholicisme intégral* (1969) shows conclusively that Pius X actively encouraged the campaign of the integrists with its spying, delations, denunciations, etc.

49

that accompanied and followed the condemnation of the movement was more black than it might otherwise have been. Thus
the fact that Giuseppe Sarto became pope in 1903 did not in
principle affect the inevitable conclusion of Loisy's relations with
the Church. In those days it was not possible for a Roman
Catholic priest to be a thoroughgoing critic in the open, however
much he might wish to be loyal to his vocations as both a priest
and a scholar. Even Père Lagrange—despite his efforts to dissociate himself from the modernists—could not publish his
commentary on the book of Genesis.[1]

The question remains whether Bremond's distinction between
mystical and dogmatic faith in the Church can be held to justify
Loisy's continued profession of Catholicism after the disintegra-
tion of his dogmatic orthodoxy, and also whether a church—
under happier conditions than those that prevailed in the Roman
Catholic Church at the beginning of this century—could reasonably be expected to accept the services of a scholar who wanted to
be free to sit as loose to its traditional teaching as Loisy did. This
is not an historical but a theological or ecclesiological question,
and I step upon its threshold hesitantly and with trepidation.

When I say that Loisy wanted to sit loose to the Church's
traditional teaching, it should be borne in mind that he did not
want to sit as loose at the time of his modernist publications as he
felt entitled to do after his rupture with the Church. In his
modernist days he did not hold what I think must be described
as the somewhat wild and arbitrary opinions in the field of New
Testament criticism to which he later subscribed,[2] nor was he
anything like as doubtful as he subsequently became concerning
how much could be known with assurance about the historical
Jesus.[3] Indeed, his opinions as a modernist about the New

---

[1] See F. M. Braun, *L'œuvre du Père Lagrange*, pp. 109–12. See also the remarks of
Cuthbert Butler quoted in my *20th Century Defenders of the Faith*, pp. 36 f.

[2] See *La naissance du christianisme* (1933), *Remarques sur la litterature épistolaire du
N. T.* (1935), and *Les origines du N. T.* (1936).

[3] But he was always a severe opponent of the Christ-myth theorists: see his *Histoire
et mythe à propos de Jésus-Christ* (1938), and *Autres mythes à propos de la religion*
(1938).

Testament and Christian origins were almost as moderate as
those that have come to be regarded as acceptable by the generality
of English New Testament critics. Even so adverse a judge of
Loisy as Père Jean Levie admitted that he 'wrote, above all in his
Commentary on the Fourth Gospel in 1903, very fine and powerful pages, of which any Catholic exegete could have been proud to
be the author'.[1]

It should be added that, even after his excommunication, he
did not hold some of the opinions that have commonly been
ascribed to him. For example, he did not separate the spheres of
faith and of history, though he distinguished them. In his last
book he wrote: 'I have never said nor professed nor insinuated
that what was not true for history could be certain for faith.'[2]
While he claimed that criticism must have an autonomy *vis-à-vis*
dogma, he did not claim that criticism could be purely objective.[3]
He did not repudiate the idea of ecclesiastical authority but held
that its proper function was educative.[4] He did not deny the
possibility of miracle, though he preferred to speak of 'mystery'.[5]

No: the real question about the sufficiency of Loisy's faith as a
modernist is whether his metaphysical agnosticism and his lack
of a firm and positive christology were tolerable in a priest. In
1892 he wrote in his journal: 'Do not embarrass yourself with
metaphysical questions. The Eternal told Job the truth about
these discussions: man had not made the world and does not
know what is at the bottom of it.'[6] Metaphysical agnosticism or
a sense of metaphysical incompetence or a lack of metaphysical
curiosity may be largely a matter of temperament or caste of

---

[1] J. Levie, *Sous les yeux de l'incroyant*, p. 205.
[2] *Un mythe apologétique*, p. 138.
[3] See Poulat, *Histoire, dogme et critique*, pp. 343, 429, 522; Loisy, *Tyrrell et Bremond*,
p. 57: 'L'historien n'est objectif que dans la mesure où il connait et comprend
exactement les témoignages, et aussi compte tenu des principes généraux, quels
qu'ils soient, d'après lesquels il croit pouvoir et devoir interpréter les faits constatés.'
See also *Un mythe apologétique*, p. 99: 'Renan a dit quelque part que l'on ne
pratique pas la critique "à genoux". Ce n'est pas avec des génuflexions qu'on
résoudra les questions d'authenticité, d'historicité, d'interprétation littérale, que
posent les écrits bibliques.'
[4] See *Tyrrell et Bremond*, p. 183.
[5] See *Un mythe apologétique*, pp. 26, 39, 168.
[6] *Mém.*, i. 209.

mind.[1] 'Let us seek to fathom those things that are fathomable', said Goethe, 'and reserve those things which are unfathomable for reverence in quietude.'[2]

Here are two lay examples. It is said that Sidney and Beatrice Webb 'never discussed religion because it bored Sidney. In his view, you might as well talk about what train to take without being in possession of a time-table.'[3] A less crude and philistine, and a more refined, example of a similar caste of mind can be seen in a distant contemporary of Sidney Webb. In one of his essays Max Beerbohm wrote:

Tell me of a man or a woman, a place or an event, real or fictitious: surely you will find me a fairly intelligent listener. Any such narrative will present to me some image, and you will stir me to not altogether fatuous thoughts...But if you are by way of weaving theories as to the nature of things in general, and if you want to try those theories on some one who will luminously confirm them or powerfully rend them, I must, with a hang-dog air, warn you that I am not your man. I suffer from a strong suspicion that things in general cannot be accounted for through any formula or set of formulae, and that any one philosophy, howsoever new, is no better than another...[4]

Except for the last clause, Loisy might have written that. I say 'except for the last clause', since he had a religious philosophy of his own which he developed after his rupture with the Church.[5] He attached much importance to it, as did some of his friends, notably Henri Bremond[6] and Maude Petre.[7] It does not directly concern us now, since we are inquiring into Loisy's state of mind during the modernist movement.

It is not enough to say that his metaphysical agnosticism was a matter of temperament and to leave it at that. Indeed, he had more to say on the subject himself, especially in the last book he wrote,

---

[1] Bremond habitually said: 'Je ne comprends pas les philosophes.' See BLE, July to September 1968, pp. 179 f.
[2] Quoted in *The Soldier's Armoury, January to June 1969*, p. 28.
[3] K. Muggeridge and R. Adam, *Beatrice Webb* (1967), p. 162.
[4] Max Beerbohm, *And Even Now* (1920), p. 304.
[5] See his books *La Religion, La morale humaine, Religion et humanité*, and *La crise morale du temps présent et l'éducation humaine*.
[6] See *Tyrrell et Bremond*.
[7] See M. D. Petre, *Alfred Loisy: his religious significance*.

Un mythe apologétique, which was a commentary on criticisms that Jean Guitton had made of his modernist views. Although at the time of *L'Evangile et l'Eglise* he could no longer subscribe *ex animo* to the traditional theistic and christological formulas, he could still speak of 'the living and true God'.[1] Reiterating what he had believed at that time and still believed, he said that 'God is the eternal mystery, above all definition, and whom one belittles if you declare that he is like man'.[2] 'God...is, before everything and above all, a mystery that transcends us. And to claim to express in human language the last word about him is in effect to blaspheme or to deny him.'[3] 'The existence of God was not called in question either in my thought or in my book' [*L'Evangile et l'Eglise*].[4] 'I have not denied the transcendence of God.'[5] Perhaps his agnosticism had more reverence in it, and even more faith, than the confident dogmatism of those who condemned him.[6]

As regards christology, he said that *L'Evangile et l'Eglise* did not deny 'tout rapport de Jésus-Christ avec la Divinité'.[7] 'I expressed no doubt about the dogma [of the divinity of Jesus Christ]; but, in speaking of Jesus, I could not represent him as if he had been God preaching publicly in Galilee and at Jerusalem, and dying on the cross.'[8] '*L'Evangile et l'Eglise* raised the historical question of Christian origins, without laying claim to a definitive

---

[1] *Un mythe apologétique*, p. 35.

[2] *Ibid.* p. 56.

[3] *Ibid.* p. 125; cf. p. 154.

[4] *Ibid.* p. 119.

[5] *Ibid.* p. 143. On 29 September 1917 he had written to Miss Petre: 'Certainly I believe in the transcendent, in the ideal and its reality, as something other in itself than humanity. But I abstain from defining this otherness, and I have endeavoured to construct my moral religion without metaphysics, without an explicit doctrine of that transcendence that escapes us, though we do not escape it.' M. D. Petre, *Alfred Loisy*, p. 83; cf. p. 89. In the expression 'the religion of humanity' which Loisy was fond of using, the genitive was subjective, not objective. See *Entretiens*, p. 235; Boyer de Sainte Suzanne, *Alfred Loisy*, pp. 133–40.

[6] Cf. Vincent Bourne, *La queste de vérité d'Irénée Winnaert* (1966), p. 39: 'Rome n'a discerné dans l'agnosticisme des modernistes l'intuition maladroite mais profondément juste de Dieu indéfinissable, impalpable, toute définition le limitant et le diminuant.'

[7] Loisy, *Un mythe apologétique*, p. 45.

[8] *Ibid.* p. 119.

solution of the religious problem.'[1] More weighty than these later testimonies is a long letter that Loisy wrote, on 29 December 1902, i.e. shortly after the publication of *L'Evangile et l'Eglise*, to a priest who had questioned him about his christology. In the course of this letter he said:

Jesus is more God than the Council of Nicaea said, and he is more really present and active in the eucharist than the Council of Trent said...Either I am quite mistaken about the final result of historical research regarding Christian origins, or the outcome will be a more real, intimate and profound conception of the divinity of Christ and of his vivifying action, not the evacuation of the Catholic dogmas.[2]

If Loisy refused to be more definite, that was partly in reaction from the over-presumptuous definitions of the scholastic theology—what Edmund Bishop called 'the Catholic "Intellectual System of the Universe"—the great intellectual system elaborated by the theologians', which, in Bishop's view as in Loisy's, was quite a different matter from Catholicity as a religion.[3] At a time when traditional theological concepts could no longer be treated as absolute or final by anyone who had become aware of their inevitable relativity, and when they needed to be reconsidered and reinterpreted, Loisy's reticence or suspense of judgment was not only creditable in itself but consistent with his intellectual integrity and continued allegiance to the Church. He still believed that the Church had a unique mission for the moral and spiritual education and guidance of humanity, whatever might be the future of its more speculative or metaphysical doctrines. This attitude may be described as pragmatic, but it was one that was perfectly respectable in a scholar who confessed his metaphysical incompetence and speculative agnosticism.

While in retrospect it is obvious that the Roman Catholic Church under Pius X could not be expected to acquiesce in such a position, it is arguable that a church ought to be able to retain the

---

[1] Loisy, *Un mythe apologétique*, p. 139.
[2] See the whole letter which is reproduced in Laberthonnière, *La notion chrétienne de l'autorité*, pp. 229 ff. Part of the letter is quoted in Boyer, p. 71, where by a slip it is dated 1907, instead of 1902.
[3] See N. Abercrombie, *The Life and Work of Edmund Bishop*, p. 376; cf. ch. 6 below.

services of scholars, or indeed of others of its members, who, while wanting to continue to serve it, confess to varying degrees of doubt about its professed doctrines. In periods of intellectual ferment and theological transition ecclesiastical authorities should bear in mind that the most mentally active and spiritually sensitive churchmen are likely not only to experience unsettlement and perplexity, but also to oscillate between faith and doubt and between doubt and faith. Loisy acknowledged that there were always fluctuations in his thought,[1] and he never claimed to have a rounded, finished system of beliefs. In 1900 he wrote to von Hügel, 'I distrust systems, because they are all false, and I prefer that in my writings there should be found only fragments of truth, without that logical continuity which is generally achieved only by getting away from facts and by looking at only one side of a question.'[2] Ought not a church to be able to provide a home and a persistent welcome for such minds as this? I would go further and say that a church should be careful not to drive its priests, when they are wrestling with the problems of belief, into a position of isolation, nor to deprive them of opportunities of pastoral responsibility, which is what was done to Loisy.[3]

When seeking to resolve the enigma that is presented by Loisy's career as a modernist, one has in the end to make a broad choice between his own autobiographical testimonies and the portrait of a tactician who practised duplicity that is displayed by Houtin and Sartiaux in their *Vie de Loisy*. My own conclusion is that Loisy's account of himself has not been seriously discredited, and I regard Mgr Mignot, Henri Bremond and Miss Petre as much better judges of his character than Houtin, Sartiaux and their followers. I had drafted this chapter before M. Raymond de Boyer de Sainte Suzanne, who knew Loisy well from 1917 onwards, kindly sent me his book, *Alfred Loisy entre la foi et l'incroyance* (1968). It provides stronger support for the

---

[1] See *Un mythe apologétique*, p. 124.
[2] See *Mém.*, i. 550.
[3] See the remarks of Abbé Louis Venard that are quoted in Poulat, *Histoire, dogme et critique*, pp. 312 ff. Cf. Duchesne's letter to Marcel Hébert that is quoted in Houtin, *Marcel Hébert*, p. 130.

conclusion that I had reached than anything that I could myself say.

As a pendant to this chapter I want to introduce Joseph Turmel, a priest and a savant who on the face of it did certainly practice the duplicity of which Loisy has been accused and whose case therefore affords a standard of comparison. Moreover, the fact that Sartiaux[1] preferred Turmel's conduct *vis-à-vis* the Church to Loisy's seems to me to put further in question the respect that one can have for his judgment.

I did not even mention Turmel in *The Modernist Movement in the Roman Church*, because I did not look upon him as a modernist. But Rivière, in *Le modernisme dans l'Eglise*, had a chapter about him, entitled 'Offensive contre le modernisme masque',[2] though at the time when he published his book—1929—the process of unmasking Turmel had, as we shall see, not yet reached its culmination. Since Turmel is still classified as a modernist by reputable authors[3] and was in any case mixed up with the movement, and since his story appears to be scarcely known in England, a brief explanation of it may be useful. It is an ecclesiastical curiosity of the first order.

Joseph Turmel was born at Rennes on 13 December 1859 of very poor parents, neither of whom could write. His home, though poor, was very pious. One of the clergy of the parish spotted the boy's ability and saw to his education. As in the case of a number of other French priests who were involved in the modernist movement,[4] this pious upbringing, this dependence on

---

[1] See his book, *Joseph Turmel, prêtre, historien des dogmes* (1931). Though Sartiaux disclaims making a *moral* judgment of Turmel's conduct, he leaves his readers in no doubt where his moral preference rested. Sartiaux's narration of the facts is not in question, and is borne out by Turmel's subsequently published autobiographical works: *Comment j'ai donné congé aux dogmes* (1935) and *Comment l'Eglise romaine m'a donné congé* (n.d.).

[2] *Op. cit.* pp. 484–505.

[3] E.g., F. Heiler, *Alfred Loisy, Der Vater des katholischen Modernismus* (1947), p. 125; E. Poulat, see p. 20 above. G. Philips writes of 'les modernistes, Turmel en particulier' in *Jean Rivière, bibliographie et souvenirs* (1952), p. 43.

[4] E.g. Houtin (see p. 24 above), Alfaric (see p. 76 below), Hébert (see p. 64 below), and to some extent Loisy. Cf. Vincent Bourne, *La queste de vérité d'Irénée Winnaert*, p. 27.

the Church for pastoral care, and this indebtedness to the Church for educational opportunity, should be borne in mind when one seeks to understand their subsequent love–hate relationship to the Church that mothered them. Paul Sabatier, at the end of his book, *France To-day: its religious orientation* (E. T., 1913), makes some perceptive remarks that bear on this point:

The Catholic says to God, 'Our Father', but when he speaks of the Church he says, 'Our Mother'; and it is she whom, from his first glance, he sees leaning over his cradle; she who teaches him to lisp the name of the Heavenly Father. The Communion of the Catholic with the Church is not the result of an act of will, or of reasoning, it is the initial fact of his moral life. He believes in her as naturally as the new-born babe believes in his mother. The Church takes possession of his soul so quickly and entirely that, in his experience, the Church and his soul are not merely inseparable, but, in a sense, they have one and the same being.[1]

Anyhow, Turmel grew up in the odour of sanctity. He became an immensely industrious student of theology. At one stage in his preparation for ordination he was a pupil of Père Louis Billot, s.j. The original motive of Turmel's intellectual industry was that he might be well qualified to defend the faith and to confound unbelievers. He was ordained priest in 1882 and was appointed to the chair of dogmatic theology at the diocesan seminary at Rennes. Within two years his faith was gravely disturbed by his study of the Old Testament. He soon came to the conclusion that the official teaching of the Church about, for example, the Pentateuch and the book of Daniel was false, and the realization of this deception led him to doubt more and more of what he had been taught until, as he says, on 18 March 1886 he became aware that he had entirely lost his faith in the Church's dogmas. He at once gave up saying the breviary offices, and he never again prayed in private.

But what about his future? No alternative profession was open to him. He decided to remain in the Church and in the priesthood and to go on supplying the cultus, while keeping his loss of faith

[1] *Op. cit.* p. 298.

entirely to himself. He justified himself on the ground that the Church had deceived him by imposing upon him its false doctrines when he was not in a position to see through them, and therefore he was now entitled to deceive the Church in his turn by concealing his infidelity. Moreover, if he left the Church he would bring incalculable suffering upon his pious parents and upon the priest who had been his principal benefactor. If he remained, only he himself would have to suffer. So he writes in his autobiography: 'Having decided to remain in the Church, I did not have to make any change in my manner of life. Nothing was modified, except that henceforth I had two more hours a day for study which had previously been taken up with pious exercises.'[1]

This initial decision was heavy with consequences that could not have been foreseen at the outset. Turmel went on both with the discharge of his professorial duties and with his intense and dedicated study of dogmatics, especially of the early history of Christian doctrine. All seemed to go smoothly until 1892 when he failed to prevent himself from imparting to a young priest, to whom he was teaching Hebrew, his critical and heretical views about the composition of the Pentateuch. The information came to the knowledge of the Superior of the Seminary and led to Turmel's being deprived of his professorship. His books were taken from him and most of his papers were burned.

After little more than a year his books were returned to him when he was appointed Chaplain to the Little Sisters of the Poor in Rennes. He now settled on the manner of life that he was to follow henceforth. He said mass and heard confessions for the women to whom he ministered, but he never preached[2] or taught the catechism. All the rest of his time he devoted to study and he became one of the most erudite patristic scholars of the time. He decided to keep himself to himself and his existence was virtually eremitical. He hardly ever left Rennes or took any relaxation from labour of the mind.

[1] *Comment j'ai donné congé aux dogmes*, p. 48.
[2] In fact, Turmel, like Houtin (see p. 24 above), never preached a sermon in his life: see Sartiaux, *Joseph Turmel*, p. 240.

He was soon publishing articles about the history of dogmatic theology in learned journals.[1] In the early days his writings were less obviously subversive of traditional orthodoxy than they became eventually. Generally speaking, they had the effect of showing that the origins and history of Catholic dogmas were quite different from what was officially alleged. In 1904, although by then he had been attacked and denounced to the Holy Office and warned that his writings should have the *imprimatur*, he was able to publish the first volume of a *History of Positive Theology* that he had written at the request of the Jesuits of the Institut Catholique in Paris. By this time he was already publishing pseudonymous articles as well.

A crisis came when he contributed in 1906–7 two series of pseudonymous articles to the *Revue d'histoire et de littérature religieuses*: one was on 'The dogma of the Trinity in the first three centuries' by 'Antoine Dupin' and the other on 'The Holy Virgin in history' by 'Guillaume Herzog'.[2] When George Tyrrell read the article on 'La conception virginale du Christ' in the issue for March–April 1907, he wrote to A. L. Lilley: 'The art. in the *Rev. d'Hist. et Lit. Rel.* on the Virgn Birth is a plain bid for excommunication. If they stand that, they are mad. I expect it means that the Review is bankrupt and wants to die gloriously.'[3] The articles were not a bid for excommunication, as will appear, but they were violently attacked as heterodox and led to the condemnation in May 1907 of the *Revue* in which they had been published and to which Loisy was the chief contributor.

Unfortunately for Turmel, he had made use in these pseudonymous articles of some material that he had previously published elsewhere over his own name. An observant divine of the Institut Catholique de Toulouse[4] detected what he publicly asserted to be a plagiarism, but with the evident implication that Dupin and Herzog were really Turmel. A heated controversy arose which was apparently terminated when, on 30 May 1908, Turmel wrote

---

[1] For a complete bibliography of Turmel's writings up to 1930: see Sartiaux, *op. cit.* pp. 269–85.

[2] The articles were also published separately as brochures.

[3] G. Tyrrell to A. L. Lilley, 29 May 1907: LP.

[4] Louis Saltet (1878–1952). He was professor of ecclesiastical history.

a letter to the archbishop of Rennes in which he not only denied categorically that he was Herzog or Dupin or knew anything about them, but went on to make the following declaration:

As a Catholic priest, I profess all that the Roman Church professes and reject all that she rejects.

As an affectionate and devoted son of the Virgin Mary, I believe in her Immaculate Conception, in her perfect and perpetual virginity, in her divine maternity; in a word, I adhere, so far as the mother of God is concerned, to the complete doctrine of the Holy Church.[1]

This thumping lie[2] put a stop to the controversy, and in due course Turmel took the anti-modernist oath.[3]

But it was not the end of the matter. While from 1908 the name of Turmel disappeared and he might have been dead so far as literary production went, he was not in truth inactive. A number of hitherto unknown authors soon began to make their appearance in theological journals[4] and later on in the rationalistic series of books, entitled 'Christianisme', edited by Dr P. L. Couchoud (1879–1959) who was an apostle of the Christ-myth theory,[5] and published by F. Rieder et Cie.[6] In the end this team of new writers numbered fourteen, for Turmel used as many pseudonyms as that.

By these means he gave his would-be discoverers plenty of employment for their detective capacities. Not until 1928–30 did they succeed in bringing things to a head. By that time they had got hold of two decisive clues.

---

[1] For the full text of this letter, see Houtin, *Histoire du modernisme catholique*, pp. 399 f.; Sartiaux, *Joseph Turmel*, pp. 87 f.; Turmel, *Comment l'Eglise romaine m'a donné congé*, p. 31.

[2] When in 1859 the authorship of *Adam Bede* was still unknown and George Eliot wanted to keep it secret, G. H. Lewes wrote to John Chapman, who had his suspicions: 'Mrs Lewes . . . authorizes me to state, as distinctly as language can do so, that she is not the author of "Adam Bede".' See G. S. Haight, *George Eliot: a biography* (1968), p. 270. A good question for a student of morals would be: were these two lies equally culpable or equally excusable or what ethical difference was there between them?

[3] See Houtin, *op. cit.* p. 401.

[4] *Revue d'histoire et de littérature religieuses* and *Revue de l'histoire des religions*: see Sartiaux, *op. cit.* pp. 278–81.

[5] See Loisy, *Histoire et mythe à propos de Jésus-Christ.*

[6] In 1926 I read *Le Quatrième Evangile* by Henri Delafosse (= Turmel) in this series without of course knowing who the author was.

On the one hand, when Abbé Paul Lejay, the eminent latinist and professor of the Institut Catholique in Paris, died suddenly in 1920, he had not secured his correspondence and papers from misappropriation. They were in the event appropriated by the ecclesiastical authorities.[1] They are said to have revealed that, although his priestly conduct had been outwardly correct and he had never published anything that disclosed his religious opinions, Lejay had in fact been without faith. However that may be, he had, as editorial secretary of the *Revue d'histoire et de littérature religieuses*, certainly maintained a correspondence with Turmel, and thus a postcard written by Turmel to Lejay in 1907 came to light,[2] which proved that Turmel had indeed been Dupin and Herzog. On the other hand, an opportunity came of comparing the handwriting of Turmel with that of one of his later pseudonyms (Gallerand),[3] and they were shown to be identical.

These clues led to the unmasking of Turmel. He attempted to make such a submission to the archbishop of Rennes[4] as would enable him to go on ministering the sacraments to his little flock of faithful women, but it was in vain. Rome was determined on his condemnation, and he was excommunicated and declared to be *vitandus* on 6 November 1930. Thenceforward he could publish his work over his own signature once more, which he continued to do until his death in 1943.

Though Turmel certainly became involved in the modernist movement, I would not myself describe him as a modernist since at no time did he hope or work for a modernizing of catholicism or believe in its possibility. I am inclined to agree with Jean Steinmann that the case of Turmel must be diagnosed as one of 'a sort of morbid schizophrenia',[5] and I am unable to follow anyone who, like Sartiaux, regards his conduct as more commend-

---

[1] See Rivière, *Le modernisme dans l'Eglise*, p. 502; Loisy, *Mém.*, iii. 559; Sartiaux, *Joseph Turmel*, pp. 144–51; Alfaric, *De la foi à la raison*, pp. 91, 128.

[2] This whole affair is treated at length by Sartiaux in *Joseph Turmel* and by Turmel himself in *Comment l'Eglise romaine m'a donné congé*.

[3] 'Hippolyte Gallerand' was the author of articles on the history of the doctrine of redemption.

[4] Cardinal Charost (b. 1860), who died suddenly on 7 November 1930.

[5] Steinmann, *Friedrich von Hügel* (1962), p. 138.

able than that of Loisy. In the final analysis it would seem to be a subject for neither commendation nor condemnation but for compassion. Loisy commented in his *Mémoires*: 'Turmel's case ... shows under what strange conditions a learned priest can manage to live—if you can call it that—in the Roman Church.'[1] After his excommunication Turmel wrote to Loisy:

The blow with which Rome reckons to have crushed me can make no change in my manner of life which, for many years, has been that of a hermit who goes out only once a week to the library (and hitherto each morning to say mass)...

Rome is causing horrible suffering to the simple souls of my entourage. That is what is embittering my life and is going to embitter it for many long months. At my age one does not move house or even renew one's linen. I am keeping my house with its modest garden, I continue to wear the soutane, I remain Abbé Turmel. (I even say mass on Sundays to reassure my housekeeper who otherwise would become crazed.)[2]

[1] *Mém.*, iii. 31.
[2] Turmel to Loisy, 16 November 1930: BN, n.a.f. 15662.

4

FRENCH MODERNISTS
TO THE LEFT AND RIGHT

I

Marcel Hébert[1] seems to have had the most attractive personality of all the modernists. He had good looks, a fine presence, and charm of manner. He had wide cultural interests—in art, history and natural science as well as in philosophy and theology—and he was an engaging conversationalist. Testimonies abound to the hold he had on those who were influenced by him. For over twenty years after his death in 1916 his former pupils used to meet annually to commemorate him.[2] Not even Albert Houtin, his biographer, could find anything malicious to say about him.

If Hébert has not had a conspicuous place in reminiscences of, or in books about, the modernist movement, that is not because there is any doubt about his having been a modernist, but for other reasons. In the first place, his own personal crisis came to a head earlier than that of any of the others. He had already broken with the Church and was, so to speak, out of the way before the movement approached its climax. Then, secondly, although M. Poulat rightly describes Hébert as one of the philosophers of modernism,[3] his system of beliefs as a modernist was peculiar to himself and the writings in which he set it forth were not much read. The influence he exercised was personal, not literary. Thirdly, though he was intellectually able, lively and stimulating, it was as an educationalist, not as a scholar or author, that he excelled, and his theological ideas are of lighter weight than those

[1] On Hébert see A. Houtin, *Marcel Hébert* (1925); J. Rivière, *Le modernisme dans l'Eglise*, pp. 140–53; R. Marlé, *Au cœur de la crise moderniste*, pp. 323–38; Poulat, *Histoire, dogme et critique*, pp. 318–26; J. Steinmann, *Friedrich von Hügel*, pp. 125–36. Except where otherwise stated, I depend on Houtin for information.
[2] See Poulat, *op. cit.* p. 319; cf. Frémont, i. 352.
[3] See p. 20 above.

of the better known modernists.[1] On the other hand, perhaps because of their comparative naivety or immaturity, they constitute a significant expression of the modernist movement which, after all, was never allowed to come to a mature development, and, as Rivière said,[2] he was a 'specimen of modernist psychology'.

Hébert was born in 1851 in modest circumstances at Bar-le-Duc in Lorraine.[3] His father died in the following year. His mother, like Hannah, appears to have given her son to the Lord even before his birth, and the boy himself always wanted to be a priest. Like other future modernist priests of humble origins, he showed brilliant promise at school—a school conducted by Marist fathers. After graduating he did not go on directly to a seminary, partly because his health was poor, and partly because the opposition of an uncle, upon whom he much depended, had to be overcome.

It was in December 1871 that he went to Issy to spend two years in the study of philosophy before going on for theology to the seminary of Saint Sulpice in Paris. Hébert was in fact dispensed from one year at Issy since he had been studying philosophy previously and had better qualifications than most of his fellow-entrants. He was influenced there by a young and enthusiastic professor who enrolled him among the disciples of St Thomas Aquinas.

When he joined the seminary in Paris at the end of 1872, he formed a close and lasting friendship with L. A. Amette (1850–1920), the future archbishop of Paris—a friendship, incidentally, which occasioned some of the attacks on Cardinal Amette's orthodoxy during what have been called 'the dog-days of integrism'.[4] It was of more consequence that at Saint Sulpice Hébert

---

[1] In 1900 von Hügel wrote to Wilfrid Ward: 'I go on liking and admiring Hébert's character and general influence so much; but do not feel he can really compare with Blondel or Laberthonnière for depth and patience of views.' See Maisie Ward, *The Wilfrid Wards and the Transition*, i. 331.

[2] Rivière, *op. cit.* p. 580.

[3] He bequeathed his papers to the municipal library at Bar-le-Duc: see Poulat, *op. cit.* p. 35.

[4] See A. Blanchet, *Histoire d'une mise à l'index* (1967), pp. 119 f.

came under the liberalizing influence of J. B. Hogan (1829–1901), the Irishman who, after 32 years as a professor in Paris, was sent in 1884 to the U.S.A. for the remainder of his life. The character of his teaching comes across in his book *Clerical Studies*, published in 1898. But, as was to be the case with Hébert himself, his influence was exercised chiefly through the impression that he made on his pupils, who included a number of other future participants in the modernist movement.[1] Hogan kept in touch with them as long as he lived. Six days before his death in 1901 Hébert lunched with him.[2] It was Hogan who weaned Hébert from his zest for thomism and made him realize the importance of history and psychology.

After his ordination to the priesthood in 1876 Hébert was an assistant curate in a rural parish near Orleans for two or three years; then in 1879 he joined the staff of the Ecole Fénelon in Paris. This was a school that provided a Catholic education for the sons of the well-to-do bourgeoisie who were attending the lycées. From 1880 to 1891 Hébert was in charge of the junior boys; from 1891 to 1895 he taught philosophy to the seniors; and in 1895 he became Director, i.e. head, of the institution.

Soon after he settled in Paris, he got to know Duchesne, and a close friendship sprang up between them. From 1880 he was a contributor to Duchesne's review, the *Bulletin critique*, and in other ways he supported Duchesne in the difficulties that he was experiencing in seeking to promote critical methods of historical study. For instance, in 1885 Duchesne wrote to Hébert: 'I want you to know that there is no one whose friendship is to me more delightful and helpful than yours. You have such a fine spirit and so noble a heart, and there are so many preoccupations that we have in common.'[3]

In a review in the *Bulletin critique* in 1881 Hébert had said that 'Kant has the great distinction of giving to philosophic minds a

---

[1] Notably, Maurice d'Hulst (1841–96) [Rector of the Institut Catholique in Paris: see MMRC, pp. 80–7]; E. I. Mignot (1842–1917) [Archbishop of Albi]; Lucien Lacroix (1854–1922) [Bishop of Tarentaise]; and Félix Klein (1862–1953) [see p. 46 above].
[2] See E. J. Dillon (who was also present) to Loisy, 24 April 1902: BN, n.a.f. 15652.
[3] See Houtin, *Hébert*, p. 55.

powerful impulsion'. The archbishop of Paris was disturbed by such a statement and called upon Duchesne to keep a watch on his collaborators. Duchesne told Hébert that he himself knew little about Kant. When Hébert explained his position, Duchesne merely smiled and said, 'If that is the case, then I too am a Kantian.'[1]

Unlike Loisy and others, Hébert came to a modernist attitude through his study of philosophy, though he soon also accepted the critical approach to the Bible. In 1885 Mgr d'Hulst invited him to join the Society of St Thomas Aquinas which had recently been founded at the Institut Catholique. When sending the invitation, d'Hulst explained that he did not want the Society to be confined to thomists or to be tied to thomism. 'I am inviting you [he wrote], whose orthodoxy is so questionable, because you will instruct us, because you will contradict us, because you will convert us, unless you let yourself be perverted.'[2] In November 1885 Hébert read a paper to the Society on 'Thomism and Kantianism' in which he claimed that Kant had made important advances on St Thomas in regard to the problems of knowledge.

From 1882 onwards Hébert's attachment to traditional orthodoxy was being undermined. He found the traditional attempts to account for the problem of evil unconvincing. Kant's rejection of the traditional proofs of the existence of God deeply impressed him. An idealist and evolutionary philosophy increasingly appealed to him. However, he still believed in the physical resurrection of Jesus. It was Duchesne who, some time before 1894, pointed out to Hébert the contradictions in the testimonies to the resurrection and so caused him to admit their legendary character. By this time Hébert had conceived the idea of treating Christian doctrines and affirmations as symbols which should be regarded as metaphors or allegories, not as prosaic statements of fact.

In 1893 he published in the *Annales de philosophie chrétienne* an imaginary conversation between Plato and Darwin in which this idea is expressed though in so cloudy a manner that it passed

---

[1] See Houtin, *Hébert*, p. 54.
[2] *Ibid.* p. 73.

without unfavourable comment. Darwin is represented as saying that the commonest fault of the pious souls who had been upset by his writings had been

the taking literally the metaphors and symbols of our sacred books. The Oriental style misled certain minds inclined to seek before all things scientific rigour, or too much accustomed to logical formalism. They failed to distinguish between parable and history; they thought they saw astronomical and geological theses in pages destined to develop the religious and moral life of the soul.[1]

Then Plato is made to say: 'Darwin, do you not realise how small an influence is exercised, in the present stage of our evolution, by pure ideas? Myths and allegories are necessary, not only to slaves and to the people, but to philosophers and men of science...'[2]

And at the end Hébert himself, who imagined he was hearing high mass in the Duomo at Pisa, concludes:

I listened, and I heard these words:—

> Sub diversis speciebus,
> Signis tantum et non rebus,
> Latent res eximiae!

I started. It was a complete expression of my own thoughts. Appearances, signs, symbols, which veil the mysterious reality, but which nevertheless adapt us to it, so that it penetrates us and makes us live—is not this one of the essential elements of all faith and of all philosophy?[3]

This article was translated into English by the Hon. William Gibson (Lord Ashbourne) and published in book form in 1899. In an introduction Gibson pointed out that Hébert's adoption of the symbolical interpretation of dogmas preceded by several years the publication of Auguste Sabatier's *Esquisse d'une philosophie de la religion d'après la psychologie et l'histoire* (1897), and therefore was not dependent on, or derived from, it. As regards his new symbolist position, Hébert wrote to Hogan in February 1893: 'I am thankful to say I have come through this

---

[1] *Plato and Darwin* (Eng. trans.), p. 20.
[2] *Ibid.* p. 57.
[3] *Ibid.* p. 72.

crisis, in which so many others have foundered, with a creed of which only the formulas have been slightly modified, but of which all that is fundamental stands.'[1]

How far that is true will appear if I quote a 'profession de foi du Vicaire Savoyard' which Hébert wrote, but did not publish, in 1894. It is a characteristic expression of the ideas that he was to embody in his published writings during his modernist period.

I believe in the objective value of the idea of God, of an absolute Ideal, perfect, distinct, without thereby being separated from the world which he draws and directs towards what is Best, principle of all physical and moral phenomena, *raison d'être* of human reason and conscience, one and threefold, for he can be called: infinite activity, intelligence and love.

And in Him in whom has been realized to an exceptional and unique degree the union of the Divine with human nature, who was aware of this intimate union and expressed it by his words and deeds, so becoming our Master and model, Jesus Christ—whose dazzling superiority so impressed the hearts of the simple that it was for them symbolized by a supernatural conception in the womb of a creature who combines the two ideal glories of woman: maternity and virginity;—who suffered under Pontius Pilate, was crucified and buried;—whose powerful action after death, persisting in this world in men's consciousness, determined in the minds of the apostles and disciples the visions and apparitions that are recorded in the gospels, and has been symbolized by the myth of a liberating descent into hell and an ascension towards the higher regions of Heaven represented in the naive imaginations of the first believers as a glorious abode situated above the clouds, where Jesus has gone up to sit at the right hand of the Father whence he will descend to judge the living and the dead.

I believe in the Spirit of love...who vivifies our souls, draws and impels us towards all that is true, beautiful and good, divine flame of Charity who alone can destroy the egotism of this world.—I believe in the holy universal Church, the visible expression of the ideal communion between all beings, of the unity which must gradually be realized by justice and charity; in the remission of sins for every soul that is penitent and of good will; I believe in the survival of what constitutes

[1] Houtin, *Hébert*, p. 92.

our moral personality, in the eternal life that already exists in every soul who is living a life above the physical level and that develops in conditions that transcend our present knowledge and that the popular imagination has symbolized by the resurrection of the flesh and eternal felicity.[1]

I must say that this 'profession of faith', like other things that Hébert wrote, illustrates Vincent Bourne's remark[2] that the religious language used at the end of the nineteenth century was 'singularly flat and colourless'.

Although by 1895 suspicions about Hébert's orthodoxy were current, no objections were raised when in that year he was appointed Director of the Ecole Fénelon. They may have been disarmed by the charm of his personality and by his popularity as a schoolmaster. He was able to continue working out his symbolist teaching in discussion with his friends and with his more questioning or responsive pupils. It was for the benefit of some of the latter that in 1899 after a visit to Italy, he composed a dialogue, entitled 'Souvenirs of Assisi'.

A young man, who is unsettled in his faith and tempted to leave the Church, visits the tomb of St Francis and converses with an old capuchin friar. The friar is not only indulgent to the doubts which the young man urges about the resurrection of Christ and the personality of God, but himself propounds views that go beyond what Hébert had said in his 'profession de foi d'un vicaire savoyard'. He tells the young man that those who are tempted to break with the Church fail to distinguish between its underlying Idea and its relative transitory appearances. 'Give this great human-divine organism time', he says, 'to eliminate certain elements that it had assimilated but are now valueless... Then at last the reconciliation of religion and science will be affected, because their reciprocal functions will be clearly understood...' 'The more humanity progresses, the more it will be understood that the Gospel [and] the Church are no longer machines for the distribution of ready-made truth and moral power, but provi-

[1] *Ibid.* pp. 91 f.
[2] In his book *La queste de vérité d'Irénée Winnaert* (1966), p. 30.

dential aids that are calculated to help and stimulate the individual in his continual striving towards the Good.'[1]

This dialogue was printed anonymously and for private circulation only.[2] Before dealing with its subsequent fate, I would observe that a more accessible and more striking revelation of Hébert's private teaching at this time, with which he sought to retain intelligent young men in the Church, is to be found in Roger Martin du Gard's novel *Jean Barois*. Martin du Gard was a pupil of Hébert at the Ecole Fénelon and always remained greatly attached to him, not least during the period when he was writing this book.[3] Abbé Schertz in *Jean Barois* is Hébert,[4] and in the chapter entitled 'Le compromis symboliste' he is seeking to commend Hébert's ideas to Jean who was troubled by the apparent incompatability between traditional Catholicism and contemporary science. Thus Jean says: 'Objections pile up around me; almost every day I encounter a new one! I have had to acknowledge, whether I like it or not, that there is not a single point of Catholic doctrine that does not today meet with innumerable contradictions...' Schertz-Hébert then explains how, when he himself had to face these problems, his faith underwent a salutary transformation.

I would say: for you, for me, and for a great number of our contemporaries...personal faith is intact. It is dogmatic belief that has been upset. We can do nothing with it. Roman religion, as it is at present fixed, is unacceptable for many cultured minds and for all minds whose knowledge is at all profound. The God whom they offer us is too pettily human: today, belief in a personal God, in a monarchical God, in a God who fabricates the universe, belief in sin and hell...ah, no! That religion is no longer for us! It no longer satisfies—what shall I say?—our thirst for perfection.

Human beliefs, like everything else, are subject to evolution; they advance...Religion must necessarily be adapted to present understanding. Rome is at fault for resisting this adaptation...

[1] See Houtin, *op. cit.*, pp. 111 f.; Rivière, *op. cit.* pp. 146 ff.
[2] There is a copy of this very rare booklet among von Hügel's papers in St Andrews University Library.
[3] See Houtin, *op. cit.* pp. 251–70.
[4] See Réjean Robidoux, *Roger Martin du Gard et la religion* (1964), pp. 105 ff.

Later Schertz continues:

One can accept the fundamental meaning which the mystery of the Incarnation contains, or that of the Resurrection, without thereby admitting that they are authentic events, historically exact,—like the capitulation of Sedan or the proclamation of the Republic...

A practical religion is a fountain of living water: it would be madness to renounce it simply because the literal meaning of its dogmas is no longer tenable.[1]

Hébert sent a copy of his *Souvenirs of Assisi* to Duchesne, telling him that he wondered whether, instead of continuing in his responsible teaching post, he would not do better to become a hospital chaplain, since his belief in a future life was unshaken. Duchesne in reply said that he would keep the booklet secret and that he did not expect to meet many people who would be interested in the disappearance of dogma into thin air. He urged Hébert not to abandon the ministry of teaching.

We are at a turning-point [he wrote on 18 January 1900]. Religious authority counts on its tradition, and the most devoted members of its personnel, who are also the least intelligent. What can be done? Hope that this will change? Endeavour to reform it? But it will not change and reform will not come about. The only outcome of such attempts would be to get oneself thrown out of the window, without any advantage to others or to oneself.

Let us then teach what the Church teaches in her name and under her responsibility. We need not deny that in all this there is a large part of symbolism that calls for explanation. But leave the explanation to make its own way privately and individually...

But I come back to my turning-point. It may be that, despite all appearances, the old ecclesiastical edifice is going one day to tumble down... Should this happen, no one will blame us for having supported the old building for as long as possible...[2]

This letter shows why Duchesne never became a modernist, and if Hébert had followed his advice *he* would have ceased to be one. But he had no intention of following Duchesne's advice. He held his ground till the summer of 1901 when one of his orthodox

---

[1] *Jean Barois* (150th edition), pp. 51, 58, 60, 63.
[2] See Houtin, *op. cit.* pp. 114 f.

colleagues furtively purloined a copy of the *Souvenirs of Assisi* from his study when he was out and sent it to the archbishop of Paris. Cardinal Richard thereupon called on Hébert to retract or to resign his office as Director of the Ecole Fénelon. Without hesitation Hébert decided to resign.

Duchesne, who happened to be in Paris at the time, urged him to submit and to take a country parish where his faith would be revived as Duchesne found that his own was by his annual vacations in Brittany. Hébert pointed out that it was Duchesne who had originally undermined his faith in the resurrection, but Duchesne said that he had been misunderstood. He did not consider that Hébert could consistently remain in the Church and maintain the negations to which he now seemed to be morbidly attached. Their longstanding friendship was severed and never resumed.

Hébert's intention was to remain in the Church and at the same time to expose all that was wrong with it. He was prepared to subscribe to its formularies while explaining that he accepted them only in a symbolical sense. He was now living with his sister in Paris and was able to continue saying mass daily in the chapel of the Ecole Fénelon and also to go on hearing the confessions of many of his former pupils. He appears to have expected Cardinal Richard to offer him a new post, and had correspondence and interviews with him in that hope. The archbishop referred the *Souvenirs of Assisi* to Rome where it was naturally regarded as heretical. At the beginning of 1902 Hébert was no longer allowed to say mass at the Ecole Fénelon and, as he had no *celebret*, he could not do so elsewhere.

He now decided to appeal to Rome on his own behalf, and he asked his old friend Baron von Hügel, who was then staying in the Eternal City, to take the matter up. Von Hügel's replies are published in his *Selected Letters*.[1] In short, von Hügel was prepared to do his best. He had already intervened on behalf of his friends Maurice Blondel and Alfred Loisy but, as he explained to Hébert, whereas in their cases he had been able to show

[1] See pp. 100–8. Cf. Loisy, *Mém.*, ii. 107 ff.

that he was in keen agreement with their views, he could not pretend that he agreed with Hébert, great as was his regard for his character. In these circumstances nothing could be expected to come of von Hügel's attempt to help.

When, after a year, there had been no further developments, Hébert decided to break silence, and in July 1902 he published a provocative article, entitled 'La dernière Idole', which was a sharp criticism of the traditional proofs of the existence of God and an argument for the impersonality of the Divine, which, together with the hope of a future life, was henceforth the idea to which Hébert was most obstinately attached. Although he had signed the article 'l'abbé Marcel Hébert', he can hardly have failed to realize that its publication must lead to a rupture with the Church. When at the beginning of September Cardinal Richard wrote asking to see him, Hébert replied, courteously but firmly, that it would be useless since he could not in conscience undertake either to retract what he had written or to publish no more. In fact, he proceeded at once to publish further articles in a similar vein.

A note attached to one of these implied that Loisy was associated with Hébert. They were indeed friends, but Loisy did not share Hébert's favourite beliefs and deplored their publication. He was himself about to publish *L'Evangile et l'Eglise*, and Hébert's manifestos might well damage its reception. Loisy therefore inserted a sentence in the introduction to his book[1] which, without mentioning Hébert, disowned his teaching, and he wrote a letter—which he subsequently regretted—to Cardinal Richard indicating that he did not share Hébert's views.[2]

Perhaps the best epitaph on Marcel Hébert as a modernist is that of Charles Guignebert who wrote of 'this good Marcel Hébert...whom everyone loved as soon as they saw him and who wanted to remain a Catholic, provided that the Church recognized the truth of opinions which he believed to be irrefutable, and which were not even open to rational debate'.[3]

[1] *L'Evangile et l'Eglise*, p. xxxiii.
[2] On this whole affair, see Loisy, *Mém.*, ii. ch. xxiv.
[3] See *Revue historique* (1933), p. 113.

Hébert was never excommunicated. He left the Church voluntarily, though reluctantly. His case did not become a *cause célèbre*,[1] nor did his writings after his laicization attract much attention. In order to earn a living he accepted a modest post as an accountant that was offered to him by one of his former pupils who owned a factory in Belgium. So in the middle of 1903 he moved to Brussels. There he identified himself with the socialists, though some of them found him much too religious. He also did some lecturing in the New University on religious questions. In 1907 he returned to Paris to live with his sister and to keep up with his friends. He continued to be preoccupied with mystical or idealistic religion. He is a type of modernist who broke with the Church but retained a nostalgia for what he had had to abandon. 'What a pity,' he said speaking of Catholic cultus and beliefs, 'what a pity, that all this is not true.'[2]

When he died in 1916, he was greatly mourned by his friends and former pupils, who regarded him more as a saint than as a philosopher. He left instructions that the words *In spe* should be inscribed on his tombstone, and that a protestant pastor or a jewish rabbi should give an address at his cremation—'to testify that, without adhering to liberal protestantism or to any other confession, I did not desire a *materialistic* burial, and that I die believing and hopeful'.[3]

To conclude this account of Hébert I am going to quote from a letter which Loisy wrote to Franz Cumont, and which perhaps tells as much about Loisy as about Hébert himself:

Did you know my old friend Marcel Hébert...when he was teaching in Brussels? He was cremated at Père-Lachaise last Tuesday...He got fuddled with philosophy, and left the Church in 1902, after

[1] As it might have done if he had married. On 14 December 1903 von Hügel wrote to A. L. Lilley (LP): 'Loisy writes me this morning that ex-Abbé Marcel Hébert has gone and married; at least that is what his allusion must mean, I think. He is quite right, I am sure, to *deeply* deplore this: it is *precisely* the kind of thing the other side will "understand", i.e. misunderstand, and lay to L's charge, more or less.' Hébert however did not marry. For more details about his affair of the heart, see Loisy to Houtin, 20 October 1903: BN, papiers Houtin, XXXI, and Loisy to von Hügel, 21 December 1903: BN, n.a.f. 15645.

[2] See Houtin, *Marcel Hébert*, p. 299.

[3] *Ibid.* pp. 213 f.

publishing an article entitled, 'The Last Idol'. By this he meant the personality of God. He believed only in the Divine, in the Ideal, in the Perfect, which he inscribed with initial capital letters...He believed also in the immortality of the soul, at least he wished to hold that it was possible, a sort of half-hope...To testify to this faith, he had decided... that a free believer, a liberal pastor or rabbi, should conduct his funeral... He would have done much better if he had written his spiritual testament and chosen a friend who had an agreable voice to read it. Pastor Wilfrid Monod, who...had agreed to officiate, began by reading us 'the psalm of Moses'—the psalm of Moses!!—that is, Psalm XC, which speaks poetically about the vanity of human life, and the *De Profundis*,—in a French protestant translation of course; then he discoursed to us about the dead man and his kind of spiritualism; after which he recited the Lord's Prayer, no doubt with a view to entering into the feelings of Salomon Reinach and of Louis Havet who were present. This was...the pattern of a protestant funeral which I saw followed four years ago for Père Hyacinthe at the Temple of the Oratory. It sounds much more false for a non-believer than the old Catholic liturgy with its *Requiem*, *Libera*, *Dies irae*, which at any rate give you a poem about death...So poor Hébert has had a protestant funeral which he had by no means foreseen.'[1]

II

My other French modernist of the left, who will make a much briefer appearance, was younger than Hébert and came into the movement later, indeed only when it was about to be dismantled. He was also a modernist of a different type who went from one extreme to the other. Prosper Alfaric (1876–1955) is not mentioned either by Albert Houtin or by Jean Rivière in their books on the modernist movement, although he was personally known to them both. This is presumably because he cannot be said to have had any influence on the course of events. He is representa-

[1] Loisy to Cumont, 22 February 1916, BN, n.a.f. 15644. Reinach was an unbelieving Jew and Havet a rationalist. In his reply to Loisy, Cumont said that he had known Hébert and had found his ideas somewhat confused. He went on to tell an extraordinary story of a French atheist who as an unbeliever had wanted to be cremated but could not be since he committed suicide, and in consequence of a strange series of misadventures ended by having not only a protestant, but a catholic, funeral as well! See Cumont to Loisy, 28 March 1916, BN, n.a.f. 15651. For the funeral of Hyacinthe Loyson, see Houtin, *Le Père Hyacinthe*, iii. 224–7.

tive of the younger adherents of the movement and of the camp followers. His autobiography, entitled *De la foi à la raison*, which was published in 1955 under the aegis of the Rationalist Union, is a document of considerable interest to students of the modernist movement.

Alfaric was, like Loisy, one of those exceptionally intelligent country boys who became a priest. Indeed, he became a member of the Society of Saint Sulpice, and was a professor of theology in three diocesan seminaries, the last being that of Albi which was presided over by Mgr Mignot, to whom Alfaric had been recommended because of his liberal or progressive views. This was in 1905. He had a rigidly orthodox and scholastic background, but it had been disturbed both by his philosophical reading and reflection and by his introduction to the critical study of the Bible through the work of Loisy and others. He became a modernist in the hope of being able to combine his inherited faith with intellectual honesty. In 1907 he told a friend that he was sure that the papacy was wrong about the Mosaic authorship of the Pentateuch, the Davidic authorship of the Psalms and the unity of the Book of Isaiah, and this made him wonder whether it had not misled him about more fundamental matters.[1]

The papal condemnation of modernism brought upon him a crisis of faith. 'The Vatican', he says, 'was pushing me to take sides for or against it by the vigour with which it was persecuting modernism. Everything went to show that one must either submit or get out.'[2] But Alfaric did not act impetuously. He eventually extracted himself from the Church by stages between 1910 and 1912, the turning-point being when he ceased to believe in the existence of God. He left the Church unobtrusively because he wanted to spare Mgr Mignot as much embarrassment as possible. His relations with the archbishop, and still more with the archbishop's secretary, Canon Rous, who advised him through-out the crisis, remained perfectly cordial.

In the ensuing years Loisy and other savants helped Alfaric to acquire qualifications for teaching in the University, and in

---

[1] See *De la foi à la raison*, pp. 177 f.
[2] *Ibid.* p. 187.

1919 he was appointed Professor of the History of Religions in the University of Strasbourg, through the good offices of C. Guignebert and Salomon Reinach and despite the religious susceptibilities of the Alsatians.[1] Henri Bremond, who was also hoping for an appointment at Strasbourg, in the course of a letter to a friend, remarked characteristically: 'Ma sainteté ferait... contrepoids à la présence, vraiment fâcheuse, d'Alfaric.'[2]

Alfaric's doctoral thesis was on 'The intellectual evolution of St Augustine and the manichean Scriptures.' When Bremond read it, he wrote to Loisy: 'Although it is a magisterial work, his Augustine much disappointed me in places. What a blessing it is never to have taught theology! It would do A. a lot of good to read Newman.'[3] A curious light is thrown on the prejudice that there was in academic circles against ex-priests by a letter that Loisy wrote to Franz Cumont in 1918, explaining why he was declining to be one of the examiners of Alfaric's thesis. 'It is to be hoped', he wrote, 'that it will make a good impression, and my presence alone [*sc.* at the oral examination]—even if I were as competent as I am incompetent on this special subject—would spoil everything. If I am not there, no one will dream of recalling that Alfaric has been a priest. If I were there, everyone would remember.'[4] Loisy himself had encountered this kind of prejudice when he was a candidate for a professorship at the Collège de France.[5]

Alfaric, as I said, went from one extreme to the other. He became an ardent, if not a fanatical, rationalist and anti-clerical.

---

[1] See L. Canet (who was then in the government service at Strasbourg) to Loisy, 9 July and 28 October 1919: BN, n.a.f. 15650. 'Ce garçon-la', wrote Canet, 'est resté terriblement scolastique et je crois qu'il ne se décrassera jamais. Le voilà nommé à Strasbourg par la grâce de Guignebert et de l'incomparable Salomon.'

[2] Bremond to Abbé Baudin, 1 December 1919: see A. Blanchet, *Histoire d'une mise à l'index*, p. 207.

[3] Bremond to Loisy, 21 January 1921: BN, n.a.f. 15650.

[4] Loisy to Cumont, 19 October 1918: BN, n.a.f. 15644.

[5] His publisher, Emile Nourry, had at that time written to him: 'Je fais campagne pour ma faible part, mais dans toutes les mesures de mes forces dans le camp anti-clérical qui vous trouve trop clérical. "Le Collège de France, disent-ils, n'est pas fait pour les Curés qui ne marchent pas." Je réponds, "Ce n'est pas un curé qui ne marche pas. *C'est un savant qui marche*".' Nourry to Loisy, 10 July 1908: BN, n.a.f. 15659.

In his latter days he used to go round France lecturing on the non-existence of God and proving his thesis with the same kind of scholastic arguments, but in reverse, that he had used earlier as a priest. He also adopted the view that Jesus was a purely mythical figure.[1]

His autobiography, however, is charmingly written and is remarkably free from bitterness. The personalities in the Church, with whom he had to do, are sympathetically portrayed. Alfaric got to know Loisy, Hébert and Houtin only after his break with the Church. He saw much of Loisy whom he used to accompany on his daily constitutional in Paris: he found him still (he says) 'altogether impregnated with theological modernism'.[2] Much of the interest of Alfaric's autobiography lies in the first-hand impression that it conveys of Mgr Mignot and his entourage during the most critical period of the modernist movement.

Mignot's affection for Alfaric was not chilled by his departure from the Church. On the contrary, there are frequent inquiries about, and messages to, Alfaric in Mignot's letters to Loisy[3] during the time when Alfaric was working for his doctorate in Paris. When he married in 1915, Mignot wrote benevolently to Loisy: 'I was a bit surprised when I heard of his marriage: I should have preferred him to be wedded to erudition, but I do not blame him, since he does not believe himself to be bound by any ecclesiastical law.'[4]

III

The 'left' and the 'right' are, in my intention, no more than a rough and ready way of distinguishing those modernists who broke with the Church after the condemnation of the movement from those who did not. The distinction does not tell very much, and in each case the more interesting question is why and how they broke with the Church or why and how they did not. The modernists of the right did not change their minds or abandon their convictions at the pope's dictation: they managed in one

[1] Cf. Loisy, *Mém.*, iii. 410 f., 530.
[2] Alfaric, *De la foi à la raison*, p. 255.
[3] See BN, n.a.f. 15659.
[4] 29 October 1915: *ibid.*

way or another to survive in the Church while deploring its contemporary policies.

Loisy was obviously the principal modernist of the left. I have chosen Marcel Hébert and Prosper Alfaric as other examples. Houtin and Turmel were certainly of the left but it is doubtful whether they should be called modernists. Anyhow, the modernists of the left have had a fair innings, so to speak, and I am going to devote the rest of this chapter, which will be a long one, to those of the right. Those of my choice fall into two classes, the philosophical and the episcopal.

Maurice Blondel (1861–1949), Lucien Laberthonnière (1860–1932), and Edouard Le Roy (1870–1954) are commonly regarded as the principal French philosophical modernists, but there were important differences between them and Blondel, although he has often been classified as a modernist,[1] should not be so accounted in my view. He was definitely not one in his own view. When I told a knowing friend that I was not going to include Blondel in my gallery of modernists, he said: 'It is just as well, for, if you did call him a modernist, he would appear from heaven and fell you to the ground.'

There are other reasons why I am not going to say much about him. For one thing, a vast amount, I might say an excessive amount, has already been written about him,[2] and I have no wish to add to it. Then again, I do not feel qualified to do justice to Blondel since I find his thought obscure,[3] his style insufferable,[4]

---

[1] E.g., see J. M. Bampton, *Modernism and modern thought* (1913), pp. 105 f.; and see MMRC, p. 186, for other examples.

[2] See André Hayen, s.j., *Bibliographie blondelienne 1888–1951* (1953). Since 1953 a substantial amount of Blondel's correspondence has been published: see Maurice Blondel and Auguste Valensin, *Correspondance* (3 vols, 1957–65); Maurice Blondel, *Lettres philosophiques* (1961); Maurice Blondel–Lucien Laberthonnière, *Correspondance philosophique* (1961); René Marlé, s.j., *Au cœur de la crise moderniste : le dossier inédit d'une controverse* (1960); Henri de Lubac, *Blondel et Teilhard de Chardin : correspondance commentée* (1965). See also Henri Bouillard, *Blondel et le Christianisme* (1961); Claude Tresmontant, *Introduction à la métaphysique de Maurice Blondel* (1963); Alexander Dru and Illtyd Trethowan (Eds), *Maurice Blondel : The Letter on Apologetics and History of Dogma* (1964).

[3] Cf. von Hügel to Loisy, 1 June 1904 (*Mém.*, ii. 391): 'Blondel est presque impossible, je ne dis pas à accepter, mais à comprendre pour plus d'une ou deux pages à la fois'; James Ward to von Hügel, 16 June 1900: 'M. Blondel's paper rather fascinated me at first but I began to feel disappointed as I neared the end: it seemed to

and his temperament uncongenial.[1] Nevertheless, I must say something about him, if only to explain his association with the modernists.

His doctoral thesis, entitled *L'Action. Essai d'une critique de la vie et d'une science de la pratique*, and presented in the Sorbonne in 1893, was the sign of the emergence in French Catholicism of a way of doing philosophy and theology that was in evident contrast to that of scholasticism. It appeared not only to go back to St Augustine and Pascal rather than to St Thomas Aquinas, but to have other novel and unfamiliar features. I do not think that I can give a more satisfactory summary indication of what Blondel was taken both by his admirers and by his critics to stand for than by repeating a paragraph from my book *The Modernist Movement in the Roman Church*.

The philosophy of action is anti-intellectualist in the sense that it denies that ultimate truth can be reached simply through intellectual processes, dialectic, etc., and finally secured by such means in abstract formulas. The attainment of truth involves the activity of the whole of our being—willing and feeling as well as knowing. The word 'action' is used to mean not one particular kind of activity, e.g. doing as opposed to thinking, but the whole of our life with all that is given in our experience, that is to say a reality that is always in movement, always incomplete, always becoming. Faith accordingly does not consist in accepting with our intellect dogmas which are revealed to us from entirely beyond our experience and, as it were, imposed upon us from outside. We approach and realize the supernatural from within. Our thinking, willing, feeling, when closely scrutinized, are found to demand an object beyond the natural, finite order. The method of

---

[1] 'Has the man no sense of humour? and is not this just what is the matter with him?' G. Tyrrell to A. L. Lilley, 27 February 1904: LP. H. Bremond wrote to von Hügel on 13 August 1909 with reference to Tyrrell's funeral: 'Blondel has sent me such an absurd careful, theological letter that—when he came to see me, I told I was out. His big argument was about the *invalidité* of my prayer on the grave! He came 3 times, and at last found his way, when the concierge was out. I must say that after the interview he altered his cathedralic views.' VHSA.

---

me to get more rather than less obscure as it went on.' VHSA. See also von Hügel, *Selected Letters*, p. 97.

[4] Cf. Illtyd Trethowan, *op. cit.* p. 120: 'His style ... is diffuse, repetitive and involved.'

immanence, as it was called, i.e. the analysis of our inmost life, is thus shown to lead to a doctrine of transcendence: it shows that the natural postulates the supernatural. Faith is not a final or static condition; it is an attitude or orientation of the whole personality.[1]

Blondel devoted the rest of his life to elaborating and refining his own form of this way of thinking. Although he was viewed with suspicion by the representatives of scholasticism, and sometimes seemed to be menaced with condemnation in Rome,[2] he never was condemned and in fact became one of the most pertinacious opponents of modernism.[3] (I shall say something about his controversy with von Hügel in the next chapter.) His 'method of immanence' should not be confused with the 'immanentism' that was condemned in the encyclical *Pascendi*. As Laberthonnière said, 'M. Blondel by the method of immanence conducted us rigorously to a doctrine of transcendence.'[4]

The fact that Blondel was never condemned undoubtedly has had something to do with the prestige that he eventually acquired and with the influence that he was able to exert. He has been cultivated by Roman Catholic intellectuals who are philosophically inclined but averse to the scholastic tradition for the same reason that Newman has been cultivated by them, that is, because both appeared to offer or open up a promising alternative to that tradition. Newman was of course lucid where Blondel was obscure, and so has naturally had a wider appeal, and his having been made a Cardinal gave his name the greater prestige.

In another respect, Blondel might be compared with Charles Gore. Robert Dell said that Blondel had 'a regular ecclesiastical

---

[1] MMRC, pp. 186 f. For a simpler indication of what Blondel's followers were taken to be saying, note that in 1907 Loisy told von Hügel that one of them 'a fait récemment un course d'instruction religieuse dans un grand collège, et les élèves eux-mêmes ont trouvé qu'il ne savait répéter qu'une chose: "il faut vivre sa foi".' Loisy to von Hügel, 19 October 1907: BN, n.a.f. 15645. For an historical account of this school of thought (by Laberthonnière), see Lecanuet, *La vie de l'Eglise sous Léon XIII*, ch. ix–xi.

[2] E.g. see George Fonsegrive, *Le catholicisme et la vie de l'esprit* (1899), pp. 64 f.

[3] See Marlé, *Au cœur de la crise moderniste*; Maurice Blondel–Auguste Valensin, *Correspondance 1899–1912*; Poulat, *Histoire, dogme et critique*. Von Hügel said that there was 'a curiously sacristan, seminarist side' to Blondel: Heaney, p. 264.

[4] See Lecanuet, *op. cit.* p. 511.

mind'.[1] Both Blondel and Gore at first appeared to be *avant-garde* Christian thinkers, and both for the rest of their lives not only refused to go any further or to budge from the positions that they had taken up in the 1890s,[2] but became extremely censorious of any who did go further in the exploration of uncharted theological territory.[3] Neither of them was endowed with liberality of temperament.[4] Blondel was painfully submissive to papal authority, although inwardly and privately he deplored many of the ways in which it was exercised. If he had been a modernist, he would have been an agonizing,[5] but not a courageous, one.

IV

Unlike Blondel, who was a layman and a professor in the University, Laberthonnière was a priest and a member of the Oratory. Son of an artisan, from his early years he was marked out for the priesthood by his piety and by his intelligence. Already in his seminary days he was assailed by an *inquiétude religieuse* which remained with him always and made him dissatisfied, and more than dissatisfied, with the confidence and complacency of the official scholastic theology.[6] Thus it was almost a matter of course that, when *L'Action* appeared, he found in Blondel a kindred spirit.[7] They were both by profession philosophers,[8] and they became intimate friends, although from an early stage differences between them began to appear which eventually led to

---

[1] Dell to Lilley, 31 March 1908: LP.

[2] Cf. von Hügel to Tyrrell, 30 June 1904: 'I feel as if [Blondel's] mind had somehow ceased to grow, except to defend and throw up ingenious reasons and hypotheses to defend a position or rather a combination of positions, taken up, apparently, for good and all.' *Selected Letters*, p. 128.

[3] See his published correspondence, *passim*.

[4] See my *Essays in Liberality*, pp. 21 f., 148–51.

[5] See, for example, the letter that Blondel wrote to Laberthonnière in April 1906 when two books by the latter were put on the Index. *Corr. phil.*, p. 195.

[6] See *Corr. phil.*, p. 90.

[7] See M. M. d'Hendecourt, *Essai sur la philosophie du Père Laberthonnière* (1947), p. 21. This book contains (pp. 145–68) a useful guide to Laberthonnière's philosophical vocabulary.

[8] From 1887 Laberthonnière was professor of philosophy at the Oratorian Collège de Juilly of which later he became superior, until in 1903 it had to be abandoned because of the French government's law against religious congregations. Thereafter he lived on his own in Paris. See *Corr. phil.*, p. 10, and M. M. d'Hendecourt's introduction to Laberthonnière, *Les fruits de l'esprit*.

a painful rupture.[1] But during the modernist movement they were closely associated, especially in working for the *Annales de philosophie chrétienne*, of which Laberthonnière became editor in 1905.

They both believed not only that it was their vocation to be Christian philosophers, but that they were called to show that Christianity was itself a philosophy with a metaphysic of its own and that it depended on no other philosophy, whether platonism, aristotelianism, idealism, positivism, or what have you. Whereas Blondel liked to speak of a 'philosophy of action', Laberthonnière spoke of a 'metaphysic of charity' or, alternatively, of '*le dogmatisme moral*'—moral dogmatism. The latter expression requires some explanation.

It did not mean that Laberthonnière was very dogmatic about morals, nor that he was a disciple of Matthew Arnold and held that creeds should give place to conduct! Moral dogmatism was deliberately contrasted with the intellectual dogmatism of the theological schools. Dogmas were not enigmatic and mysterious formulas that God promulgated by his almighty power in order to humble man's pride. They had a moral, a practical, a vital meaning: they show 'what we are and what we ought to be and how we can become what we ought to be'.[2] On the other hand, 'theological dogmatics (*la dogmatique théologiste*) is a collection of abstract propositions that present themselves either as fallen from heaven or as officially drawn up once and for all, from which those who manipulate them mean to make for other people an intellectual iron collar.'[3] Or again, 'moral dogmatism should be regarded above all as a method. What it combats is the claim to make truth a system that one can get hold of only by reasoning, whereas *truth is a life*.'[4]

---

[1] See Claude Tresmontant in *Corr. phil.*, p. 383 *et passim*; L. Canet in Laberthonnière, *Esquisse d'une philosophie personnaliste*, p. viii.

[2] Laberthonnière, *Théorie de l'Education* (1935 edition), p. 77. See also *La notion chrétienne de l'autorité*, pp. 43 f.; *Corr. phil.*, p. 14.

[3] *La notion chrétienne de l'autorité*, p. 65.

[4] Laberthonnière, *Essais de philosophie religieuse*, p. 118. The most serious consideration of Laberthonnière's teaching in English is D. M. Eastwood's chapter on 'The "New Apologetic" represented by Father Laberthonnière with reference to Pascal as an apologist' in her book *The Revival of Pascal* (1936). See also L. Susan Stebbing, *Pragmatism and French Voluntarism* (1914), pp. 83–92.

I have said enough to indicate that there was a broad similarity between the teaching of Laberthonnière and that of Blondel. It is quite beyond my scope to attempt a full exposition and critique of either. All that I want to do is to point to those differences between Laberthonnière and Blondel that justify one in regarding the former as, in some respects, a modernist while acquitting the latter. In this one is following the lead of Pope Pius X, though he was not exactly discriminating in his approbations and disapprobations and in his application of the term 'modernist'.[1] It is relevant, in the first place, to recall that Laberthonnière's books, *Essais de philosophie religieuse* and *Le réalisme chrétien et l'idéalisme grec*, were put on the Index in 1906, and that in 1913 the *Annales de philosophie chrétienne*, which he was still editing, together with two other books of his, were also put on the Index. He himself was then forbidden to publish anything more. This did not, however, prevent him from continuing to write, nor did it prevent the Vatican from pursuing him in his grave, for some of his posthumously published works were put on the Index in 1936 and 1941.[2] Laberthonnière, like Blondel, could very reasonably claim that he was not touched by the *Lamentabili* or the *Pascendi* since, although the papal documents contained some of their characteristic expressions, they failed, whatever the intention may have been, accurately to represent any of their opinions;[3] especially was this the case in what the encyclical said about 'immanentism'.[4]

There were various differences both of temperament and of opinion between Laberthonnière and Blondel. As regards

---

[1] As Laberthonnière said after the promulgation of the *Pascendi*: 'Le modernisme? Mais c'est tout le monde?' Laberthonnière to Loisy, 11 October 1907: BN, n.a.f. 15658.

[2] See *Index librorum prohibitorum* (1948), pp. 17, 248.

[3] Cf. Loisy, *Simples Réflexions*, p. 19.

[4] 'Quant à moi, dans ce qu'on appelle "l'immanentisme", en toute sincérité, je ne reconnais que le contraire exactement de ce que j'ai pensé . . . J'ai toujours protesté, et Blondel aussi, contre cette manière de comprendre la méthode d'immanence.' Laberthonnière to Loisy, 11 October 1907: BN, n.a.f. 15658. *The New Catholic Encyclopedia* (viii. 277) describes Laberthonnière as a 'French Modernist philosopher and theologian'.

temperament, von Hügel observed, at the time of his christological controversy with Blondel, that Laberthonnière kept
'remarkably free...from Blondel's curious absolute-minded-
ness',[1] which was to say that Blondel was more 'dogmatic' in the
pejorative sense of the word. Some of their differences may
appear at first sight to have been mainly verbal: for example,
Laberthonnière disapproved of Blondel's acceptance and use of
the distinction between 'natural' and 'supernatural'.[2] But this was
part and parcel of Laberthonnière's belief that Blondel became
too appreciative of, or at least insufficiently hostile to, the whole
aristotelian–thomistic tradition.[3] Laberthonnière was almost
fanatical on this subject. The opposition between Greek and
Christian ways of thinking had been the theme of his book *Le
réalisme chrétien et l'idéalisme grec* (1904). Where Greek idealism
was abstract, static, impersonal and individualistic, Christian
realism was concrete, dynamic, personal and social. They were
quite incompatible and the attempt to combine them had disastrous results. This was indeed a constant theme of Laberthonnière's writing, and he was always ready to denounce any
tendency to compromise about it. His sharpest tirade on these
lines that I have come across was addressed to von Hügel in
1924, taking him to task for having praised Aquinas in the
preface to his *Essays and Addresses on the Philosophy of Religion.*[4]

I was astonished (he wrote) to find St Thomas figuring among those
to whom you express your spiritual gratitude...To me—I say it to you
in all simplicity—he appears to stand doctrinally for a radical anti-
Christianity. In place of the Gospel's God of love he put an egocentric
God. In the final reckoning he accepts predestination in its most brutal
form. His metaphysic justifies the Inquisition and slavery. In a word
he is the theologian par excellence of theocracy. For him the Church

---

[1] *Selected Letters*, p. 128. Cf. *Corr. phil.*, p. 175 f. On the other hand, C. Tresmontant
writes: 'Laberthonnière plus farouchement prophète. Blondel plus conciliant, plus
philosophe, plus historien' (*Corr. phil.*, p. 383). It would not have occurred to me
to apply the first and third of these epithets to Blondel. Von Hügel once described
Blondel's writing as 'implacably heresy-hunting': see *Dublin Review*, 1953, p. 182.
[2] See *Corr. phil.*, pp. 241, 310, 326–30, 350.
[3] See 'Blondel et le thomisme' in C. Tresmontant, *Introduction à la métaphysique de
Maurice Blondel*, pp. 315–29.
[4] *Op. cit.* I. xv.

consists essentially in the ecclesiastical organization regarded as a *domination* that is to be exercised under the direction and to the advantage of the theologians...I have found that Buchez had a way of characterizing him that seems to me perfectly just. In St Thomas, says Buchez, all the questions are asked in Christian language, but all the answers are given with a pagan meaning. And in fact—and this is what in the end irritates me against him most—he jealously retains the letter of the Christian tradition, but always in discarding its spirit...'[1]

I am not saying that Laberthonnière's view of St Thomas is to be preferred to Blondel's, von Hügel's or anyone else's.[2] That is not the question. My point is this. If we bear in mind that in those days St Thomas and thomism were regarded with almost exclusive favour at Rome and in the theological schools,[3] then it will be evident that Laberthonnière's persistent and violent anti-thomism was one of the factors that caused him to be looked upon as subversive by the ecclesiastical authorities and to be linked with the modernists who were all more or less anti-scholastic.

A still stronger reason for associating him with the modernists was his extremely critical attitude to papal authoritarianism, or '*romanisme*' as he called it. He recognized the need for organs of authority in the Church including the papacy, but he held that the function of authority was to serve, not to dominate. Its purpose was educative, not to suppress intellectual initiative but to develop it, not to negate but to guide and encourage personal autonomy and liberty.[4] '*Romanisme*', which had been rampant for centuries, was a profound distortion of Christianity.[5]

Though Laberthonnière was far from being an undiscriminating admirer of Luther, he once told Blondel that, as a result of years of reflection on the history of the Church, he had come to

---

[1] Laberthonnière to von Hügel, 1 April 1924: VHSA. Cf. M. D. Petre, *My Way of Faith*, pp. 175 ff. On the other hand *The New Catholic Encyclopedia* says that Laberthonnière was 'a severe critic of Church authority and of scholastic philosophy (but *not of St Thomas Aquinas*).' See *op. cit.*, VIII. 277 (my italics).

[2] See Tresmontant, in *Corr. phil.* pp. 50 f., on Laberthonnière's prejudices and limitations with regard to St Thomas.

[3] Cf. F. Heiler, *Der Katholizismus*, p. 319.

[4] See the essay on 'Théorie de l'éducation: rapport de l'autorité et de la liberté' in *Essais de philosophie religieuse*, pp. 233–89; *La notion chrétienne de l'autorité*, p. 66; *Esquisse d'une philosophie personnaliste*, p. 707.

[5] *La notion chrétienne de l'autorité*, p. 174.

the conclusion that what Luther and others had said about Rome was less than the truth. Rome had ended up with a doctrine of obedience 'according to which one ought to act as though one no longer had even the right to have a conscience when one was faced by ecclesiastical authority. Obsequiousness had become the supreme virtue.'[1] After Laberthonnière's condemnation in 1913 Louis Canet said to Loisy that the unforgivable sin was that men should suppose that they had the right to be more than sheep led by the shepherd of Rome and his dogs. Whatever divergence there was between Loisy, Laberthonnière and Tyrrell, they met at that point, and 'because he most of all has insisted on it, Laberthonnière is the most hated although of the three he is the most attached to Catholicism'.[2]

That may have been so, but Laberthonnière was not a rebel against authority as Loisy and Tyrrell were in their different ways. When condemned he submitted, though not unconditionally. He told Blondel that he differed from him in that he would not practise 'unconditional obedience'.[3] He stood for resistance, but not for revolt. He considered that revolt reflected a desire to dominate and so was the obverse of authoritarianism.[4] When Laberthonnière tried to dissuade Loisy from publishing his commentary on the *Pascendi* (i.e. *Simples réflexions*), he wrote:

It is not for reasons of 'prudence' that I say this. It is because of a sense of Catholic discipline. And I am convinced that what appears and is affirmed in the encyclical and what is repugnant to you will be rather consolidated than weakened by the scandal you will cause. Silent, persevering, mortified work will do more than anything else.[5]

Resistance, not revolt: despite his apparent obedience, from 1913 until his death in 1932, to Rome's prohibition of his publishing anything whether over his own name or anonymously, Laberthonnière may yet be said to have resisted with some success. He continued to write a great deal, for posthumous

[1] *Corr. phil.*, pp. 252 f.
[2] L. Canet to A. Loisy, 17 August 1913: BN, n.a.f. 15650.
[3] *Corr. phil.*, p. 283.
[4] See *La notion chrétienne de l'autorité*, pp. 78, 149.
[5] Laberthonnière to Loisy, 11 October 1907: BN, n.a.f. 15658. Cf. *Corr. phil.*, p. 215.

publication if the ban should not be lifted in his life-time, and after his death a whole series of volumes came out, edited and annotated by his literary executor, Louis Canet.[1] They contained, in addition to hitherto unpublished work, a republication of writings that had appeared before 1913 over his own name and some for which he was responsible but which had appeared over other names. Also during his life-time he had a curious, though secret, revenge upon his detractors.

In 1915, during the first world war, Mgr Chapon, bishop of Nice, was eager to induce the French hierarchy to issue a pastoral letter that would deal with German doctrines and atrocities, and he persuaded Laberthonnière to draft for him such a document which he hoped to persuade the French bishops to adopt and sign. Cardinal Amette, the archbishop of Paris, to whom the document was submitted, warmly approved of it but said that it was not possible to have it signed by the bishops. Instead, he urged that it should be published as an article by Mgr Chapon in the *Correspondant*, and this was done. After its publication sixty French bishops announced their adhesion to it.[2] Thus, ironically, a priest who was forbidden to publish anything became the spokesman of the bishops, all unbeknown to them.

This was not the only occasion on which Laberthonnière was able to publish what he had written. The three chapters on religious thought in Lecanuet's *La Vie de l'Eglise sous Léon XIII*, which was published in 1930,[3] were the work of Laberthonnière. Again, from 1925 to 1927 the Lenten conferences or sermons at Notre Dame in Paris, while nominally preached and subsequently published by Père Sanson of the Oratory, were actually composed almost entirely by Laberthonnière, who was thus enabled to broadcast his message.[4]

---

[1] *Œuvres de Laberthonnière publiées par les soins de Louis Canet* (1935–).

[2] See Laberthonnière, *Pangermanisme et Christianisme*, pp. vii–xiv.

[3] Chapters ix, x and xi. See Laberthonnière, *Esquisse d'une philosophie personnaliste*, p. 426.

[4] See *Corr. phil.*, p. 323; P. Sanson, *Le christianisme, metaphysique de la charité* (1927). Although forbidden to publish, Laberthonnière was not forbidden to speak or preach, and some of his addresses were published posthumously: see *Les fruits de l'esprit : instructions pour une retraite*, edited by M. M. d'Hendecourt, (1961). In 1919 he was the preacher at the wedding of Louis Canet's brother,

French Modernists to the Left and Right

I hope that I have shown on what grounds Laberthonnière may be regarded as a modernist or be included in a gallery of modernists. He was not a biblical or doctrinal modernist. While he disclaimed competence as a biblical critic,[1] on principle he accepted the critical approach to the Bible, valued it for bringing out the human and relative aspects of the divine revelation,[2] and deplored the decisions of the Pontifical Biblical Commission.[3] But he did not allow that biblical criticism should upset the Catholic believer's confidence that the christological miracles, e.g. the virginal conception, had really occurred. Even if the historical critic seemed to be led to a negative conclusion, in the case of 'dogmatic facts' religious experience afforded sufficient evidence for them.[4]

Laberthonnière's last years were saddened by a sense of isolation and somewhat embittered. After his death, Bremond wrote to Loisy:

Poor Laberthonnière!...Perhaps you do not know that...he wished several of his former friends as much ill as he did to St Thomas or Pius X. I think that he did not forgive me for having kept afloat. He had a bit of Houtin's state of mind. Besides I will acknowledge to you that I never properly understood his position... He was neither rebellious nor submissive. And then so many useless subtleties in order

---

[1] See Laberthonnière, *Critique du laïcisme*, p. 419. The whole of book viii in this volume deals with his attitude to criticism.

[2] Ibid., p. 409. He allowed that there were errors in the Bible, ibid., p. 421.

[3] See *Corr. phil.*, p. 214.

[4] See *Critique du laïcisme*, pp. 408 f., 432, 434, 437. Cf. *La notion chrétienne de l'autorité*, p. 70.

---

which was almost a modernist reunion. Loisy described the occasion, in a letter to Cumont, as follows: 'J'ai vu Canet mercredi dernier. Il était venu à Paris pour le mariage d'un sien frère avec la fille de Paul Bureau, professeur à l'Institut catholique .. La cérémonie religieuse, célébrée à l'église des Carmes, devant le Cardinal Baudrillart, fut d'un modernisme touchant. Laberthonnière fit le discours et donna la bénédiction nuptiale; un prêtre de Rouen—le seul prêtre de France qui ait refusé de prêter le serment antimoderniste, et que Pie X a autorisé ensuite à y faire toutes les réserves qu'il voudrait,—disait la messe.' A. Loisy to F. Cumont, 25 November 1919: BN, n.a.f. 15644. Bureau had a book of his put on the Index in 1908; the priest who refused to take the anti-modernist oath was Abbé E. Maubec.

to evade the historical problem. But all the same they treated him shamefully.[1]

V

I said that Edouard Le Roy was commonly regarded, along with Blondel and Laberthonnière, as one of the principal French philosophical modernists. It is true that all three were professors of philosophy but, whereas Le Roy was a disciple of Bergson (and his successor both at the Collège de France and in the Académie française), Blondel and Laberthonnière were, to say the least, highly critical of bergsonism.[2] A few years ago in my Robertson Lectures[3] I gave some account of Le Roy's anti-intellectualist and pragmatic interpretation of the nature of dogma, which was his chief contribution to the modernist movement, and I will not repeat that here. Blondel, when writing to Laberthonnière, did once speak of '*notre pragmatisme*', but it was in order to say that there was an 'abyss' between that and what he called Le Roy's '*practicisme*',[4] and in the ordinary usage of the term 'pragmatism' fits Le Roy's teaching much more closely than that of either of the other two.[5]

Another reason why I do not want at present to add to what I have previously said about Le Roy's pragmatic interpretation of dogma is that M. Emile Poulat has promised to provide a full documentation of it, and of the controversy it caused, in the second volume of his *Histoire, dogme et critique dans la crise moderniste*,[6] which is sure to be very illuminating and therefore is prudently to be awaited.

---

[1] H. Bremond to A. Loisy, 29 October 1932: BN, n.a.f. 15650. Cf. Bremond to Loisy, 16 July 1920: BLE, October to December 1968, p. 283.

[2] Blondel considered that his philosophy had nothing in common with that of Bergson and his disciples: see, e.g., M. Blondel–A. Valensin, *Correspondance*, i. 320, ii, 298, 300. For Laberthonnière's opposition to bergsonism, see his *Esquisse d'une philosophie personnaliste*, pp. 163–346.

[3] *20th Century Defenders of the Faith*, pp. 51–5. See also 'M. Le Roy on the Nature of Dogma' in A. L. Lilley, *Modernism*, pp. 149–62.

[4] See *Corr. phil.*, p. 186. For Blondel's disagreement with Le Roy, see *Entretiens*, p. 90; *Corr. phil.*, pp. 190 ff.; *Mém.* ii. 529 f; for Laberthonnière's, *Corr. phil.*, p. 211.

[5] For Blondel's use of the term 'pragmatism', see L. Susan Stebbing, *Pragmatism and French Voluntarism* (1914), p. 84.

[6] See *op. cit.* i. 27 f.

There are, however, some other points about Le Roy that are suitable for brief attention here. First, I would recall a revealing interchange in the *Times Literary Supplement* in 1906. The reviewer of the English translation of Paul Sabatier's book, *Disestablishment in France*, cited the following passage from Le Roy's famous article 'Qu'est-ce qu'un dogme?', which Sabatier had incidentally quoted:

No authority can compel me to hold a given argument sound or unsound: above all, no authority can make this or that conception with or without meaning to me. I do not say merely that authority has not the right to do this, but that the thing is radically impossible, for ultimately it is I who think, not the authority that thinks for me. Against this fact nothing can possibly prevail. Nor can I force or forbid myself to find the evidence satisfactory in this or that case.[1]

On the basis of this quotation the *Times Literary Supplement* reviewer, who evidently knew nothing much about Le Roy, charged him with being 'a neo-Catholic whose standpoint was Voltairean in everything but name'. In the following issue there appeared a letter from Oxford, signed 'J. A. Leger', i.e. Augustin Leger, a former pupil of Blondel, one of the younger modernists, who was at that time studying in Oxford.[2] He was able to put the ill-informed reviewer to rights.

Voltaire [he wrote], on his own principles, could not but make light of dogma; M. Le Roy, on the contrary, finds it justified by its fruitfulness in directing our will (if not in informing our mind), and in promoting a better, fuller, more spiritual life. He believes all the dogmas that are taught by the Catholic Church. He and his friends, therefore, do not style themselves 'neo-Catholics', but Catholics, and claim to stand by the genuine Catholic tradition.[3]

Le Roy was indeed not only a professing Catholic but a devoutly

[1] See Sabatier, *op. cit.* pp. 115 f. For the French original of the passage quoted, see Le Roy, *Dogme et critique*, pp. 13 f.
[2] I have some letters, written in 1908, from Leger to G. W. Young of Oxford which imply that he had previously been studying or staying there. He translated Tyrrell's *External Religion* into French.
[3] *Times Literary Supplement*, 27 April 1906, p. 146; 4 May 1906, p. 161.

practising Catholic[1] who was irrevocably attached to the Church. Later in the same year, when he was taunted with being a quasi-Catholic by a correspondent in the Liberal Catholic paper *Demain*, he wrote to say that he wanted always to belong to the body as well as to the soul of the Church and, whatever happened, he intended to live and die in communion with Rome. Religious individualism was a contradiction in terms. He realized that identification with the Church involved being apparently identified with elements in it which one deplored, but that was not a sufficient reason for breaking away: on the contrary, reform was possible only from within.[2]

He was, however, under no illusions about the treatment that the modernists were likely to receive in what he called the 'terrible crisis of reaction that was sweeping across Catholicism'.[3] He explained in a long letter to von Hügel what line he would take if he were called upon to subscribe to the expected syllabus (i.e. *Lamentabili*). He would be against maintaining an unbending attitude. They would be dealing with people who did not constitute an infallible authority and who did not at all understand them. Any formulas *officially* promulgated should be received with no more than *official* submission and should be so interpreted as to bear an acceptable meaning. In other words, he would sign them, and at the same time continue his work so as to show that they did not hit him. To jib at such formulas, which would not be based on an accurate understanding of what they were aimed at, would be to treat them as important when it would be better to view them with indifference. Even if called upon like Galileo to sign a quite definite proposition, he would do so and publicly explain why and in what sense. Anything would be better than excommunication, for that would make one powerless to work for reform or to bear an effective witness to the faith.[4]

When the *Lamentabili* and the *Pascendi* were promulgated and when, in December 1907, his book *Dogme et critique* was put on

---

[1] See Daniel-Rops, *Edouard Le Roy et son fauteuil* (1956), pp. 11, 24.
[2] See *Demain*, 26 October 1906, p. 11.
[3] Le Roy to von Hügel, 9 June 1906: VHSA.
[4] See *ibid*.

the Index, Le Roy acted on these determinations. He gently bowed his head, as it were, in submission, and went on with his work without changing his mind.[1] He followed the same course when, in 1931, four more of his books were put on the Index.[2]

There are two more points about Le Roy that should be mentioned here. While, unlike Loisy, he was primarily a philosopher, he was much more in sympathy with Loisy than either Blondel or Laberthonnière. At the time of Loisy's excommunication Le Roy told him how much he and many others felt indebted to him for having strengthened their Christain faith.[3] He said he had read *Quelques lettres* (one of Loisy's most outspoken modernist books) with as much edification as instruction and could accept it all with only some slight reserves.[4] He also said that he had thought for a long time that there was a kind of concordance and concurrence between Loisy's thought and Bergson's, and Loisy agreed that this was so.[5]

The other point is that Le Roy and Teilhard de Chardin were very close friends who certainly influenced one another considerably.[6] There was an obvious concordance and concurrence in their ideas about the meaning of history and the cosmos. They discussed such matters as the philosophy of evolution so constantly that Le Roy confessed that he could not be sure which ideas were his own and which he had derived from Teilhard.[7] As a layman, Le Roy was able to publish what Teilhard, as a priest and a Jesuit, was prevented from doing.

[1] See Le Roy to von Hügel, 1 August 1907: VHSA; Le Roy to Loisy, 20 September 1907: BN, n.a.f. 15658. Although the archbishop of Paris obliged the publishers to stop selling *Dogme et critique*, Le Roy went on selling it from his own house: see von Hügel to E. Bishop, 16 June 1908: *Dublin Review*, 1953, p. 426. See also E. Barbier, *Histoire du catholicisme libéral*, v. 247 ff.

[2] *L'exigence idéaliste et le fait de l'évolution; Les origines humaines et l'évolution de l'intelligence; La pensée intuitive;* and *Le problème de Dieu.* For the text of Le Roy's submission, see Daniel-Rops, *op. cit.* p. 34.

[3] See Le Roy to Loisy, 12 March 1908: BN, n.a.f. 15658. Cf. *Demain*, 26 October 1911, p. 11.

[4] See Le Roy to Loisy, 15 April 1908: BN, n.a.f. 15658.

[5] See Le Roy to Loisy, 26 November 1908: *ibid.* Cf. *Mém.*, iii. 381.

[6] See Daniel-Rops, *op. cit.* pp. 19–23; Robert Speaight, *Teilhard de Chardin*, pp. 135, 140, 143, 328.

[7] See Daniel-Rops, *op. cit.* p. 19.

VI

There were two episcopal modernists in France, Mgr Mignot, archbishop of Albi, and Mgr Lacroix, bishop of Tarentaise, but they were so different from one another that I will consider them separately. Mignot played a central, whereas Lacroix played only a marginal, part in the movement.

Eudoxe-Irénée Mignot, son of a village schoolmaster in northern France, was born in 1842. He received his theological education at the seminary of Saint Sulpice, where he came under the stimulating and liberalizing influence of Professor J. B. Hogan, to the French edition of whose book, *Clerical Studies*, he was later to contribute a preface. Mignot served in a large variety of ministerial offices in the diocese of Soissons before being appointed bishop of Fréjus in 1890.

Though he was never a professional scholar, he never neglected his studies, and he became one of the most cultivated and open-minded divines of his time and the most intellectually distinguished member of the French hierarchy. He was specially well-versed in the critical and historical study of the Bible and aware of the questions it raised for the received theology. Georges Goyau, the well-known Liberal Catholic layman, said (in a private letter of 1893) that Mignot was a great and good and intellectually audacious bishop, who spoke of the progress that was due to protestant exegesis and declared that dogma ought to be taught historically. 'An extremely modern mind.'[1] When Père Hyacinthe Loyson had a long and friendly talk with Mignot in 1899, he noted next day in his journal: 'Il a une sorte de culte pour Richard Simon.'[2] Mignot did not read German but he was a diligent reader of English theological works. For instance in 1898 asking Loisy for information about books in English, he said: 'I have Montefiore, Bruce, Driver, Sanday, Ryle, Kirkpatrick, etc.'[3]

Mignot's close friendship with both Loisy and von Hügel dates

[1] See *La Revue de Paris*, February 1967, p. 15.
[2] See A. Houtin, *Le Père Hyacinthe*, iii. 273.
[3] E. I. Mignot to A. Loisy, 26 December 1898, BN, n.a.f. 15659.

from early in the 1890s. He met them from time to time, and all three were in frequent correspondence about the possibilities of intellectual revival in the Church and indeed about everything that bore on what was to be known as the modernist movement. Von Hügel later recalled that when he first met Mignot in 1893 he was 'a tall, erect, handsome man of fifty-one...with dark eyes and finely modulated voice'.[1] Alfaric who first met Mignot in 1905 and also became closely attached to him found him somewhat reserved, cold or distant at first, but very soon afterwards cordial and indeed paternal.[2] Hyacinthe Loyson was captivated by him at their first meeting in 1899. Loisy was devoted to Mignot and has nothing but praise for him in his *Mémoires*. He could say little about him in *Choses passées*, since he did not want to embarrass the archbishop during his lifetime. When I read Loisy's *Mémoires* and the quotations from Mignot's letters therein, I confess that I wondered whether he had not picked out what was most favourable to his enterprises and so conveyed an exaggerated impression of Mignot's enthusiasm for, and involvement in, the modernist movement, but now that it has been possible to read the whole correspondence I can say that there is not the least exaggeration.

In Mignot's case, even more than in that of other modernists, it is necessary to look behind their published works to their private correspondence for the fullest evidence of their opinions. Mignot, who was anything but aggressive or reckless and who had a lively sense of pastoral solicitude, used to point out to his modernist friends how cautious he had to be in his public utterances so as to avoid scandalizing the faithful.[3] Thus he told

---

[1] *Contemporary Review* (May 1918), p. 519

[2] See P. Alfaric, *De la foi à la raison*, p. 154. See also L. Birot in *Monseigneur Mignot* by L. de Lacger, p. xv.

[3] His successor as archbishop of Albi (Mgr Cézerac) supposed that Mignot had destroyed his papers before his death: see his letter of 29 October 1919 to Mgr Lacroix who wanted to write about Mignot: BN, n.a.f. 24403. It was only in 1964–5 that the discovery was made that a considerable amount of Mignot's correspondence had survived in addition to his letters to Loisy, von Hügel, Loyson, etc., which were already known. See BLE, January–March 1966, pp. 3 f. For Loisy's letters to Mignot, see BLE, 1966; for his letters to Loyson, *ibid*. April–June 1968.

von Hügel that it was very difficult for a bishop to express novel opinions without causing scandal, which he did not want to do at any price,[1] and for that reason he was not publishing anything for the time being, seeing that what he would have to say would be much more serious than what he had said.[2] This was in 1898. Subsequently he did publish a number of articles and letters on subjects that were at issue in the modernist controversy, and these were collected in his volumes, *Lettres sur les études ecclésiastiques* (1908) and *L'Eglise et la critique* (1910).

In 1899 M. Vigouroux, the doyen of French biblical scholars, asked Mignot to contribute a preface to a polyglot edition of the Bible that he was editing. Mignot did this with his customary caution only to find that Vigouroux was so scared by what he had said in favour of literary criticism of the Bible that he suppressed it.[3] In the following year Vigouroux begged him not to call in question the Mosaic authenticity of the Pentateuch saying that, the further he went into the question, the more convinced he was that Moses was the author and that it had been written only in his time.[4]

Mignot's zest for the critical study of the Bible, which was the driving force behind his participation in the modernist movement, gave him a feeling of intellectual isolation. 'It is a great trial', he wrote to von Hügel in 1901, 'to feel oneself intellectually isolated among people with whom one should form only a great family.'[5] He received no sympathy from his fellow bishops. 'Most of the bishops', he told Loisy in 1896, 'are incompetent as regards biblical criticism... Many are hostile to what they look upon as dangerous novelties, as are also most of the Consultants of the Index and of the Holy Office.'[6] He himself was evidently fascinated by the critical work that was being done on both the

---

[1] Mignot to von Hügel, 24 May (1896?), VHSA.

[2] Mignot to von Hügel, 27 February 1898, VHSA.

[3] Mignot to Loisy, 28 October 1899: BN, n.a.f. 15659. Cf. *Mém.*, i. 530 f.

[4] Mignot to Loisy, 26 December 1900, BN, n.a.f. 15659. Cf. *Mém.*, ii. 13. Mignot had abandoned the Mosaic authorship of the Pentateuch by 1886: see Mignot to Hébert, 19 March 1886. Houtin, *Marcel Hébert*, p. 57.

[5] Mignot to von Hügel, 21 August 1901, VHSA.

[6] Mignot to Loisy, 13 September 1896: BN, n.a.f. 15659. See also Mignot's letter to Loisy of 31 December 1898 (about Cardinal Mathieu) in *Mém.*, i. 509.

Old and New Testaments and eager to promote its assimilation by Catholics. His mind was also actively engaged in thinking out in what ways dogma should be recast or reinterpreted so as to take account of the new understanding of the biblical history. Thus in 1898 we find him writing to Loisy:

I should like to write. . . a history of the religion of Israel which would show that the revelation of God did not fall down in one piece from heaven to earth; that the Bible is not a gramophone on which the word of God is recorded; that men played a large part in the development of the divine thought; that it was only at quite a late stage that the idea of God was disengaged from the darkness of polytheism. . . I should like to show how the history of Israel logically leads on to Christianity without at the same time explaining it like the theologians as a mechanical fulfilment, so to speak, of the prophecies.[1]

Later in the same year he adumbrated a similar view of the New Testament and, in doing so, anticipated the theme of Loisy's *L'Evangile et l'Eglise*:

From the historical and critical point of view it is difficult to admit that Our Lord established the Church as we know it today with its cultus, its hierarchy, its dogmatic theology, its sacramental life. No doubt everything developed in conformity with the thought of the Saviour, but Jesus did not explicitly formulate this thought, and its development has been the work of God, of human consciousness, and of circumstances. In this sense there will have been less objective truth in the Revelation than the theologians assign to it. In consequence the *theology* of our dogmas is only a framework, the best that we have found until now, to enshrine the revealed truth; that the propositions, the definitions, the affirmations of the theologians are far from exhausting the doctrine and expressing it adequately.[2]

Mignot regarded it as axiomatic that history must be constructed from documents and not from preconceived theories.[3] He also sought to grapple with particularly delicate theological

---

[1] Mignot to Loisy, 13 March 1898; BN, n.a.f. 15659.

[2] Mignot to Loisy, 15 November 1898: BN, n.a.f. 15659. See also Mignot to Loisy, 13 January 1901: *ibid.*

[3] E.g. Mignot to von Hügel, 3 January 1903: VHSA.

questions that the historical approach posed, such as that concerning the knowledge possessed by the incarnate Lord. In 1896 he wrote to Loisy about this:

All the evidence shows that Our Lord's knowledge which was not infinite had a limit. Why want to ascribe to Our Lord a knowledge which he declared he did not have? He knew at least as well as the theologians what to believe about the extent of his knowledge. But we are always up against the same system of *a priorisme*, the 'inferential theology'.[1]

This implies, what is indeed the case, that Mignot shared the common modernist aversion to the scholastic theology and to thomism. Years before, he had written to Marcel Hébert: 'How right you are to see only words in the scholastic metaphysic! They are *a prioristes*... They invent a definition out of nothing, then they finish by believing in its objective truth...'[2] So now he wrote to von Hügel: 'I really do not understand the general craze for the scholasticism of St Thomas. It is absurd! What can philosophical arguments and affirmations that are *a priori* or often wrongly deduced have to do with purely critical and historical inquiries?'[3]

In the light of what we have seen so far, it comes as no surprise that Mignot, the only one of his friends to whom Loisy submitted the manuscript of *L'Evangile et l'Eglise*, pronounced enthusiastically in favour of publication.[4] Loisy's line of thought was already congenial to Mignot, to whom the idea of development was vitally important and also the idea that the Catholic faith depended on tradition rather than on the Bible and so was not shaken by the discoveries of the critics. In the event, the reception of the book was much more controversial than he had expected.

---

[1] Mignot to Loisy, 3 January 1896: BN, n.a.f. 15659. Cf. Mignot to Loyson, 12 July 1902: 'Que Jésus n'ait eu qu'une science limitée, cela n'a rien de contraire à la vérité catholique; on peut, selon moi, soutenir que Notre Seigneur n'a su que ce qui était nécessaire à sa mission; mais qui mesurera les nécessités, les exigences de cette mission unique au monde?' Houtin, *Le Père Hyacinthe*, iii. 277. See also BLE, April to June 1968, pp. 105 f.

[2] Mignot to Hébert, 19 March 1886: Houtin, *Marcel Hébert*, p. 80.

[3] Mignot to von Hügel, 27 February 1898: VHSA.

[4] See *Mém.*, ii. 125, 132 f.

Four months after its publication, he wrote to Loisy: 'Your "Evangile et l'Eglise" would have done a great deal of good if a pack of jackals had not attacked it.'[1]

All the same, from the outset Mignot had some reservations about *L'Evangile et l'Eglise* on account of what it did *not* say. Commending the book to Père Hyacinthe in January 1903, he said that its exposition of doctrine was 'insufficient',[2] and he made the same point in public in his article 'Critique et Tradition'.[3] What Mignot admired in Loisy at this time was his genius as an exegete of the Bible and as an apologist for Catholicism. Indeed as late as in 1915, when of course he had been saddened by Loisy's break with the Church and abandonment of the Catholic faith, he wrote to him: 'I have just re-read for the third or fourth time your Synoptics...What problems! what difficulties are concealed in these narratives that look so clear and simple!'[4] Still, Mignot was far from going all the way with Loisy in his critical conclusions. Whereas in May 1906 he told Père Hyacinthe that he regarded as assured various conclusions which the Pontifical Biblical Commission would disallow, a year later he told him that his opinions in exegesis were not more advanced than those of Lagrange, Genocchi and Fleming, all of whom were members of the Commission.[5] But these two statements were not necessarily inconsistent. As regards the Fourth Gospel, his opinions lay somewhere between those of Loisy and Lagrange. 'As for my personal opinion,' he wrote to Loisy in 1913, 'while I regard the Fourth Gospel as symbolic and do not attribute it to St John, I believe—*notwithstanding the difficulties which I fully realize*—in the resurrection of Lazarus, in *spite* even of the *inexplicable* silence of the Synoptics.'[6] That is a fair indication of the position which

---

[1] Mignot to Loisy, 3 February 1903, BN, n.a.f. 15659. Cf. *Mém.*, ii. 209. For an account of the attacks and of the whole controversy, see Poulat, *Histoire, dogme et critique*.

[2] Mignot to Loyson, 19 January 1903: Houtin, *Le Père Hyacinthe*, iii. 282.

[3] Extrait du *Correspondant*, 10 January 1904, p. 7. The passage in question was omitted when the article was reprinted in *L'Eglise et la critique* (1910).

[4] Mignot to Loisy, 29 October 1915, BN, n.a.f. 15659. Cf. *Mém.*, iii. 320.

[5] See Houtin, *Le Père Hyacinthe*, iii. 296, 301.

[6] Mignot to Loisy, 21 November 1903, BN, n.a.f. 15659. See also his letter of 30 October 1903 to von Hügel, VHSA.

Mignot occupied and from which he did not retreat despite the mounting conservatism of Roman decrees.

As time went on, he came to feel, as many others did increasingly, that there was a considerable element of arbitrariness in Loisy's critical conjectures, and his considered judgment may be taken as having been expressed in a letter of March 1908 to von Hügel:

I pay tribute to his erudition which is almost impeccable, to his prodigious knowledge of the texts which he analyses with astonishing skill; but I find that he himself falls into subjectivism, into hypotheses and conjectures. I believe that he ascribes to the evangelists more ingenuity than they possessed...Not that I contest all his statements, but I ask myself whether there are as many microbes as he believes he sees in his microscope.[1]

Although Mignot was far from going all the way with Loisy in his critical conclusions or conjectures, he did not regard the radical opinions, e.g. about the burial and resurrection of Jesus, which Loisy set forth in his *Evangiles synoptiques*, as incompatible with profession of the Catholic faith. In February 1908 he had written to Loisy: 'The ordinary readers [of your *Evangiles synoptiques*] do not understand that a fact can be true without being historically demonstrated...one could wish that you had written a 4th little book[2] to show to the *Christian public* how and why one can and should believe in the Christain dogmas independently of the Gospels.'[3] This letter shows, on the one hand, how much of a modernist Mignot himself was,[4] and, on the other hand, that he had failed to realize that Loisy could not conscientiously do what was suggested, least of all now that his break

---

[1] Mignot to von Hügel, 9 March 1908, VHSA. See also Mignot to Loisy, 27 December 1915, BN, n.a.f. 15659; Mignot to von Hügel, 31 March 1916, VHSA.

[2] I.e. in addition to *L'Evangile et l'Eglise*, *Autour d'un petit livre*, and *Simples réflexions*.

[3] Mignot to Loisy, 13 February 1908: BN, n.a.f. 15659. Cf. *Mém.*, ii. 621. See also Mignot to Loisy, 12 July 1907: BN, n.a.f. 15659.

[4] It is quite insufficient and misleading to say, as Louis de Lacger does in his unsatisfactory book about the Archbishop: 'On voit en quel sens il était "moderniste", c'est-à-dire simplement progressiste.' *Monseigneur Mignot* (1933), p. 66. Cf. Bedoyere, p. 75, who says that Mignot 'could hardly be called a Modernist'!

with the Church was imminent.[1] When Loisy was excommunicated (7 March 1908) and declared to be *vitandus*, Mignot told
him that he would never be a *vitandus* for him,[2] and in fact they
maintained a cordial correspondence until Mignot's death in
1918.[3]

We have still to consider how Mignot himself was affected by,
and responded to, the condemnation of modernism. Even in the
time of Leo XIII he had been regarded with disapprobation by
the ecclesiastical authorities. In February 1902 he told von
Hügel that both the nuncio in Paris and Cardinal Richard viewed
him with a lively displeasure. 'I am loudly blamed', he wrote,
'for constituting myself the protector of men like Loisy, Hébert,
Blondel, etc. etc. etc. I am as near as anything to deserving
condemnation by the Holy Office!! It is as lamentable as it is
absurd!'[4] It may have been lamentable, but it was not absurd, and
it became still less so in the time of Pius X. For Mignot actively
opposed papal policy in regard to such matters as the separation of Church and State, the *associations cultuelles*, and the Sillon,
as well as the papal treatment of doctrinal modernism.[5]

When the syllabus *Lamentabili* and the encyclical *Pascendi*
appeared, Mignot acknowledged that both contained propositions
that were apparently directed against his teaching, though like
the other modernists he considered that his opinions were
misrepresented. On 1 August 1907 he wrote to Loisy: 'I think...
that the Holy Inquisition, in its 6th proposition, has had in view
my discourse at Toulouse; but if I am "in eâdem damnatione"
they have aimed at you more than at me. Assuredly they have
misrepresented my thought, as they have yours in many of the
propositions.'[6]

---

[1] See Loisy to Mignot, July 1907: BLE, 1966, p. 269.
[2] Mignot to Loisy, 12 April 1908: *Mém.*, iii. 19.
[3] Loisy had no difficulty in respecting the decision of those modernists who remained
in the Church. In 1909 he had written to Félix Klein: 'Je ne vois nul inconvénient
à ce que vous restiez un bon catholique. L'Eglise serait un trop mauvais lieu si on
n'y rencontrait plus que des Baudrillart, ou même des Batiffol.' Loisy to Klein,
9 June 1909: BN, n.a.f. 14039.
[4] Mignot to von Hügel, 1 February 1902: VHSA.
[5] Cf. L. Birot's preface to L. de Lacger's *Monseigneur Mignot*, pp. viii f.
[6] Mignot to Loisy, 1 August 1907: BN, n.a.f. 15659. See also *Mém.*, ii. 554; Poulat,

The sixth proposition of the decree *Lamentabili* reads as follows: 'In defining truths the *Ecclesia discens* and the *Ecclesia docens* collaborate in such a way that it only remains for the *Ecclesia docens* to sanction the opinions of the *Ecclesia discens*.' In an allocution of 'The Method of Theology', which he had delivered at the Institut catholique of Toulouse in November 1901, Mignot had said something of the kind. But, whether intentionally or otherwise, the Holy Office had not accurately represented what he had said,[1] and he was able with an easy mind to say that he adhered to the condemnation of the proposition as stated in *Lamentabili*.[2]

When the *Pascendi* appeared, Mignot wrote to von Hügel: 'All our friends are struck; we are ourselves, more or less.'[3] Not until three years later did he have to decide upon his own personal response to these documents. After Pius X had in September 1910 promulgated the anti-modernist oath,[4] which included adhesion to the *Lamentabili* and *Pascendi*, Mignot wrote a long letter to von Hügel in which he developed a highly sophisticated argument that was calculated to justify taking the oath as an act of respect which did not necessarily imply an assent of the mind to all the propositions contained in it—a standpoint similar to that which had been anticipated by Le Roy.[5] Bedoyere, in his biography

[1] Poulat, *loc. cit.*, points out that E. Dimnet, in a book published in 1906 and placed on the Index in July 1907, had stated the condemned proposition almost exactly.
[2] See Mignot, *Lettres sur les études ecclésiastiques*, pp. 314 ff.
[3] Mignot to von Hügel, 5 October 1907: VHSA. Mignot also said: 'J'ai regretté... que le Souverain Pontife regard les "modernistes" comme des orgueilleux. Ceux que je connais aiment Dieu de tout leur coeur, cherchent sa gloire et la gloire de l'Eglise, rien de plus. C'est une grosse épreuve pour les âmes intelligentes et sincères.' Bedoyere, p. 202, does not quote either of these passages, but he does quote some other criticisms of the encyclical that the letter contained. For other comments of Mignot on the encyclical, see Mignot to Loisy, 3 October 1907 (deploring the disciplinary section which would open the door to delations, etc.), BN, n.a.f. 15659; and Mignot to Loyson, 3 November 1907 (pointing out how helpless the bishops were), Houtin, *Le Père Hyacinthe*, iii. 307.
[4] *Motu proprio Sacrorum Antistitum*, 8 September 1910. For an English translation, see M. D. Petre, *Modernism*, pp. 241–6. See also *ibid.* pp. 178–85.
[5] See p. 92 above.

Histoire, dogme et critique, p. 479; Mignot to Loyson, 26 July 1907: Houtin, *Le Père Hyacinthe*, iii. 307.

of von Hügel,[1] supplies an English translation of the main part of Mignot's letter so that I need not quote it here.[2] I will however translate a concluding passage from this letter which shows that Mignot was able to view what he had already called 'a white terror'[3] with a certain imperturbable good humour:

There you have, my venerable friend...the sense in which I should take the oath if it were imposed on me.

But it appears that there is still more to come. According to news which I receive from a pretty reliable source, the Pope is suffering from brain-fag. His entourage is much taken up with Pius X's *idée fixe* which is to pursue modernism into its last entrenchments. He has, it seems, on his table ten or twelve 'motu proprio'. After social modernism he is going to condemn literary modernism; then mathematical modernism...[4]

As long as Pius X lived, countenancing and encouraging as he did 'the white terror' and the campaign of the 'integrists', Mignot felt an increasing sense of isolation and sadness. 'It is no good deceiving ourselves: we are the defeated and there will be no reaction in Rome during the lifetime of Pius X at least', he wrote to von Hügel in October 1910,[5] and again in April 1914:

---

[1] Bedoyere, pp. 210 f.

[2] Here is the French original of a passage that follows that translated by Bedoyere and indicates the line of Mignot's argumentation: 'Le serment... ne peut rien abolir du droit naturel, ni de la force de l'évidence. Adhérer de toute son âme au décret *Lamentabili* c'est adhérer à ce décret qu'il a *par lui-même*; ce n'est pas lui en conférer une nouvelle; adhérer à l'Enc. *Pascendi* c'est en recevoir chaque partie avec le degré de vérité qui lui appartient, et non supprimer d'avance *tout le travail de discernement* qui *s'impose*.

'Et il importe peu ici de savoir qu'elle est actuellement l'intention personnelle du Pape: car par-là il n'est qu'un homme. Ainsi il faut prendre les choses *en soi*, avec la rélativité inévitable que la critique et l'histoire feront ressortir en elles. Le Pape ne peut pas nous demander de jurer autre chose que ce qui est *effectivement* contenu dans ses actes. Nous recevons ces actes pour ce qu'ils sont; et s'ils ne sont pas infaillibles, s'ils ne contiennent ni définition précise, ni condamnation expresse; s'ils n'expriment que des directions, une doctrine officielle mais non garantie; s'ils ont une programme pédagogique plutôt qu'un formulaire de foi, c'est comme tels que nous les prenons, comme tels que nous y adhérons, et il est impossible d'y adhérer autrement.' Mignot to von Hügel, 28 October 1910, VHSA.

[3] 'C'est une *terreur blanche* qui s'organise'. Mignot to von Hügel, 7 January 1908: VHSA.

[4] Mignot to von Hügel, 28 October 1910: *ibid*. At the head of this letter von Hügel wrote 'A Détruire?'

[5] Mignot to von Hügel, 17 October, 1910 *ibid*. Cf. Bedoyere, p. 250.

How much there is to make one sad, but it is no good speaking about it, for no good purpose would be served!...I feel...isolation developing around me. However faithful we are, we are looked upon with distrust; we are almost taken to be bad Christians; there is no room except for the sycophants, the turn-coats, the hyper-orthodox, the self-styled *integrists*...We shall soon have to return to geocentrism... There is sadness too in seeing those whom we love separated from us...[1]

So the old archbishop buried himself, so far as he could, in his books and in reflection upon the everlasting questions,[2] for he was a man of thought rather than of action.[3] After the death of Pius X in August 1914, he wrote to von Hügel:

Pius X was a saint, and exceptionally disinterested for an Italian: it is said—and I believe it—that he died a poor man; but his hard and fast ideas paralyzed his heart. He took no account of *contingencies* which nevertheless played so great a part in his life. He crushed many souls whom a little goodness would have kept in the right way; he allowed too much scope for delation...May his successor do something to gladden our hearts![4]

The accession of Benedict XV, who was expected to follow in the steps of Leo XIII rather than of Pius X, somewhat raised Mignot's spirits, and in October 1914 he submitted a memorandum to Cardinal Ferrata, the new Secretary of State, about what he considered to be the needs of the Church in the new

---

[1] Mignot to von Hügel, 23 April 1914: VHSA.
[2] Abbé Jean Desgranges, when staying at Albi in June 1913, wrote in his *Carnets intimes* (p. 329): 'L'Archevêque voit toutes les difficultés, en fait le tour, les résout ou ne les résout pas, et se réfugie dans la vieille foi héritée de sa mère. Après avoir ainsi gambadé dans l'impénétrable forêt des contradictions, il récite pieusement son chapelet en inclinant sa belle tête majestueuse, couronnée de cheveux blancs.

'On l'estime pour sa prudence qui est consommée et pour sa bonté qui est exquise. Il vit dans la cité de ses livres, toujours accueillant, n'entrant en campagne que sur les instances de son audacieux vicaire général, mais tout heureux de se replier sous sa tente.'

Mignot's last letters to Loisy reveal him as still very much alive to the fundamental questions of theology: see Mignot to Loisy, 19 July 1917, 15 January 1918: BN, n.a.f. 15659. Cf. *Mém.*, iii. 339 f., 354.
[3] Cf. L. Birot in L. de Lacger, *Monseigneur Mignot*, pp. xii f. In 1905 Mignot told Hyacinthe Loyson of his longing for solitude: see *ibid.* p. 145.
[4] Mignot to von Hügel, 9 September 1914: VHSA.

pontificate, of which not the least was a relaxation and correction of the anti-modernist campaign.[1]

The closing years of the archbishop's life—he died in March 1918—were further saddened by France's ordeals in the world war, and in the autumn of 1914 he was himself found to be suffering from cancer. Operations could defer but could not prevent the inevitable end.

Let me bid farewell to Mgr Mignot with some words written about him by Henri Bremond in 1931:

Less of a genius... than M. Loisy and than Tyrrell, but no less honest; less petulant than the latter, more flexible than the former; less bitter, or rather more gentle, than either of them, not only with persons but still more with ideas—he is the modernist *par excellence*, and in all that he did the most decisive justification of modernism: as a churchman he is and will remain, for future historians, the living antithesis and the condemnation, not only of the 'jackals' against whom he so often inveighed, but also, and still more, of Pius X, that narrow and gullible [*borné et berné*] pontiff, who always had the name of Jesus Christ on his lips, and who, nevertheless, laboured unceasingly to prove to the world, and even more perhaps to France, that 'the Roman Church has no heart'.[2]

VII

Lucien Lacroix (1854–1922), like Mignot, was a scholar. His scholarship, however, was not theological or biblical, but historical. He was a doctor not of divinity, but of letters.[3] Before becoming bishop of the mountainous diocese of Tarentaise in 1901, he had been chaplain to the Lycée Michelet and so in the service of the University, which was not a normal recommendation for ecclesiastical preferment. But he had friends in government circles, notably the Waldeck-Rousseaus.[4] He had also

[1] See L. de Lacger, *op. cit.* pp. 120–6.

[2] Sylvain Leblanc, *Un clerc qui n'a pas trahi*, p. 97. The last expression is a remark that Loisy made when Pius X condemned the Sillon: see *Mém.*, ii. 363. F. Heiler (in his *Alfred Loisy*, p. 14) is mistaken in saying that S. Leblanc applied the words 'Modernist *par excellence*' to Loisy and the page reference that he gives is wrong too.

[3] *Docteur ès lettres* at the Sorbonne in 1891: his thesis was on Richelieu.

[4] René Waldeck-Rousseau (1846–1904) was prime minister from 1899 to 1902.

founded the *Revue du clergé français* and had edited it for three and a half years.

Tarentaise was the smallest of the French dioceses and had only about 60,000 inhabitants. Lacroix's relations with the Roman curia were never happy. He was viewed there with disfavour[1] because of his University background and his republican associations. His active opposition to Pius X's policy at the time of the separation of Church and State led to such a chill that he was glad to resign his see in October 1907. The reason that he gave to Cardinal Merry del Val in his letter of resignation was the state of his health, but that was a diplomatic reason.[2] In a letter, which he drafted but did not send and which he retained among his papers, he said that, while he would gladly submit to papal authority in the religious sphere, it was repugnant to him to accept in the political sphere the decisions of a pope who 'intervened between a nation and its government and preached insurrection against the laws'.[3] Further, in a letter to M. Briand, informing him of his resignation, he said that his real motives were a resolution to dissociate himself from the war of reprisals in which Rome was engaging against the Government of the Republic and a desire to safeguard the right to freedom of thought against which the encyclical *Pascendi* had been directed.[4]

After his resignation Lacroix was appointed to a professorship of church history at the Ecole des Hautes Etudes—thus succeeding to a chair that Duchesne had held from 1885 to 1895. Lacroix ceased to have any ecclesiastical status or functions, but he did not break with the Church and shortly before his death in 1922 Benedict XV nominated him to a titular bishopric.

Although Lacroix apparently liked to describe himself as 'the

---

[1] See his draft of a letter of resignation, 12 October 1907, which specifies the ways in which he considered that the curia had treated him badly: BN, n.a.f. 24402.

[2] 'Evidemment ce ne sont pas les neiges des Alpes, ni le froid, ni les mauvais jours, ni le diabète qui ont fait démissioner notre ami de Tarentaise. Toutes ces raisons sont vraies, mais insuffisantes.' Mignot to Loyson, 3 November 1907: Houtin, *Le Père Hyacinthe*, iii. 306.

[3] BN, n.a.f. 24402. He was alluding to Pius X's prohibition of the *associations cultuelles*, which a majority of the bishops had been prepared to accept.

[4] Lacroix to Briand, 21 October 1907, *ibid.*

bishop of the modernists',[1] his connexion with the movement was not as central as that suggests. Nevertheless, he was rightly regarded as at least a sympathizer and a supporter.

In September 1901 Loisy sent him a copy of his book *The Babylonian Myths and the First Chapters of Genesis*, remarking that it was 'a very dull book'. 'Although in that respect', he added, 'it resembles *good* ecclesiastical books, I don't think you should recommend it at present to your seminarists.'[2] He would not have written like that to an unsympathetic prelate. When *L'Evangile et l'Eglise* was threatened with condemnation in Rome, Lacroix persuaded Waldeck-Rousseau to make representations there in Loisy's interest,[3] and after Cardinal Richard had condemned the book Lacroix wrote to Loisy that he was not pleased with all of it but looked upon himself as incompetent in such matters. He went on to say that he retained all his esteem and affection for Loisy, and concluded: 'You can then be sure that there will be at least one bishop who will not turn his back on you.'[4]

Again, when Houtin was refused a *celebret* in 1903,[5] Lacroix told Loisy that he would gladly have supplied him with one, but since he was the youngest and most recently appointed bishop such an action would be considered a piece of bravado.[6]

Then, when Loisy was driven to make his most unqualified act of submission in March 1904, Lacroix told him that it made him furious to think that 'the imbeciles' were triumphing.[7] In November 1907, telling Loisy about his resignation of his see, Lacroix wrote: 'You can be sure that I shall employ my leisure otherwise than in delivering panegyrics in honour of the Encyclical

---

[1] E.g., see Loyson to Loisy, 7 February 1908: BN, n.a.f. 15658.

[2] Loisy to Lacroix, 16 September 1901: BN, n.a.f. 24401.

[3] See Loisy, *Mém.*, ii. 271.

[4] Lacroix to Loisy, 21 January 1903: BN, n.a.f. 15658. Likewise Lacroix wrote to express his sympathy with Antonio Fogazzaro when *Il Santo* was placed on the Index. See Fogazzaro to Lacroix, 16 April 1906: BN, n.a.f. 24402. See also Poulat, *Histoire, dogme et critique*, pp. 264 ff.

[5] See p. 25 above.

[6] Lacroix to Loisy, 9 October 1903: BN, n.a.f. 15658.

[7] Lacroix to Loisy, 2 April 1904, *ibid.*

Pascendi.'[1] As soon as Loisy's excommunication was announced, Lacroix wrote to him:

I read this morning, in *La Croix*, that one is forbidden to correspond with you. That inspires me with an irresistible desire to write to you, to tell you again of my lively and profound sympathy. It is beyond my comprehension that, in the twentieth century,...such antiquated proceedings should be brought into play: it is childish, grotesque and odious.[2]

Lastly, when he had read *Choses passées*, Lacroix wrote to Loisy in terms that are most revealing of his attitude to the modernist movement:

I am not going into the fundamental question, that is the biblical question, first because I am incompetent to do so, and secondly because I have made an invariable rule to keep to myself alone my personal opinion on these delicate matters...But I want you to know that your book has moved and affected me as perhaps no other book has ever done till now. Yes, certainly, these pages are infinitely sad; but after all they do honour to your love of truth...Above all, they testify to your perfect sincerity...and to the nobility of your character.[3]

It may be inferred from this letter that it is anyone's guess what Lacroix himself thought about the doctrinal issues that were at stake in the modernist movement, but he was undoubtedly a participant in it. It should be added that he was closely associated with the *abbés démocrates*, and also with Paul Sabatier, the great busybody of the movement.

[1] Lacroix to Loisy, 5 November 1907, BN, n.a.f. 15658.
[2] Lacroix to Loisy, 10 March 1908, *ibid.*
[3] Lacroix to Loisy, 4 May 1913, *ibid.*

5

TWO MAJOR ENGLISH MODERNISTS

Of those whom I would call the four major English modernists, only one, Maude Petre (1863–1942), was born in England. George Tyrrell (1861–1909) and A. L. Lilley (1866–1947) were both Irish by birth, and Friedrich von Hügel (1852–1925), who was born in Italy, had an Austrian father and a Scottish mother. But they were all based in England during the modernist movement, though they all went abroad periodically—a circumstance to which we owe some of their correspondence.

During the course of the movement Tyrrell was undoubtedly the most conspicuous, and he has been the most renowned ever since. When people speak about modernism, the names that most promptly come to mind are those of Loisy and Tyrrell. I will explain at once why I am not writing about Tyrrell, except indirectly, in this book. One reason is that he is already better known and better understood in the English-speaking world than any other of the modernists. I do not mean that there is no need or scope for further work to be done on Tyrrell. In fact, a considerable number of students are engaged in research that is centred on him, and I should wish to profit from the outcome of their labours before I myself added to what I have previously written about him. That is a second reason for omitting him now. Thirdly, if I have any inclination and energy left for the composition of more books after this one, I might write about Tyrrell at greater length than would be possible here, and also about Miss Petre who was a major modernist in her own right but whose life and thought were so closely bound up with Tyrrell's that they could not be satisfactorily considered apart. If I were to turn to such a task, it might take the form of an extended commentary on their letters to Lilley and others. But at present I am doing no more than explain why, of the four major English modernists, I am going to attempt an appraisal of only Baron von Hügel and Archdeacon Lilley.

I

Paul Sabatier happily described von Hügel as 'the lay bishop of the Modernists',[1] but he was of course much more than that. Whereas Loisy, Tyrrell, Maude Petre and others will be remembered and discussed principally by reason of their parts in the modernist movement or of their modernist writings, von Hügel has a broader title to enduring fame. He would have been highly esteemed as a religious philosopher, as an authority on mysticism, as a guide[2] of souls, and as a great Christian character, even if he had had no part or lot in the modernist movement. There is no question here of my considering the whole range of his thought and action of which valuable studies already exist[3] and others are, I believe, in preparation.

I am concerned here only with his role as a modernist, about which there has been much misunderstanding, not to say misrepresentation. In 1951 H. J. T. Johnson rightly remarked that 'the tendency to minimize von Hügel's modernism has been apparent for many years'.[4] In 1933 a Jesuit reviewer went so far as to assert that 'the Baron always opposed Modernism'![5] Bernard Holland, the editor of von Hügel's *Selected Letters*,[6] did not go anything like so far as that, but Dr D. A. Binchy justly noted that the letters were 'carefully selected with the object of portraying him in as orthodox a position as possible', and he added that 'to deny that von Hügel was a Modernist would be

---

[1] P. Sabatier, *Modernism* (1908), p. 42. Cf. 'Vous êtes notre père à tous': Sabatier to von Hügel, 10 May 1908: VHSA; 'Vous avez vu et vécu tout le mouvement': Houtin to von Hügel, 18 October 1911: *ibid.*

[2] A. A. Cock may be right in saying that the Baron 'would have repudiated the term "director" applied to himself'. See *The Faith in Wales*, October 1948, p. 9.

[3] *The Religious Philosophy of Baron F. von Hügel* by L. V. Lester-Garland (1933); *Von Hügel and the Supernatural* by A. H. Dakin (1934); *La pensée religieuse de Friedrich von Hügel* by M. Nédoncelle (1935) [the French original of this work is to be preferred to the English translation: see p. 112 below]: *A Critical Examination of von Hügel's Philosophy of Religion* by A. A. Cock (n.d.); *Friedrich von Hügel* by Jean Steinmann (1962); *The Modernist Crisis: von Hügel* by J. J. Heaney (1969). There are bibliographies in the books by Dakin, Nédoncelle and Heaney.   [4] See *The Tablet*, 16 June 1951.

[5] See *The Month*, June 1933, p. 563.

[6] Baron Friedrich von Hügel, *Selected Letters 1896–1924*, edited with a memoir by Bernard Holland (1927).

rather like refusing to include Pusey among the leaders of the Oxford Movement because he did not follow Newman over to Rome'.[1]

The official biography of von Hügel by Michael de la Bedoyere[2] is much more satisfactory in this respect, though even this, I should say, tends to reduce von Hügel's perduring heterodoxy.[3] I note that Professor Clement Webb, who was one of the Baron's closest friends and sympathizers, in a predominantly favourable review of de la Bedoyere's book, corrected his statement that 'the baron...was all for the objective historical facts—at least a "kernel" of them—as absolutely essential'.[4] Webb said that von Hügel did not subscribe to the doctrine of a 'kernel' or 'hard nucleus' of revealed truth which for believers must be beyond criticism,[5] and he recalled that von Hügel told him personally that 'he was to the end...wholly impenitent in his adherence to modern critical views of the sacred books'.[6]

Though in my book, *The Modernist Movement in the Roman Church*, I devoted only a few pages directly to von Hügel, I certainly intended to emphasize his part in the modernist movement. But I must acknowledge that, after its publication, Miss Maude Petre, in a kindly letter (13 September 1934), said to me: 'There is one gap in your history, and that is a more emphatic presentation of the hidden, but pervasive and persistent influence of the Baron...He is essential to any account. Without him Fr Tyrrell would have been a *spiritual* and *moral* pioneer, but not strictly a Modernist.'

The English Roman Catholics seem to have been particularly

---

[1] D. A. Binchy on 'The Modernist Movement' in the *Cambridge Journal*, January 1948, p. 225.
[2] *The Life of Baron von Hügel* (1951). I reviewed this book in *Theology*, July 1951, pp. 241 ff.
[3] Cf. H. J. T. Johnson's article 'Baron von Hügel and the Catholic Religion' in *Studies*, XXXIX (1950), pp. 373–84, which was evidently written with an awareness of what de la Bedoyere was going to say in his book.
[4] Bedoyere, p. 145.
[5] See, however, what von Hügel said in *Du Christ éternel et de nos christologies successives* (1904), p. 6; *Eternal Life* (1913), pp. 346 f; and *Selected Letters*, p. 349. Cf. also J. J. Heaney on 'The Enigma of the later von Hügel' in *The Heythrop Journal*, April 1965, pp. 145–59.
[6] *Journal of Theological Studies*, April 1952, pp. 144, 148.

anxious to minimize von Hügel's modernism. Only last year, when unveiling a memorial plaque to him at 4 Holford Road, Hampstead, Bishop B. C. Butler was careful to speak of him as 'a devout Catholic who was *the friend of* Modernists' (my italics).[1] But a much more glaring instance of this anxiety is to be seen in the English translation of Maurice Nédoncelle's admirable book *La pensée religieuse de Friedrich von Hügel*.[2] In the French original von Hügel's part in the modernist movement had been frankly acknowledged. The censors of the English translation were not content to insist on the insertion in the Foreword of the statement: 'From first to last von Hügel was a convinced and devoted Catholic. True he was *to some extent involved* in the Modernist controversy' (italics mine). They also required a large number of alterations to be made in the text of the book and the addition of many footnotes which were aimed either at reducing von Hügel's deviations or at correcting them by reference to the standards of orthodoxy.[3]

As I said, I am not going to consider the whole range of von Hügel's thought or activity. I want only to make some points about his characteristics as a modernist, points both of a positive and of a negative or qualifying kind.

[1] See *The Tablet*, 25 May 1968, p. 537.

[2] *Baron Friedrich von Hügel: a study of his life and thought*. Translated by Marjorie Vernon (1937).

[3] Here are just two instances (which I cited when reviewing the English version of Nédoncelle's book in *The Church Times*, 5 March 1937): 'On p. 114 of the French original M. Nédoncelle, when dealing with von Hügel's opinion about the limitation during the Incarnate life of our Lord's knowledge about the date of his second coming, says: "Cette opinion n'est certes pas conforme à la doctrine commune des théologiens; elle est discutable, mais elle n'est pas non plus, semble-t-il, contraire aux données de la foi." In the English version it is surprising to find this translated: "Still, this thesis does certainly *differ widely* from the usual doctrine of theologians and *even from the doctrine formally approved by the Church*" (p. 106; italics mine). And a long footnote is added which explains that a decree of the Holy Office "has forbidden the teaching that it is not theologically certain that the soul of Jesus was all knowing". Again, on p. 121 of the French original M. Nédoncelle reports von Hügel's view that the material fire of hell is not a dogma defined by the Church, but a common opinion of theologians against which the opinion of more than one of the Fathers and even of the scholastics might be adduced. On p. 113 of the English translation this statement is modified, and a note added which says that "Catholic theologians hold that the idea that the fire of Hell is material is common and certain".'

Two Major English Modernists

The first point to be made, on the positive side, is that von Hügel was the chief engineer of the modernist movement. He made it his business to seek out potential modernists, to stimulate and encourage them in their intellectual pursuits, and to introduce them to one another's work, especially to writings and ideas that would enlarge their understanding of what would be involved in a renewal of Catholicism. To many of the modernists he had the status of guide, philosopher and friend—the venerated leader or, as Miss Petre said, 'arch-leader'.[1] He was an indefatigable correspondent and traveller. He took great trouble to comment in detail on what his friends wrote, to inform them about what others were doing or planning, and to urge them on if he considered that they were inclined to withdraw or to give up the struggle. He was also at pains to see that his friends' publications were sympathetically reviewed in appropriate journals.

Several of these characteristics are illustrated in the first of many letters that he wrote to A. L. Lilley. This was on 6 April 1903, when Lilley had published two articles about Loisy soon after the appearance of *L'Evangile et l'Eglise*. I reproduce the larger part of this letter:

'Dear Reverend Sir,
　　　　　　If I venture to write to you (all unknown to you as I am pretty sure to be) it is because your two papers on my close friend and fellow-worker, abbé Loisy, in the 'Guardian' and 'Commonwealth',[2] have given me a pleasure which I feel I ought to express to your own self. There is no doubt that I am by far the most intimate friend of Loisy's living on this side of the Channel: I hear from him sometimes two and three times a week; and his admirable letters now fill the greater part of my tin letter-box. You can, then, easily imagine with what pleasure I read your papers. I think what specially struck, and indeed delighted me in them, was the way in which you appeared conscious throughout of the first-class quality of his mind and of all

---

[1] See her article in the *Hibbert Journal*, October 1925. Cf. what she said at the *Congrès d'histoire du Christianisme, Jubilé Alfred Loisy* (1928), iii. 227: 'Von Hügel était, non seulement moderniste, mais archi-moderniste, en tant qu'il a été, sûrement, le pionnier du modernisme en Angleterre, son premier maître et son chef.'
[2] See *The Guardian*, 25 February 1903, and *The Commonwealth*, March 1903: also A. L. Lilley, *Modernism*, pp. 55–64, 185–94.

that he has got to teach anyone and everybody; and then the manner in which, throughout again, the problems and solutions discussed and propounded by him, were felt by you as, practically, quite inter-confessional, as concerning all Christians of any and every kind, who find that they must and do *think*. My good, most honest and distin-guished friend, Prof. Gardner,[1] has just published a review of the little–great book in the April 'Hibbert Journal', but in both respects I am sorry to find it distinctly inferior to your articles. In reading it, one never gets the impression that L. is more than, after all, one scholar amongst many others, with largely 'schematic' views, in part superior, in part certainly inferior to Harnack's; and everywhere one feels a kind of grudging, crusty tone as if, after all, the old question of Rome *versus* Geneva...were again on the *tapis*. — And yet close friends of mine, so little Roman as Prof. Eucken[2] of Jena, and Prof. Troeltsch,[3] of Heidelberg, write to me with a warm, ungrudging admiration of the book [*sc. L'Evangile et l'Eglise*], and its quite un-doubted superiority to H., precisely in the great, universally religious and Christian fundamental questions. Thank you then, again, very much.'

Then, after proposing to call on Lilley one day in the following week, von Hügel continued:

I also venture to send you a copy of a book by my close friend, the Revd George Tyrrell, a truly deep and brilliant Irishman, and a Jesuit as liberal as his close friend Père Bremond, the Frenchman. The book[4] was approved by the Censors of his order, but met with diffi-culties of approbation from the *entourage* of our good Cardinal: hence its non-publication. I cannot but think that you will find it *full* of deep and delicate thinking and experience about and of religion...

This letter was sent to Lilley, whose address von Hügel evidently had not known, in an envelope addressed by Henry Scott Holland who, in an accompanying note to Lilley, wrote: 'This is a rare noble testimony to have won, from a rare and scholarly soul like Von Hügel. I am exceedingly glad. The letter is a real

---

[1] Percy Gardner (1846–1937).
[2] Rudolf Eucken (1846–1926).
[3] Ernst Troeltsch (1865–1923).
[4] *Oil and Wine.* See *Autobiography and Life of George Tyrrell*, ii. 175.

possession—there could not well be a finer judge. It will greatly enhearten you. Do *see* him...'

Needless to say, they did soon meet, and thereafter met often. In his next letter (13 May 1903), which began 'Dear Mr Liley [*sic*]', von Hügel wrote:

I venture to hope that when (as will happen now any day) Laberthonnière publishes his collected Papers[1] (there are simply *grand* ones among them) and Miss Petre brings out her essays in subjects connected with the interior life,[2] you will be able and willing to give them both a warm and sympathetic welcome in the 'Guardian'. I shall take care that copies of both books get sent to you: for, in any case, I am quite sure you will like them. I, for one, simply feed on their work. I find it so entirely drawn from life itself, the deep, hard, sweet 'Paedagogue to Christ'

So Hügel went on, with elaborate explanations, to invite Lilley to come as his guest to a meeting of the Synthetic Society.[3]

As regards von Hügel's disposition to urge on other modernists or possible modernists when he considered that they were inclined to retreat or to be too submissive to ecclesiastical authority, there are some instances of this in his letters to Lilley. Thus, when after the appearance of the encyclical *Pascendi* Laberthonnière and Blondel published in the October 1907 issue of *Annales de philosophie chrétienne* (for which they were responsible) an extremely submissive article, signed 'La Rédaction', von Hügel wrote to Lilley (28 October 1907):

I do wish (if the chance turns up of doing the thing on an occasion which wd prevent your act looking as in any way done in collusion with me) you could let Laberthonnière know how distressed you are at that 'La Rédaction' thing of his.[4] I now see your objections even to that 'Immanence' bit there; still, I continue to feel the other, the

---

[1] L. Laberthonnière, *Essais de philosophie religieuse.*

[2] M. D. Petre, *Where Saints have Trod: some studies in Asceticism.* With a Preface by the Rev. George Tyrrell, s.j.

[3] See *Papers read before the Synthetic Society 1896–1908* (privately printed, 1909); Maisie Ward, *The Wilfrid Wards and the Transition* (1934), i. 417–20.

[4] It is now known that Blondel composed this article. For the circumstances in which he decided to write it, see Blondel–Valensin *Correspondence 1899–1912*, i. 367–70; part of the text of the article is reproduced in *Corr. phil.*, pp. 203 f. Bremond defended Laberthonnière: see Lilley to Young, 31 January 1908: YP.

general, unlimited acceptance and submission to be the worst feature. But we will all deal most gently with Lab. and Bl. Yet by some kindly, tactful protests, we may help towards their doing better, a little later on.

Again, on 16 July 1908 von Hügel wrote to Lilley about one of the young Italian modernists who was on a visit to Britain:

> Let me ask you to write... at once to Signor A. di Soragna, Carlton Hotel, Pall Mall, S.W., and invite him to come and see you...He is one of the chief collaborators at 'Rinnovamento'[1] and a most promising young man; but (between ourselves) wanting bracing up and encouraging to continue without further modifications. You will do great good if you praise, back, press, encourage (and do not show that you have been set up to this, at all)...He knows all about you.

This connects with what Miss Petre wrote to me on 13 September 1934 with regard to something I had said, or rather not said, in my book:

> I regretted that you did not fully know how largely von Hügel was responsible for the action and conduct of the Rinnovamento. I look on it as one of his greatest failings that he hid his action in this matter— *that he actually blamed them for submitting*—Tomaso Scotti's mother spoke to me about it, and almost apologized for her son not continuing in response to von H's instigations. *I* told her to let him do as he thought right, and that he had no call to suffer martyrdom unless his own conscience told him to. I have, on more than one occasion, defended those who submitted when von H. blamed them.

The second point to be made on the positive side is that von Hügel was not only the chief engineer of the modernist movement but himself held advanced modernist opinions as a biblical critic, and also in his aversion to the scholastic theology[2] and in his

---

[1] On this periodical, see L. H. Jordan, *Modernism in Italy*, pp. 24 ff.

[2] See his letter of 26 May 1896 to Blondel: 'Si la scolastique me ruine la philosophie, elle m'est aussi l'implacable ennemie sur le terrain historique et biblique. Nulle connaissance réelle des stades passés de la pensée humaine, même (peut-être surtout) de la pensée religieuse, sans les trois éléments du *relatif*, du *développement*, du *moralisme*. Or ces trois éléments manquent, au fond, complètement à la scolastique: elle cesserait d'être le jour où elle les accepterait en leur vraie étendue.' Quoted in Poulat, *Histoire, dogme et critique*, p. 534. Von Hügel once remarked that he had 'not had to go through an early training in those rigid, and now largely

distrust of papal authoritarianism.[1] The simplest illustration is his article on the Fourth Gospel in the eleventh edition of the *Encyclopedia Britannica* which denied the apostolic authorship and emphasized the symbolic, non-historical character of the work, and which persuaded Professor William Sanday that he must abandon the conservative position which he had hitherto defended.[2] It so happened that von Hügel completed this article a fortnight[3] before the Pontifical Biblical Commission issued its decree of 29 May 1907, affirming that external and internal arguments prove that the Apostle John was the author of the Fourth Gospel, and that the deeds of Christ related in it are not merely allegories or symbols for religious truths just as the discourses are not free theological compositions of the author.[4]

The most remarkable illustration that I can give of the lengths to which von Hügel's heterodoxy could go in private is contained in a letter which George Tyrrell wrote to A. L. Lilley on 14 August 1908. Perhaps this should be accepted with some reserve. I confess that it surprised me, but when I told a Roman Catholic interpreter of von Hügel about it he said that it was quite credible. Tyrrell is recording the Baron's conversation during a visit to Storrington when Bremond was also there.

The Baron has just gone. Wonderful man! Nothing is true; but the sum total of nothings is sublime! Christ was not merely ignorant but a téte brulé [*sic*]; Mary was not merely not a virgin, but an unbeliever and a rather unnatural mother; the Eucharist was a Pauline invention—

---

[1] See his paper 'Official Authority and Living Religion' which was composed in 1904 and published in *Essays and Addresses* (1928), ii. 3–23. Bedoyere (pp. 164 f.) regretted the publication of this paper which, in his view, 'came perilously near confounding the inevitable one-sidedness of official authority, together with the errors and faults of human officials, with the rights of authority itself in Catholic doctrine and tradition'.

[2] See W. F. Howard, *The Fourth Gospel in recent criticism and interpretation*[2] (1955), p. 7.

[3] See Bedoyere, p. 191.

[4] See A. Wikenhauser, *New Testament Introduction* (1956), p. 279; cf. propositions 16–18 of the Syllabus, *Lamentabili sane exitu* (3 July 1907).

---

childish, metaphysics of the Neo-Scholastics': see his letter of 11 June 1907 to Lilley: LP.

yet he makes his daily visit to the Blessed Sacrament and for all I know tells his beads devoutly. Bremond's French logic finds it all very perplexing.[1]

A third feature of von Hügel's modernism was his readiness on occasion publicly to champion venturesome causes or views. An early instance of this was his paper on 'The Historical Method as applied to the study of the Hexateuch',[2] which was read to the fourth International Congress of Catholics at Fribourg in August 1897, and he was to reiterate what Father Crehan, s.j., has called 'his advanced views on the Old Testament'[3] in 1906 after the Pontifical Biblical Commission had decreed the Mosaic authorship and authenticity of the Pentateuch.[4] As his biographer says, 'he found it quite impossible to square the decree with his findings as a scholar'.[5]

Another instance was von Hügel's rejoinder to the articles that Maurice Blondel published in 1904 on 'History and Dogma'.[6] These articles, though they were cast in an abstract, impersonal form, constituted a scarcely veiled attack on Loisy's supposed teaching about the relations between faith and history. The whole affair is an important chapter in the discussions that were provoked by *L'Evangile et l'Eglise* and it is treated at length in Poulat's *Histoire, dogme et critique.*[7]

Blondel contrasted what he called 'Extrinsicism' with 'Historicism'[8] and put forward his objections to both, particularly to the latter, to counter which was his main object in writing. Under the term 'Extrinsicism' he was getting at the official apologetic of the schools, for which the truth of the Bible was certified as a whole

[1] Tyrrell to Lilley, 14 August 1908: LP.
[2] *La méthode historique en son application à l'étude des documents de l'Hexateuque* (1898).
[3] Joseph Crehan, s.j., *Father Thurston* (1952), p. 54.
[4] C. A. Briggs and F. von Hügel, *The Papal Commission and the Pentateuch* (1906).
[5] Bedoyere, p. 185.
[6] 'Histoire et dogme. Les lacunes philosophiques de l'exégèse moderne.' *La Quinzaine*, 1904, pp. 145–67, 349–73, 433–58. Eng. trans. in Dru and Trethowan, *op. cit.* pp. 219–87.
[7] *Op. cit.* pp. 513–609. See also Lilley, *Modernism*, pp. 112–20.
[8] On the many different senses in which the term 'historicism' has been used, see A. Richardson, *History, Sacred and Profane* (1964), p. 104.

by the argument from miracle, i.e. extrinsically. 'The Bible', he wrote, 'is guaranteed *en bloc*, not by its content, but by the external seal of the divine: why bother to verify the details? It is full of absolute knowledge, ensconced in its eternal truth; why search for its human conditions or its relative meaning?'[1] Extrinsicism resisted the findings of biblical criticism to the utmost, and concessions were made to it only in the last extremity.

The impression given will be one of uninterrupted defeat, of the disillusioned obstinacy of men who imagined that they knew everything without having examined anything, of mystical ideologists claiming to impose their systems upon the concrete truth of history, and of men who end by taking refuge in an ostrich-like policy, shutting their eyes and not even allowing themselves to face too plainly the embarrassing literalness which they continue to teach the simple.[2]

The fact that Blondel could write like that about the conventional apologists for Catholicism goes to explain why he was *suspected* of modernism.

On the other hand, although he would follow a tortuous route of his own in accordance with his 'philosophy of action', Blondel could always be depended on to arrive at orthodox conclusions. So, in his involved treatment of what he called 'Historicism', he appeared to grant that historical criticism of the New Testament did not by itself show that there was sufficient ground, in what could be known of the earthly life of Jesus, for the dogmas of christology. But he maintained that tradition, understood as that which articulates the continuous and living experience of the Church, could legitimately supplement the deliverances of the critical historian. 'The Church', he wrote, 'is a proof of itself: *index sui est*; for it supplies the verification of what it believes and teaches in its age-old experience and its continuous practice...it has within it a power of self-justification which is independent of historical proofs or moral probabilities.'[3] For instance, Blondel allowed that from the synoptic Gospels, when critically examined,

---

[1] Dru and Trethowan, *op. cit.* p. 229.
[2] *Ibid.* p. 230.
[3] *Ibid.* p. 269.

it could not be inferred that Jesus was conscious of his divinity in the way that christological dogma asserted, but from the Fourth Gospel and subsequent Christian experience it could reasonably be concluded that he really was so.

There was much else, and much that was obscure, in Blondel's argument, but this was the issue on which von Hügel fastened in his reply,[1] in which he explicitly aligned himself with Loisy. He himself of course attached great importance to Christian experience of the eternal Christ, and he said that one could speak of 'the earthly life of the heavenly Christ',[2] that is, of what the eternal Christ has done on this earth or the *gesta Christi* in the history of the Church and in the experience of the faithful. But these phenomena 'do not complete our critical knowledge of the earthly life of Jesus. Of this earthly and phenomenal life we shall learn nothing new, so long, at least, as no new document is discovered or a more penetrating analysis of the documents already known to us is not forthcoming.'[3] Von Hügel proceeded to challenge Blondel's use of the Fourth Gospel and also his view that the incarnate Jesus must be shown to have been fully aware of his divinity if the faith of the Church was to be justified.

It should be borne in mind that Blondel himself had never submitted to the discipline involved in historical criticism, as von Hügel had. He evidently did not realize that, in the words of Professor Dennis Nineham, 'the modern historian's procedure depends on a refusal to treat any sources, whether written or otherwise, as more than primary data, data which have to be rigorously criticized and cross-examined, compared and contrasted with other data... before anything they contain or suggest can be used as the basis for an historical account which deserves that name.'[4] Looking back in 1912 on this discussion, von Hügel wrote to Maude Petre: 'B [londel] wrote as one with little sense or

---

[1] *Du Christ éternel et de nos christologies successives* (1904); extrait de 'La Quinzaine' du 1er Juin 1904.

[2] *Op. cit.* p. 23.

[3] *Ibid.* p. 24. Cf. von Hügel to Clement Webb, 9 March 1908: 'I feel, as strongly as ever, that what claims to be history cannot escape being judged by historico-critical methods and tests.' *Selected Letters*, p. 146.

[4] D. E. Nineham in *Christ for us Today*, ed. by Norman Pittenger (1968), p. 50.

knowledge of historical method and the precise historical documents and facts; and my mind and hand were and are nearly as
much in those things as L[oisy]'s own.'[1]

But now there are several things to be said on the other side
about von Hügel's position as a modernist.

First, although he had once been indifferent or even averse to
metaphysics and transcendentalism, by the time the modernist
movement really got under way he had become resolutely and
obstinately metaphysical and transcendentalist to an extent that
marked him off from other modernists whose interests were,
primarily if not exclusively, historical, ecclesiastical or psycho-
logical. Thus in 1902 he wrote to Percy Gardner about the 'no
metaphysics' tendencies of William James and others:

Ten years ago, there is hardly a statement as to this point, made...
even by James, which I would not have echoed, which I did not in
good part anticipate, *con amore* or *furore*. But now the close study of
such independent modern philosophical writers as Vaihinger, Volkelt,
Eucken, Wobbermin on the one hand, and of such deeply and finally
historical investigators as H. J. Holtzmann, Johannes Weiss, Ernst
Troeltsch on the other hand, and the living intercourse with living
members of each group, have persuaded me, gradually throughout these
last ten years, that there is a certain demonstrable, utterly irrepressible
metaphysical cognitive element in all, even the most elementary
'experience'...[2]

And in 1905 we find von Hügel writing, about his book on St
Catherine of Genoa, to Tyrrell:

I feel as I get on with my book, with a certain sadness, how few, I do
not say of the old school, but of the new, will be with me... For not
in the least to get rid of all Metaphysic, all Transcendence, is my aim;
but on the contrary to show how Metaphysics and Transcendence of
some, indeed a definite, kind are in all religion: and how these are still
imperative and possible.[3]

Von Hügel regularly deplored the indifference to, or neglect of,
metaphysics by many of his friends and acquaintances. For

---

[1] F. von Hügel to M. D. Petre, 12 February 1912. BM, Add. MSS 45362.
[2] Von Hügel, *Selected Letters*, pp. 111 f.
[3] *Ibid.* p. 131.

example, of Duchesne he said: 'I have, I think, never yet known him to praise, or indeed carefully to read through, anything philosophical.'[1] Cuthbert Butler he described to Bremond as 'my friend Dom Butler, the Cambridge Benedictine scholar...a thoroughly scientific historical worker, and on friendly terms with most of the European scholars of the same type, but with a curious systematic non-care about all things philosophical'.[2] Again, he lamented to Blondel in 1902 that Pierre Batiffol wanted to restrict himself to textual criticism and insisted on keeping clear of 'all philosophy, of all general thought or doctrine': and that even Newman was too much for him.[3]

A second distinguishing feature of von Hügel's modernism was the degree and the depth of his mystical attachment to the Church of Rome, of which the consequence was that, however much his loyalty was tried, he was never tempted to revolt. Alfred Fawkes was being perceptive when in 1922 he wrote to Alfred Loisy:

No two men could be more unlike [than Duchesne and von Hügel]: but to each the great name of Rome was, as it may well be, irresistible; and neither (I suppose) felt the position of a rebel possible—which one can quite understand. Perhaps, however, people who feel in this way should not lead reform movements...

It always seemed to me that von H. had two unreconciled sets of principles: from one, *subesse Romano Pontifici* would seem to be a secondary matter, from the other an essential one...[4]

And after von Hügel's death Fawkes wrote to the same correspondent: 'He seemed to me to feel strongly that in the R. C. Church was the main current of the spiritual experience and life of mankind: and that, in comparison with this, the excesses of the Papacy and the breach with knowledge were secondary—and would, probably, be temporary.'[5]

His style of piety at once reflected and sustained his unshakeable attachment to the Church—his daily visit to the Blessed

[1] Von Hügel to Tyrrell, 4 December 1899: *Selected Letters*, p. 77.
[2] Von Hügel to Bremond, 7–9 October 1900: VHSA.
[3] Von Hügel to Blondel, 4 March 1902: VHSA. See also von Hügel's regrets about Edmund Bishop, p. 145 below.
[4] A. Fawkes to A. Loisy, 13 July 1922: BN, n.a.f. 15653.
[5] A. Fawkes to A. Loisy, 18 February 1925: *ibid.*

Sacrament, his recitation of the rosary, etc. 'I love to trust that you will *not* be pressed out of the visible Church', he wrote to Maude Petre in 1910. 'Its helps are *great* things, we both of us know well.'[1] Yes, but he was more dependent on them than she was. Louis Canet, who was himself a practising Catholic, was puzzled by von Hügel's piety. In 1927 he wrote to Loisy:

It is true that I saw a lot of the Baron in 1915...in Rome... He did not say anything to me that enabled me to understand his spiritual condition. He went to confession every week: I found that disconcerting, and no more intelligible in the case of the Baron than in that of Joan of Arc (who made her confession daily).[2]

Thirdly, there was what Maude Petre called 'the diplomatic and temporizing quality'[3] of von Hügel's mind, which distinguished him from those modernists who were determined, in one way or another, sooner or later, to force issues to a head. This characteristic was no doubt connected with what Maude Petre also called his 'timidity as to his own safety'.[4] His aptitude for constructing elaborate arguments and for making patient qualifications, and—let us add—the experience and wisdom that enabled him to see all round a problem, made it easy for him to exercise caution and restraint when others were driven to exasperation. These considerations partly, though only partly, justify Mr Martin Green's description of him as 'the Erasmus of the Modernist movement'.[5]

Fourthly, it is a fact that in the last period of his life, after the modernist movement had petered out or been driven underground, von Hügel's attitude to it changed, and it is this fact that has lent some plausibility to attempts to minimize his part in it. His plainest statement of his change of attitude is given in a letter that he wrote to Maude Petre in 1918 when she was writing her book *Modernism*. He then distinguished between 'Modernism' as

[1] Von Hügel to M. D. Petre, 9 February 1910: BM, Add. MSS 45361.
[2] Canet to Loisy, 17 July 1927: BN, n.a.f. 15650. See also Cuthbert Butler, *Religions of Authority and the Religion of the Spirit* (1930), pp. 184 f.
[3] M. D. Petre, *Alfred Loisy* (1944), p. 32.
[4] M. D. Petre to Loisy, 22 February 1921 (?): BN, n.a.f. 15660.
[5] M. Green, *Yeats's Blessings on von Hügel* (1967), p. 8.

the necessary and ever-recurring need and duty to interpret 'the old Faith... according to what appears the best and the most abiding elements in the philosophy and the scholarship and science of the later and latest times' and 'Modernism' as the particular series of attempts to do that during the pontificate of Pius X. While he hoped still to contribute to the former, he had revised his attitude to the latter which was a closed chapter. He still considered that the action of the Church authorities with regard to it had been 'very largely, violent and unjust' and he could not have subscribed 'to this or that document without express reservations', but had now come to see, more clearly than before, 'how much of serious unsatisfactoriness and of danger there was especially in many of the philosophical (strongly subjectivist) theories really held which *Pascendi* lumped together'.[1]

Maude Petre dated the change in von Hügel from the time of Fr Tyrrell's death. 'As to the Baron,—have you not seen it for a long time, dear M. Loisy?' she wrote in 1921. 'I myself date the most definite *recul* from the death of Fr Tyrrell.'[2] In November 1909, four months after Tyrrell's death, she had written to von Hügel himself: 'I have felt in my intercourse with you since his death...that you seemed more conscious of things to be excused than of things to be admired.'[3] And in the following month she wrote to A. L. Lilley: 'I am in a strangely isolated position, and have literally no Catholic of whom I can ask authoritative advice. It would have been the Baron, but *between ourselves* I simply cannot understand his present attitude.'[4] So it came about that when she was preparing Tyrrell's biography she depended more on the advice of Lilley than of von Hügel who 'would have liked every strong utterance omitted'.[5]

An early and significant, and to me an astonishing, indication

---

[1] Von Hügel to M. D. Petre, 13 March 1918: *Selected Letters*, p. 248.
[2] M. D. Petre to Loisy, 22 February (1921?): BN, n.a.f. 15660. Cf. 'Je dois vous dire que, tout en restant amis, mes relations avec von Hügel diminuèrent beaucoup de sympathie et de *confiance* après la mort de Tyrrell.' M. D. Petre to Loisy, 21 December 1927: BN, n.a.f. 15660. See also M. D. Petre, *Von Hügel and Tyrrell* (1937); and *Congrès d'histoire du Christianisme, Jubilé Alfred Loisy* (1928), iii. 227.
[3] M. D. Petre to von Hügel, 17 November 1909: BM, Add. 45361.
[4] M. D. Petre to Lilley, 10 December 1909: LP.
[5] M. D. Petre to Lilley, 17 July 1912: *ibid.*

of the way in which von Hügel began to get cold feet after Tyrrell's death, or rather after the funeral, is to be seen in his telling Henri Bremond, less than a month afterwards, that he now considered 'it would have been better if, at the Funeral, you had simply read the Prayers, and had invited all to follow your example, at the end, in the sprinkling of Holy Water on the coffin',[1] which must mean that he would have dispensed with Bremond's sublime address.[2] Indeed, if he had had his way, Catholics would not have accompanied the coffin to the cemetery.[3]

The change that came over von Hügel is further illustrated by the change that took place in Bremond's appraisal of him. In or about 1906 he wrote to von Hügel as follows:

I want some months of reflection and quietness to be myself again and to be able to go to *Jerusalem and see Peter*. But I really want you to realise how truly you are our *Peter* and we are living upon your thoughts and from your inspirations. I could easily draw the *courbe* of my intellectual and spiritual life and mark your influence at all the important ascensions...[4]

In 1927, however, we find Bremond writing to Loisy in quite different terms: 'Personally, I have always found—when one came to the critical points, to decisions whether theoretical or practical—that this bronze turned into a reed. But I can explain this phenomenon only by the fear of blows, and I should not have believed that this progressive capitulation of his mind was possible.'[5] And again in the following year: 'He was always very good to me—but I could not be his man. He often said to me that I represented French frivolity to a high degree. We had long conversations in the public gardens of London—but as soon as he launched into metaphysics, he could see quite well that I was not following him.'[6]

[1] F. von Hügel to H. Bremond, 10 August 1909: VHSA.
[2] For the full text of it, see Petre, *Autobiography and Life of George Tyrrell*, ii. 443 ff.
[3] Bremond to Loisy, June 1913: BLE, 1968, p. 176: 'Ma soumission lors des funérailles Tyrrell...l'a irrité et cependant si nous l'avions écouté, les catholiques n'auraient pas accompagné le corps au cimitière, ce qui me paraissait plus odieux.'
[4] Bremond to von Hügel (summer 1906?): VHSA.
[5] Bremond to Loisy, 20 August 1927: BN, n.a.f. 15650.
[6] Bremond to Loisy, 8 February 1928: *ibid.*

It was indeed his preoccupation with metaphysics and what has not unfairly been described as his obsession[1] with 'The Transcendent' that came between von Hügel and some of his closest modernist friends. In the case of Loisy and others he had some reason to regret the subjectivist or immanentist tendency of their thought, though he exaggerated it. In 1927 Maude Petre wrote to Loisy: 'As regards immanence, let me tell you that it was not only your writings that excited his mistrust. He saw it everywhere in what he read and in what he did not read.'[2] In a letter of 1921 von Hügel brought this, his favourite, indictment not only against Loisy and the Italian modernists, Buonaiuti and Minocchi, but against Tyrrell and even against Blondel and Laberthonnière.[3]

Let me conclude what I have to say about von Hügel with a recent piece of testimony from Mgr Maurice Nédoncelle, with whom I am always happy to find myself in agreement. It was given during a series of discussions in 1965 about Bremond. Nédoncelle was asked whether he thought Bremond shared von Hügel's views about subjectivism, and he replied:

That is not my impression. To make myself understood I am going to say something outrageous, but von Hügel already anticipated Maritain in this respect. He was the advocate of the Transcendent. He was always talking about Reality (with a capital R). Did von Hügel influence Bremond? In exegesis, yes certainly; in religious experience also. But when von Hügel talks as a metaphysician, as a philosopher of religion, his position in the modernist movement is an isolated one. Bremond is with the rest.[4]

II

I come now to Alfred Leslie Lilley, and I will say something about him in general, before bringing out his characteristics as a modernist and his part in the movement. Lilley was born at Clare in County Armagh in 1860. He had a brilliant career at Trinity College, Dublin. After two years as an assistant curate in the

---

[1] See M. D. Petre, *Alfred Loisy*, p. 36; *My Way of Faith*, p. 196.
[2] M. D. Petre to Loisy, 21 December 1927: BN, n.a.f. 15660.
[3] Von Hügel to R. Guiran, 11 July 1921: see *Selected Letters*, p. 334.
[4] *Entretiens* p. 63. For Maritain's latest views, see his *The Peasant of the Garonne* (E.T. 1968).

Church of Ireland he came to London, and from 1900 to 1912 he was Vicar of St Mary's, Paddington Green. In 1911 he was appointed to a residentiary canonry of Hereford Cathedral and two years later to the archdeaconry of Ludlow, and so came to be known as 'Archdeacon Lilley'.

This was the title of a chapter that A. G. Gardiner devoted to him in his book *Pillars of Society* (1913). Gardiner lamented the withdrawal from London of 'the chief ornament of the Church's pulpit', whose preaching had 'made the little church on Paddington Green a very well of living water to many to whom the appeal of the churches has grown sterile and unreal'.[1] Lilley's life and teaching, he said, were a protest against the petrification of the Church. 'It is not the protest of the rebel or the bitter controversialist, but of the seer who stands aloof in some spacious solitude of the spirit, catches the vision, and utters it in grave, abstracted speech. There is no note of the popular preacher in his style.' Moreover Lilley was 'the ideal parish priest, simple in manners and tastes, happy in the lowliest company'.[2]

He was indeed, as his private papers which were entrusted to me show, a man greatly beloved of all sorts and conditions of people, and not least by his many friends among the modernists. I myself met Lilley only in his old age when he was living in retirement in Oxford, but one felt at once what a singularly engaging personality he had. He had other qualities too that enabled him to enter into close relations with the modernists, and not only in England. He was a man of much learning and extensive culture, and he was fluent in French, German and Italian.[3] His ecclesiastical and theological orientation was congenial to the modernists, for he had graduated from ulster protestantism via anglo-catholicism (neither of which was conducive to width of sympathy) to a churchmanship that was liberal without being Liberal Protestant. Von Hügel quoted

<hr />

[1] Several volumes of his sermons were published, notably *The Soul of St Paul* (1909), *The Religion of Life* (1910), *The Nation in Judgment* dedicated to Henry Scott Holland (1911), and *Nature and Supernature* dedicated to M. D. Petre (1911).

[2] A. G. Gardiner, *Pillars of Society*, pp. 142, 143, 148, 149.

[3] See H. D. A. Major, 'In Memoriam: Alfred Leslie Lilley' in *The Modern Churchman*, March 1948, p. 14.

Lilley to G. E. Newsom as having said: 'The pressing divisions
are no more *vertical*, denominational,—they are *horizontal*, inter-
denominational.'[1]

Lilley's final theological orientation comes out in the conclusion of an unpublished address that he gave in 1933 to mark the
centenary of the Oxford Movement. After referring to Dean
Church's characterization of anglicanism as embodied in John
Keble,[2] he continued:

From that position, indeed, we have all of us, including those who
were and are most directly the spiritual descendants of the Trac-
tarians, the men of *Lux Mundi* and of *Essays Catholic and Critical*,
been forced to advance very fast and very far. The critical study of
history has made us much less sure of a consistent witness among even
the earliest interpreters of the faith, has indeed revealed to us among
them especially a most disconcerting variety of interpretation even on
the most central points of faith. An infallible authority in the old sense
we are less able to find, or indeed to conceive of as existing, anywhere.
Yet we who still survive from an older generation are grateful for
having been led by the inspiration and example of their stedfast faith
through what seemed a growing darkness and confusion towards the
dawn of a new day which will be so different from their yesterday. We
can just remember Church and Liddon facing bravely the coming of a
change which, to the latter at any rate, seemed in the last degree
ominous and menacing. And then we knew Scott Holland and Gore
as, the one with high cheer, the other with a more grim resolve, they
advanced into the new strange world of knowledge to convince it that
the integral substance of the ancient faith could still survive within its
categories and was even needed to give ultimate meaning to its most
confident certainties. Naturally the accommodation which they
effected left many a frayed edge and opened up perhaps some new and
disturbing problems for their successors to solve as best they might.[3]

In facing those problems Lilley certainly considered that he
had derived immense help from the modernists, and not only
from Tyrrell and von Hügel with whom he was in constant
communication during the course of the movement. Thus, for

[1] *Selected Letters*, p. 167.
[2] See R. W. Church, *Occasional Papers* (1897), ii. 303.
[3] LP.

instance, in 1903 he wrote to Loisy, thanking him for *Autour d'un petit livre*: 'For those of us who feel with something like despair the shivering hesitation which has come to mark the representative Anglican theology of the moment, your work and its certainty of principle and method are a proclamation of deliverance.'[1] And again, a few weeks later:

To me [your thought] has been as much of an inspiration or more than that of the later Ritschlians. It corrects in a Catholic sense the something of rigid and unhistorical simplicity which there is in their return to the Gospels. I feel that you have done for actual historical Catholicism what Pfleiderer has sought to do for religion in the air and apart from all historic 'cadres'.[2]

And, five years later, writing to Loisy just after his excommunication, he contrasted what seemed to him the anglican poverty of thought at that time:

In the main there is a portentous hush in Anglican circles. Our so-called scholars are, I feel sure, radically unfriendly and bitterly resent the slightest concession to the positions demanded by honest criticism ...Meanwhile the younger men are profoundly disturbed, and are not to be satisfied by the dogmatic assurances of Gore & Co. that criticism is tending more and more to conservative conclusions![3]

Similarly, he acknowledged his sense of indebtedness to Maude Petre, when dedicating his book *Nature and Supernature* (1911) to her, 'from whose writings I have learned so much, from whose quiet boldness in the faith I have still so much to learn'.[4]

What Lilley owed to Tyrrell may be inferred from the 'Epistle Dedicatory'[5] that he prefixed to his volume *Modernism: a record and a review* (1908). It contains expressions like these:

[1] Lilley to Loisy, 30 October 1903: BN, n.a.f. 15658.
[2] Lilley to Loisy, 17 December 1903: *ibid.*
[3] Lilley to Loisy, 4 April 1908: *ibid.*
[4] *Op. cit.* p. v. Cf. 'Dear Miss Petre, I would offer this book to you as to one from whom I have learned that the closed mind and the closed heart are the only things which are absolutely fatal to the life of religion.' *Ibid.* p. vii.
[5] Von Hügel to Lilley. 12 October 1907 (LP): 'Only this morning did I properly realise both the beauty and nobility of your writing and act, in that Dedication to Tyrrell...I do not see how the tone of it could be finer and more to the credit of both him that gives and him that takes.' This refers to a draft that Lilley had shown

You and your friends have written an inspired and inspiring page in the history of religious thought. . .

Through you the dawn has at last broken for thousands of wearied souls who have battled all their lives, and battled hopelessly, with the spectres of doubt and darkness. You have spoken for them the word of hope, so simple and obvious that, till you spoke it with the calm confidence of assured conviction, they dared not believe it to be true. . .

You have taught us both the necessity of an organised religious system and its inevitable imperfection as something whose life and growth forbid finality, petrification, and exclusiveness, and demand elasticity and an unlimited power of assimilation. . .[1]

Lilley's book, which he modestly described as 'some stray notes' consisted for the most part of articles and reviews that he had published during the preceding five years and it constituted the best contemporary account of the movement that appeared in English, and perhaps in any language. It moved von Hügel to designate Lilley, if he lived long enough, as the providential historian of the movement.[2] The book shows how closely Lilley was *en rapport* with the thinking of the modernists on the continent: he did not include what he had written about English publications.

So much for the way in which he viewed the modernists and identified himself with them. But how did they view him? Their letters that are now accessible leave no doubt about the answer to that question. 'Indeed you are to me no "outsider"!' Maude Petre once wrote to him,[3] and they would all have said the same. On another occasion she wrote: 'I know it is because you feel, as few on our side feel, and, perhaps, even fewer on your side, how closely our deepest interests are interwoven, that you work for our

---

[1] *Op. cit.* pp. vii, x ff. The precise wording of the last sentence was suggested by Tyrrell. See his letter to Lilley, 13 October 1907: LP.

[2] See von Hügel to Lilley, 22 February 1908: LP.

[3] M. D. Petre to Lilley, 25 July 1909: LP. At one time she hoped that Lilley and Bremond would be her literary executors: see *ibid.* 4 February 1910.

---

to von Hügel, who went on to boggle at one point, a too favourable allusion to the Church of England, which Lilley modified in the final version. On another occasion von Hügel spoke of his 'envious admiration' of Lilley's 'ever lucid, winning style': von Hügel to Lilley, 15 January 1912: LP.

Church almost as you work for yours.'[1] Lilley was the confidant
not only of the principals but also of their adherents. For instance,
after Tyrrell's death not only did Miss Petre depend on Lilley for
advice, much more than she depended on von Hügel,[2] but long
letters to him have survived from two other of Tyrrell's women
friends, Norah Shelley and Katherine Clutton (who were by no
means well disposed to Maude Petre), taking him into their
confidence.

The modernists regarded Lilley not only as a trustworthy
friend in whom they could safely confide, but also as exceptionally
well qualified to interpret and disseminate their message through
his articles and reviews. Thus Loisy told him that in his review of
Autour d'un petit livre, what he had written about the divinity of
Christ had interpreted his thought most accurately and at certain
points had even expressed it more clearly and forcefully than he
himself had done.[3] Similarly, Laberthonnière told von Hügel that
he had been delighted to find in Lilley an interpreter so sympathetic, so well-informed, broad-minded and penetrating.[4]
Bremond told von Hügel that Lilley was their best popularizer.[5]
Tyrrell wrote to him: 'Let me thank you most heartily and
affectionately for all you say; and for understanding me so
thoroughly and helping me to understand myself still better.'[6]

Again, in thanking Lilley for his review of *Medievalism*,
Tyrrell wrote: 'As a review it is quite admirable seizing as it does
the very point and heart of the book in a manner to which one is
not accustomed. Of course that is because our minds are one, and
you know your own mind.'[7] Von Hügel too was lavish in his
appreciation of Lilley as an interpreter of the modernists' cause.

---

[1] M. D. Petre to Lilley, 17 August 1907: LP.
[2] 'The Baron simply puzzles and astonishes me, so I cannot look to him for light,
though I keep him *au courant*.' M. D. Petre to Lilley, 10 December 1909: LP.
[3] Loisy to Lilley, 6 December 1903: LP. The review appeared in *The Guardian*,
2 December 1903. See *Modernism: a record and a review*, pp. 65–75.
[4] Laberthonnière to von Hügel, 1 March 1905: VHSA.
[5] Bremond to von Hügel, 10 March 1904: VHSA. See also Bremond's review of
Lilley's *Adventus Regni* in *Annales de philosophie chrétienne*, February 1908, pp.
526 f.
[6] Tyrrell to Lilley, 13 October 1907: LP. This was apropos of the draft of Lilley's
'Epistle Dedicatory'.
[7] Tyrrell to Lilley, 8 August 1908: LP. The review appeared in *The Daily News*.

'It is indeed a great consolation and one to thank God for,' he wrote, 'the finding in you, one more of the few minds and souls that understand the situation!'[1] And again: 'I was talking with Tyrrell about you...and we were spontaneously confiding to each other what a downright *calamity* it would be to our cause if you were, even for any appreciable time, be [*sic*] put *hors de combat*.'[2]

On Maundy Thursday 1911 von Hügel wrote a long and remarkable two-pointed letter to Lilley. He began by saying: 'For some time now...I have been pursued by the sad feeling that you, a very dear friend, to whom my friends and I owe so very much, are passing through much interior trouble and trial, much depression and loneliness.' (He appears not to have kept Lilley's letters,[3] but they frequently met, especially in connexion with the London Society for the Study of Religion.) Lilley, it seems, must have said something to him that implied doubt about whether he was doing any good as an anglican vicar. So von Hügel's first point was to give him an exceedingly emphatic assurance about '*the reality, the breadth and depth, of the good that, in Paddington, as a Church of England Vicar, you are doing. I am very,* VERY *sure of this.*' After enlarging on this, he concluded:

If I could, by lifting my little finger, or again, by making some great sacrifices, move you exteriorly or interiorly from where you are, —unless it were to some other, more fully appropriate and more cheering, Anglican clerical post, I would not lift it or make them. But I would gladly do all I could to help you to realise in your mind the good you are doing, and the ever increasing good that *you* can and will do, you, yes, but you *in and by means of institutional, i.e. Anglican religion.*

Von Hügel's second point is another instance of his preoccupation or obsession at this time with 'immanentism', which, as Maude Petre said, he saw everywhere 'in what he read and in what he did not read'.[4] So he said to Lilley, 'I notice, of course,

---

[1] Von Hügel to Lilley, 14 December 1903: LP.
[2] Von Hügel to Lilley, 27 October 1908: LP. Cf. *ibid*. 20 March 1908: 'You... are, out and out, the most helpful non-R.C. friend and ally we have got in England.'
[3] There are only two letters from Lilley to von Hügel in VHSA.
[4] See p. 126 above.

your *very* strong attraction, I think, temptation, to sheer Immanentism', and proceeded to read him an agitated and severe lecture
on the subject,[1] which contrasts unpleasantly with the generosity
of what he had said under his first point.

The words 'of course' in the foregoing quotation reveal von
Hügel's state of mind rather than Lilley's. For I fail to see any
warrant, in the three volumes of sermons that he published in
1910 and 1911,[2] for charging him with being attracted to 'sheer
Immanentism'. Indeed, one can say more than that, for in 1909
he had actually published a sermon on 'Immanence and Transcendence'[3] in which, while he explained why God's transcendence
and immanence were both vitally important for Christian faith,
his stress on the divine transcendence was the more emphatic.
Moreover, his other sermons show that he was not on that
occasion striking an unfamiliar note, in the way that some
preachers, when Michaelmas Day falls on a Sunday, affect a
hearty belief in angels, of which at other times you would never
suspect them. Nor is it credible that Lilley, when preaching,
sought to conceal the extent of his modernist sympathies or
opinions. On the contrary, while his preaching was characteristically positive, expository and practical, he did not disguise the
fact, for example, that in his view the truth of the Incarnation did
not depend on the historicity of the virginal conception[4] nor the
truth of the Resurrection on the evidences for the empty tomb.[5]

One might speculate on what would have happened to Lilley
if he had been a *Roman* Catholic modernist. I should say that he
would have been most likely to follow the course not of Loisy, of
Tyrrell, or of von Hügel, but of Mgr Mignot.

[1] Von Hügel to Lilley, 13 April 1911. VHSA.
[2] See p. 127 above.
[3] *The Soul of St Paul*, pp. 104–11.
[4] See *Practical Questions: lectures on modern difficulties in church life* (1905), p. 35.
Again, he treated the legendary character of the visit of the Magi as axiomatic: see
Nature and Supernature, p. 3.
[5] See *Nature and Supernature*, pp. 233–9; *Practical Questions*, p. 34.

6

AN UNRECOGNIZED MODERNIST

In the books about the modernist movement Edmund Bishop has not even been mentioned. He is not mentioned by Houtin nor by Rivière nor in my own book, *The Modernist Movement in the Roman Church*.[1] It was Dr Nigel Abercrombie's *The Life and Work of Edmund Bishop* (1959) that made the first public revelation of Bishop's modernism, although for good reasons it was no more than a subordinate theme in that book. Dr Abercrombie had worked through Bishop's papers which are preserved at Downside Abbey, and he made copious use of them. Even so, after reading his book, I was still somewhat perplexed about Bishop's position, that is, about his attitude to, and his relations with, the modernists. I was therefore glad to be allowed an opportunity to work through the papers at Downside for myself, and I am grateful to the Abbot for permitting me to quote from them. The information that I derived from them, and the extracts that I made, have, I believe, made clear to me what Bishop's position was and will, I hope, have enabled me to make it clear to others.

I will first briefly recall the main facts about Edmund Bishop, whose dates are 1846 to 1917. He was the son of a Devonshire hotel keeper. He received no more than a secondary education though part of it was at a school in Belgium. He became a minor civil servant. That was his professional occupation until he retired at the age of 39 on a very modest pension. He had been converted to Roman Catholicism when he was 21. At one time he tested his vocation to the monastic life at Downside Abbey, to which he became permanently attached and where he is buried.

---

[1] I did not at that time connect Bishop with the modernists, though he is once quoted in Maude Petre's *Modernism* (p. 169), which I had of course read. There are two references to him in Loisy's *Mémoires* (i. 377, 402), but only in connexion with the condemnation of anglican orders. He is mentioned a few times in Bedoyere, but not in such a way as to show where he stood *vis-à-vis* the modernists. See also Maude Petre's *My Way of Faith*, p. 213.

From 1903 onwards he lived a secluded life with a sister and niece at Barnstaple in his native county.

But the most important fact about Bishop is that, as Dom David Knowles says in his foreword to the biography by Dr Abercrombie, he 'was one of the last great English autodidacts'.[1] He was one of the most erudite and influential scholars of his time in the field of the history of liturgy. Naturally the greater part of his biography is taken up with the story of his researches, discoveries, publications and learned communications in that field as well as in the history of the Benedictine Order on which also he became a leading authority. I leave all that on one side, since I am here concerned only with the modernist aspect of his life.

The first point to be observed is that, in private though not in public, Bishop acknowledged, and acknowledged emphatically, that he was a modernist. Thus on 6 September 1908, a year after the promulgation of the *Pascendi*, he wrote to his anglican namesake, W. C. Bishop, who shared his liturgical interests: '(...*tell it not in Gath—or anywhere else*: I *seriously* mean this caution), of course I am an irredeemable modernist from long before the days when modernism was thought of'.[2] Earlier in the same year he had written to von Hügel: '...you know I am a modernist of before modernism; and the only person of the (then) young generation that was (I have ever heard of as being) really affected (but that profoundly and permanently) by "H and F-ism"...'[3] This was to say that he had been irrevocably captivated by the Liberal Catholicism of the *Rambler* and the *Home and Foreign Review*,[4] and had adopted the intellectual standards of Acton,

[1] *Op. cit.* p. xi.
[2] This letter is deciphered and quoted, though not dated, by Abercrombie, pp. 381 f.
[3] BP.
[4] See Josef L. Altholz, *The Liberal Catholic Movement in England : the 'Rambler' and its contributors 1848–1864* (1962). On 29 November 1922 von Hügel wrote to Mrs Lillie: 'I knew Mr Bishop well, a great scholar, one of Lord Acton's disciples, whose only faults, in my mind, were those of his master. He had a persistent irritation against Philosophy, or what he took to be such; and again, his suspicion and antipathy towards the Vatican were...distinctly excessive.' *Selected Letters*, p. 362.

Simpson and their group, particularly with regard to the critical study of history.

Even if Bishop had not made his confession in private, it would now be apparent that, on more than one count, he was a dyed-in-the-wool modernist[1] although, as we shall see, he was a singular and a detached one.

In the first place, he was an historical positivist or an historicist. He distinguished sharply between the theological and the scientific or critical attitude to history. In 1899 when reviewing Langlois and Seignobos, *Introduction to Historical Studies*, he said:

The writers begin by emphasizing in the strongest manner a truth which must be perfectly obvious to all, but which seems but dimly perceived by only too many writers—the truth, namely, that it is utterly impossible for us ever to know more than the extant documents tell us. Whatever airs or graces historians may give themselves, whatever their *allures* of mastery or freedom, it is by this inexorable necessity that they are cabined, cribbed, confined. Any past, or any part of the past, not witnessed to by documents is for us as though it had never existed.[2]

Bishop considered that there was a deep antagonism between this position and that of the theologians of his time. So, in a privately printed paper of the following year, significantly entitled, 'History or Apologetics', he wrote:

The historical and the theological methods of mental training are, in fact, here and now, different, and so different, as to be, at this time of day, almost—I fancy I may say quite—antagonistic... The business of the modern historian, the mere historian, the condition on which depends the utility of his labours, is precisely the ascertainment and

[1] Writing to Maude Petre on 14 September 1909, after he had spent several days with Bishop, von Hügel spoke of his 'experience, wisdom, and *union of ideas with us*' (italics mine). *Selected Letters*, p. 168.

[2] Art., 'Historical Critics on the Critical Art', *Downside Review*, July 1899, p. 191. It may be noted that G. C. Rawlinson said that he learned more about historical criticism from Langlois and Seignobos' book than from any others. See Rawlinson to von Hügel, 16 May 1908: VHSA. On G. C. Rawlinson, see Knox and Vidler, *The Development of Modern Catholicism*, pp. 191 ff.; MMRC, pp. 251 f.; and pp. 178 ff. below.

presentment—as nearly as the material conditions will allow—of the mere truth, on the evidence...'[1]

Writing to von Hügel in 1906 he spoke of his 'profound and permanent conviction that the "redemption" of the modern Catholic on the intellectual side can be wrought out only through the scientific pursuit of history,...through the positive not the speculative'.[2] History was not to be regarded as the *ancilla theologiae*, and the historian, to do his work aright, must be free.

In Bishop's view the condemnation in December 1903 of *L'Evangile et l'Eglise* and other books by Loisy showed unmistakably that the scientific or critical study of the Bible was ruled out of court for Catholics. Thus he wrote at the time to Dom Cuthbert Butler, who was having to consider whether he could go on with the study of the New Testament:

The condemnation of Loisy I quite expected: I have never seen why the renewed 'scientific' movement among Cathcs shd meet with a better fate that the old one when I was young. The differences in the Cathc schools are a matter of *principles* starting from an *antagonism of method*. The antagonism is in the things themselves: there is no reconcilement. See what I said in *History and Apologetics*...

To come to your own particular case...I have always said—keep hands off Scripture (i.e. as a *subject*). I think the path for a Cathic ecclestiastic who will be sincere & candid is not *viable*. An overpowering sense of vocation in that direction like Loisy's is another question: such a man must decide for himself: yours is certainly not such a case...[3]

And in another letter to Butler, written a few days later, he enlarged upon this advice:

I look on it that a Catholic worker on pure critical lines in N.T. and quite early things still has to work, it appears by Loisy's condemnation, with a rope round his neck. Moreover the people who hold the end of it and can at any moment tighten the noose & strangle a man, or half, hold all such work in suspicion...

[1] *Op. cit.* pp. 4, 6. This paper was prepared for a meeting of the Rota dining club on 4 December 1900.
[2] Bishop to von Hügel, 6 May 1906: BP.
[3] Bishop to Butler, 29 December 1903: BP.

Now the work *in itself* is tedious, trying, distressing enough to a Cathc in any case...and needing all possession of self, & one's powers & an even mind to make one's way... A man needs to work through it all in a sense of security, a sense that even a slip on his part will be viewed with indulgence in considn of the good end aimed at. But to subject oneself to all this trouble & distress with the knowledge that so far from being looked on with a benevolent eye one is regarded *ipso facto* with suspicion by the Authority one wd serve, by others of the common run as 'unsound' or 'temerarious', and has always at one's heels denouncers (Houtin says that *everything* Loisy has done the last 10 or 12 years has been denounced at Rome by some one or other), only too glad to seize hold of any slip to shut one up and render one useless—I say that such a position is an impossible one, and that unless driven by positive vocation and an overwhelming sense of duty —a position to be absolutely avoided.[1]

Secondly, Bishop's concord with the modernists is shown in the fact that he was extremely critical of papal and clerical authoritarianism. He deplored the character that the papacy had given to the Church during the nineteenth century, especially its treatment of liberal movements and its hostility to critical scholarship. It seemed to him that the pontificate of Leo XIII had been a misleading interlude and that its apparent or comparative liberality had been due to the personal qualities of the pope, and not to any change in the determined policy of the Vatican. At the end of 1903 he wrote to Cuthbert Butler: 'We are entering with Pius X on a *normal* state of things. The younger generation don't seem to have realized *what* a Pope, how great a Pope, they had grown up under in Leo XIII.'[2] He enlarged on the point a few days later:

However things may have seemed in the 50ies/60ies, and 80ies/90ies, I don't think that any one competently informed & looking back at the scientific–liberal movement among Catholics can have any doubt

---

[1] Bishop to Butler, 4 January 1904: BP. This letter, by an obvious slip, was dated 4 January 1903.

[2] Bishop to Butler, 29 December 1903: BP. Cf. Bishop to von Hügel, 2 July 1909 (*ibid.*): 'My own view, or sense, you know, is that our present state & condition is no temporary phase, but is *irreformable* & settled. It was (as I conceive) planned & the end clearly pursued since the early fifties. Leo XIII's Pontificate was indeed in practice a breathing time—no more—& one due exclusively to him *personally*.'

whatever that it is on principle & as a settled policy viewed with as much suspicion and disfavour as political liberalism. Certain hopes were justified in the 50ies/60ies, but the then generation experienced how they had deceived themselves by their very generosity of good will and high aspiration. It might be and were excusable that a new generation that had not 'known' those things shd be filled with the same high hopes and generous aspirations—which I hold most strongly still were good in themselves—but I think it must be allowed on a full survey of the century that the Authority's policy is just the same as before, is consistent throughout, and the Authority is itself subject to just the same (as I think pernicious and fatal) influences as in the times of the older generation.

Then, after remarking that the pontificate of Leo XIII had obscured this state of affairs, he continued:

It is a wonderful thing to think that this great old man on his very deathbed with all kinds of influences urgent upon him as the spirit was quitting the body still resisted to the last the efforts to induce him to censure *L'Evangile et l'Eglise*...This great personality has excusably enough prevented many persons from observing how in fact single uniform consistent has been the policy of 'Rome' during all the last century in regard to the matters that interest us.[1]

During the first world war Bishop likened the despotic policy and methods of the papacy to those of Prussian militarism.[2]

Thirdly, Bishop shared the common modernist attitude to the official or scholastic theology and to those who cultivated it. In 1905 von Hügel sent him a copy of the pseudonymous and privately printed booklet, *The Church and the Future* by Hilaire Bourdon,[3] which purported to be a translation from French. Bishop evidently had no suspicion that George Tyrrell was the author.[4] It was in fact one of Tyrrell's most forceful

---

[1] Bishop to Butler, 4 January 1904: BP.
[2] See his comments on the newspaper cuttings of the time which he inserted in his scrap book: BP.
[3] It was *published*, after Tyrrell's death, in 1910 with an introduction by M. D. Petre.
[4] Von Hügel wrote about it as follows: 'Since you are so utterly trustworthy and understanding a reader of Catholic writings of the *coming* type, I venture to send you a booklet...which I cannot help hoping you will find deeply stimulating. I know that I can count upon your absolute discretion.' Von Hügel to Bishop, 29 September 1905. See *Dublin Review*, 1953, p. 187.

modernist writings. In thanking von Hügel for it, Bishop wrote:

At once I may say that I find in it so much that corresponds to my own solitary musings... I find myself arrested by a master hand... The side on which it naturally appeals to me most is as a solution for the individual Catholic of the personal difficulties of his position. Herein I may say that the writer's general lines & conclusions are those I have been led to adopt for my own help guidance support.[1]

In the booklet Tyrrell had argued that a Catholic could reasonably and honestly remain in the Church while rejecting the doctrine of its official representatives or spokesmen. One passage which Bishop will have especially savoured read as follows:

In practical working... it is not the pope personally who governs Catholic thought and opinion, but the various congregations and commissions whom he 'consults' and whose decisions he may adopt or reject. These commissions again are under the influence of what is, I think, *the* great tyranny of the modern Church, *sc.* the theological schools—the 'consensus theologorum'. If this meant the free and independent agreement of qualified experts *au courant* with all the data of the problems in question, it would indeed be a valuable, if a purely natural, criterion of religious truth. But in point of fact it is a purely artificial consensus enforced from without, as little worthy of consideration as the uniformity of a regiment of soldiers...

Metaphysics (and scholastic theology is chiefly metaphysics), by reason of its necessary obscurity, is the department where mediocrity and slovenliness of thought can most easily mask itself under the semblance of profundity, and where the intellectual charlatan can lie longest undetected. Yet in the ecclesiastical *milieu* it shares with theology the glory of being the queen of sciences to whose rulings all must submit, and it offers a short cut to all human knowledge; or at least is conceived to give a right and power of universal criticism independent of any laborious study and inquiry into the positive and concrete.[2]

Writing of this kind was calculated to appeal immediately to one of Bishop's positivist cast of mind. In June 1904 he had written to von Hügel:

[1] Bishop to von Hügel, 8 October 1905: BP.
[2] H. Bourdon, *The Church and the Future*, pp. 25 ff.

in a society of 'thinkers' I am out of place, if only by the very constitution of my mind which has all the native English weakness of incapacity for abstract thought and tendency towards the positive or
verifiable.... I venture to believe, that the tendency of the pure
'thinkers' is towards the methods of authority and of the schools, and
herein betrays... a curious kinship of spirit with the theologians... I
am... (perhaps unduly) alive to the possibilities of danger on this score
through observing how readily in our own communion expositors and
apologists, official and unofficial, make assumptions and take up
positions that are unwarranted or untenable; and how this often
proceeds from mere ignorance, or indisposition... to follow the results
attained, or in the way of being attained, by the application to the
'evidences' of the past of modern 'historical and scientific method'. I
quite recognize the humble place of these results as compared with the
realm of thought. But they have their use; and not their least use to my
mind is the check they place on the absolutism which so often manifest
[*sic*] in the thinker...[1]

While, in the respects which I have illustrated, Bishop was
certainly at one with the modernists and was justified in privately
describing himself as one of them, yet, on the other hand, he
differed from them in that he did not believe, or even hope, that
any such reform in the Church as the modernists advocated
could come about. There was no possibility within the foreseeable
future of loosening the fatal grip of the ecclesiastical authorities
and of the scholastic theologians. Thus, on 28 June 1908, he
wrote to von Hügel: 'I do *not* believe, have long not believed, in
those party, or non-party, efforts for "reform" in the Church, as
I think they originate in an entirely false estimate of the situation
& want of realization of what the modern "R. C. Church" has
constituted itself as being.'[2]

---

[1] Bishop to von Hügel, 7 June 1904: BP. For further light on Bishop's view of
'theologians', see the quotations from his letter to Dom Ethelbert Horne in
Abercrombie, *op. cit.* pp. 436 f.

[2] Bishop to von Hügel, 28 June 1908: BP. On 12 February 1913 Bishop told Miss
Petre that he agreed with her in thinking that reform of the Church must come
eventually from without, and on 22 October 1914 he wrote to her: 'All my whole
feeling & outlook are thoroughly summed up in the last reported words of "*John
Inglesant*"... "The sun is set", said Mr Inglesant cheerfully, "but it will rise again.
Let us go home."' Bishop to M. D. Petre: BM, Add. MSS 45744. See J. H.
Shorthouse, *John Inglesant* (1900 edn), p. 445.

And, a year later, he said to the same correspondent: 'My own view, or sense, you know, is that our present state or condition is no temporary phase, but is *irreformable* & settled.'[1]

Pius X's condemnation of modernism, therefore, neither surprised nor depressed Bishop. On the contrary, its immediate effect was to make him thankful,[2] not because he approved of the papal acts, but because they afforded unmistakable evidence that reform was out of the question. On 19 January 1908 he wrote to his friend, Everard Green: 'I can't imagine any one "leaving the Church" on a/c of this Pope his ways & works. It comes all under the rubric—that scandals must needs come.'[3] Not the least of the scandals was that, as he said to von Hügel later in the same year, Pius X had 'extended to the whole Church the special "religious" discipline of the "Society" [i.e. the Jesuits], spying & delation; &...raised these to the dignity & state of religious duty.'[4]

Was there then nothing that laymen such as Bishop could do about the situation? This was the question to which he addressed himself in a paper that he prepared for the Rota dining club[5] a few months after the *Pascendi* was promulgated. It was called 'A Paper without a Title'. In a survey of past history Bishop noted how, while lay Catholics had been able to contribute to the revival of the Church in the first half of the nineteenth century, after 1850 those who had attempted to serve the Church directly had come to grief, since all power and authority were now concentrated in the pope, and the help of the laity was neither asked for nor desired. His conclusion therefore was that laymen must forgo 'honourable and well-meaning attempts' to interpret the Church to the modern world or to reconcile the modern world to the Church. Laymen, who had leisure, disposition and opportunity for intellectual labour, must make up their minds to

---

[1] Bishop to von Hügel, 2 July 1909: BP.
[2] See Abercrombie, *op. cit.* p. 374.
[3] Bishop to Green, 19 January 1908: BP.
[4] Bishop to von Hügel, 28 June 1908: BP. Cf. p. 150 below.
[5] In the event the paper was read for him, as he was not present at the meeting on 4 December 1907. Several drafts of this paper (which was never published) exist at Downside. I have used the draft from which the final copy was made.

do their work—whether it be in the field of philosophy, science, criticism, or what not—as intellectuals, not as Catholics. That is to say, their contributions to learning must claim, and expect to receive, attention only on the ground of their intrinsic quality, and not because they were in any way representative of Catholicism. Since the Church authorities wanted no help, they should be left to manage things in their own way. In 1903 Bishop had written to Cuthbert Butler: 'My own feeling strongly has been for some years past that the only possible course for a Catholic, self respecting, "scientific", is to throw back on the Eccl[l] Authority & those whom it trusts the defence of the whole position?'[1]

It was in this light that, at any rate from about 1900 onwards, Bishop had viewed his own contributions to learning. He was in the habit of saying that it was no use doing anything for the Church as it was only misunderstood.[2] In 1904 he had written to von Hügel:

With us the Church *authority* for any time I can remember has shewn itself pervasive and omnipresent, and at the same time peremptory and professedly irresponsible. I will express my conclusion on our situation in the words of another man; they exactly express my view; but, as not being mine, may come with a confirmatory force: viz. that for us Roman Catholics 'pour obtenir la tolérance, les travailleurs ont dû se borner à étudier les faits, à publier des documents, dont ils ne tiraient point les conséquences, ou dont ils paraissaient même ne point comprendre l'importance'.[3]

The case of those members of the clergy who knew and reflected was, in Bishop's view, much more delicate and difficult, since they could not altogether steer clear of theological and ecclesiastical issues. We have seen how he warned them to keep off Scriptural questions and 'quite early things'.[4] As regards wider questions such as those that Father Tyrrell handled, Bishop's

[1] Bishop to Butler, 29 December 1903: BP.
[2] 'What you commonly say—that it is no use doing anything as one is only misunderstood...I am much more optimistic about the Church than you are.'—H. C. Corrance to Bishop, 4 May 1905: BP.
[3] Bishop to von Hügel, 12 June 1904: BP.
[4] See p. 137 above.

consideration for the embarrassing position in which clerics with modernist sympathies were placed is revealed in the following letter in which he told von Hügel that he felt 'little, if any, temptation to talk out even e.g. to our friend [Cuthbert] Butler' about the fundamental matters that were dealt with in Hilaire Bourdon's *The Church and the Future*, which von Hügel had just sent him. He went on:

You know that personally I feel that it is incumbent on one to remember the difficulties of an enlightened and 'liberal' minded ecclesiastic in the present state of things & I believe often he is best 'helped' by his 'best' friends by not being forced or pressed to sound the depths of his own mind in a time of transition such as is our present age: & while I quite enter into, and highly share, the reasons of your 'discretion' in not giving our friend E. C. B. a copy, I feel also no 'temptation' to entertain him, by so much as a word, with it in the way of conversation.[1]

Although Bishop himself took so negative a view of the prospects of a modernist movement in the Church, he was not only greatly respected by, but regarded almost as a leader, by more committed modernists. I will give a few examples.

H. C. Corrance, about whom I shall have something to say in the next chapter, was a convert clergyman who became a thorough-going modernist. Writing to Bishop in 1905, he said:

I always feel very grateful to you, among others, for the assistance you were to me, when groping my way in the Church soon after my conversion, in giving me the right clue... You prepared the way for my acceptance of Loisy's position...[2]

The 'clue' you gave me was the distinguishing of dogma from its history, which, though a simple enough principle in itself and, when one came to think of it, merely an elementary and obvious truth, is one that is not at all recognised in the Anglican milieu in which I had lived ...Had I not been prepared by your ideas I do not think I should have appreciated [Loisy] as much as I did, but having been so prepared I found in him the proper fulfilment of that preparation. You were in

---

[1] Bishop to von Hügel, 8 October 1905: BP.
[2] Corrance to Bishop, 19 April 1905: BP.

my case, and I think in that of others as well, 'the pedagogue to lead one to Loisy'...[1]

The only *prominent* modernist with whom Bishop was in close personal relations was von Hügel. What von Hügel thought of him is shown in the card he addressed to Bishop when sending him a presentation copy of Loisy's *Evangiles synoptiques*. It read as follows:

> To Edmund Bishop,
> in grateful admiration of the fearless sincerity
> of his mind, the persistent laboriousness of his
> life, the competence of his scholarship,
> and the thoroughness of his Catholic faith,
> from his Friend and Well-wisher
> Friedrich von Hügel.
> 20th Febr. 1908.[2]

Von Hügel had previously told Bishop that 'the only point of even *apparent* divergence' between them was in regard to philosophy. He said that he looked upon Bishop's aversion to philosophy as an entirely intelligible recoil from Neo-Scholasticism ('*the* foe of all serious historico-critical liberty and re-interpretation of thought and of religion in the Church') and from the post-Hegelian German philosophical systems ('so abstract, short-lived, and mutually contradictory'). 'In your case, as (I venture to think) with all deep and complete natures, the aversion to philosophy is, I am very sure, but to certain conceptions and habits going under that name.'[3]

Perhaps Bishop's most interesting modernist liaison was with the young Frenchman, Louis Canet (1883–1958),[4] who was to become the literary executor both of Lucien Laberthonnière and of Alfred Loisy. Canet got into touch with Bishop in 1912 when he wanted to consult him about his work as a research student. In an early letter Canet told Bishop about himself, and I will

[1] Corrance to Bishop, 4 May 1905: BP.
[2] BP.
[3] Von Hügel to Bishop. See *Dublin Review*, 1953, pp. 292 f.
[4] Cf. Abercrombie, *op. cit.* pp. 438, 455 f., and p. 31 above.

translate what he said, since he was an important adherent of the modernist movement. He wrote on 18 July 1912:

I am 29 years old today. I was born at Rouen, where my father teaches a small class at the Lycée... I was educated at Rouen, then at Paris. Three years ago I passed the *agrégation* examination and became a student at the Ecole des Hautes Etudes. Finally, I have just been appointed for *two* years a member of the Ecole Française at Rome.

I am a Catholic, but this calls for some explanation. I was taught at the Lycée in Rouen by Abbé Vacandard;[1] later I came under various influences, notably those of Loisy, of Laberthonnière and above all of Tyrrell whom however I didn't know personally. I am still today affectionately attached to M. Loisy, although I have not gone all the way with him; and I am Père Laberthonnière's secretary and live with him while I am far from altogether sharing his outlook. For a long time I preached the modernist gospel, but for several months now I have kept quiet, not that I am going back to the official doctrines; far from it. But I thought it would be a good thing to get a respite by abstaining at least for some time from philosophical, theological or apologetic speculations. There is in me a being who works and a being who believes; I mean by that one who wills to be united to the Church understood as the mystical society of those who are of the spirit of Christ. A day may come perhaps, and I hope it will, when I shall be able to give a more precise definition of my religious attitude. Meanwhile, without any longer seeking to convert other people, I hold myself to be a Catholic, I say that I am one, and I act as one.[2]

In the following year, during a visit to England when he also saw von Hügel and Miss Petre, Canet spent a week with Bishop at Downside. Among other things, Bishop evidently explained his settled view that it was impossible to do anything directly towards the renewal of Catholicism, for afterwards Canet wrote to him as follows:

You are the first person to have made me understand that our struggles and our sacrifices may be able to do nothing for the renewal of Catholicism and that it may well be at once more intelligent and more Christian to work unobtrusively at the tasks of pure science. There

---

[1] Elpège Vacandard (1849–1927) was a theological savant.
[2] Canet to Bishop, 18 July 1912: BP.

too you may have given me, even for my inner life, a precious pointer...[1]

It should of course be borne in mind that this was the time when the campaign of the integrists was at its height and the so-called white terror prevailed in the Church. Canet went on to tell Bishop that he had been greatly moved when attending Evening Prayer at Westminster Abbey on the previous Sunday, and in the following week he wrote and told him of a visit he had made to Oxford: 'On Sunday I went to Oxford and heard Morning Prayer at Magdalen College. This liturgy is really admirable. I think I can now see better what a wrench your conversion [i.e. from anglicanism] must have been, and what an appeal "the Church of his baptism" must have continued to make to Tyrrell.'[2]

Bishop approved warmly of Le Roy's practical or pragmatic interpretation of dogmas.[3] So we find him writing to von Hügel: 'Personally I "think highly" of the substance of Le R.'s contention. Towards the end he jumps one without warning into an abyss—or is it *chaos*?'[4] This refers to Le Roy's *Qu'est-ce qu'un dogme?*,[5] where towards the end he turns from the practical to the speculative aspects of dogma. In the same letter Bishop told von Hügel that he had been very glad to see that Le Roy had been defended in the *Times Literary Supplement*.[6]

Towards Loisy and Tyrrell Bishop's attitude was more ambivalent. Obviously he would approve, and did approve, of the distinction that Loisy drew between the sphere of scientific history and that of theology, apologetics and faith. This was the distinction that Bishop himself had drawn in his paper 'History or Apologetics' and on many other occasions. It did not follow that he found Loisy's mind in other respects congenial or that he agreed with his conclusions (as distinguished from his methods) as an historian.

[1] Canet to Bishop, 18 July 1913: BP.
[2] Canet to Bishop, 23 July 1913: BP.
[3] See p. 90 above.
[4] Bishop to von Hügel, 6 May 1906: BP.
[5] Extract from *La Quinzaine*, 16 April 1905.
[6] See the letter from J. A. Leger in the *T.L.S.* of 4 May 1906, which is quoted on p. 91 above.

When in 1906 von Hügel and others were proposing that an address to Loisy, expressing sympathy with him from other Catholic scholars, should be prepared for presentation in the likely event of his excommunication, von Hügel wrote to Bishop asking him to draft such an address. The facts that the request was made and that Bishop was disposed to comply with it are evidence of his approval of the stand that Loisy was making for the rights and duties of a scientific historian. (Actually the proposed address was abortive, since not enough signatures could be secured.) The invitation also led Bishop to explain with some care how he regarded Loisy. Thus he wrote to von Hügel:

I ought to explain my position in regard to 'Loisy'. I do not know him; have no particular or special sympathies with him—with the 'self' of him so far as I can guess it from what I have read of his: if anything perhaps my leaning might be the other way. Moreover my own lines of study are removed & apart from his, in which I have no competence or special knowledge whatever. Harnack's *Wesen* I read, *enjoyed*, felt the force of...very soon after it came out: & quite felt how it might affect some young Catholics. Loisy's reply I did not read—I was not interested; nor I think did I even see it until after the '*Autour*' [*d'un petit livre*] came out...I am even now indifferent to the Reply itself *except* in one of its aspects. The one aspect is this. Whilst every one else among us Catholics was helpless and so would in fact (though not in will) have left intelligent young Catholics to the influence of Harnack's book,—would have left the 'wolf' to ravage the 'fold', —Loisy, Loisy alone, stood up and did the work of a Shepherd of the flock: and so effectively that even Harnack or Harnack's friends recognized and allowed the force and power of the defence.

And it is our relation as *laymen*, as of the 'flock'—to this one fact that gives us an opening, a right—and I am not sure whether it may not impose upon us a duty—to speak, should he in some way be excommunicated. For as laymen deserted at the moment of danger by the professional theologian, we have a duty of gratitude to one who (it would seem to my mind, whatever be the mixture of human weakness in his work and workings) has in fact laid down his (spiritual) life for the sheep—has become anathema for our sake.[1]

[1] Bishop to von Hügel, 6 May 1906: BP. Part of this letter is quoted by Abercrombie, *op. cit.* p. 355, where it is combined with part of another letter (of 25 May 1906).

At the same time, Bishop is unusual among the modernists in having considered that Harnack's view of the origins of Christianity was probably more true than Loisy's.[1] Soon after he had begun to read Loisy's *Evangiles synoptiques*—'*the* book of his I wanted to consider'—he wrote to von Hügel: 'You know I am not & never was of the least mood or capacity to swallow Loisy whole. I am not at all clear, or indeed disposed to think that in the main contention he is all right and Harnack all wrong. Far from this. . .'[2] This preference for Harnack's view was probably connected with, if it did not arise from, a strain of simple evangelical piety that was deeply rooted in Bishop's spirituality and also the fact that his profound attachment to the Catholic cultus was combined with a strong aversion to the ecclesiastical and theological developments which had become dominant in historical Catholicism and which Loisy's modernist apologetic seemed too much calculated to justify.

Among many other illustrations that might be given from Bishop's papers of his anti-ecclesiastical animus, I give one that is also interesting on another account. In a letter of 1905, H. C. Corrance said that the modern High Church movement in the Church of England (out of which he had himself come) had 'been built up on the theory of the necessity of tracing dogma in its present form to as early a period as possible, which of course does not conduce to creating the detached state of mind necessary to an historian'. And he went on:

The reason for this state of things I have long recognised is the fact that they have to create some sort of artificial support for their personal beliefs, have no general faith of the Church to fall back upon, which, as you say, is the strength of our position and the reason why the Catholic Church, alone among 'the Churches', can be at once both Christian and critical.[3]

In the margin of Corrance's letter, against this passage, Bishop wrote: 'What I said was the *Catholic religion*'—i.e. not the Catholic *Church*.

---

[1] Cf. Abercrombie, *op. cit.* p. 345.
[2] Bishop to von Hügel, 3 March 1908: BP.
[3] Corrance to Bishop, 10 May 1905: BP.

As regards Bishop's attitude to Father Tyrrell, we have already noted the warm concurrence he expressed with Tyrrell's pseudonymous booklet, *The Church and the Future*.[1] Incidentally, so far was Bishop from discountenancing the use of pseudonyms by theologians who wanted to avoid aggravating their ecclesiastical superiors that, after the condemnation of modernism, in June 1908 he wrote to von Hügel:

The present Pope by his *Lamentabili* has...extended to the whole Church the special 'religious' discipline of the 'Society' [*sc.* the Jesuits], spying & delation; & has raised these to the dignity & state of religious duty...Of one thing experience of the past twelve months has convinced me—that the 'modernist' is quite justified in mystifying the new inquisitors by any kind of anonymity,—by any amount of ambidextrousness that may render difficult identification of persons &c &c.[2]

In 1908 when the principal modernists were being denounced and vilified, Bishop, who had sympathized with them and agreed with much that they had said but had not shared their hopes or publicly supported them, said to von Hügel: 'It is not I who am going to make any reserves, or depreciatory comment, on *any*thing men like Tyrrell & Loisy may say. They have earned the right to our respectful silence *at the very least* even in points where we do not in fact sympathize.'[3]

When Tyrrell died in July 1909 Bishop wrote to the Baron:

You know how & what I feel in regard to him & others like him. They have been to me not (as I fancy some have regarded them) as pioneers & forerunners in a new day for 'the Church'; —it is not so that I have looked on them;—but as men who had compassion upon the multitude,—the unhappy multitude (& they are more numerous I take it than most of us, & particularly the clergy realize) who either 'know' or reflect, or both...[4]

In 1914 he said to Miss Petre that Tyrrell's 'great work was to put in a clear plain unmistakable form what so many persons—

[1] See p. 140 above.
[2] Bishop to von Hügel, 28 June 1908: BP.
[3] Bishop to von Hügel, 18 February 1908: BP.
[4] *Ibid.* 18 July 1909.

may I say conspired?—to blur & confuse. And it cost him his life.'[1] This was after Bishop had read and been greatly moved by Tyrrell's *Autobiography and Life*.[2]

One reason why Tyrrell appealed to Bishop more than Loisy was that he somehow conveyed an impression of the clouds and darkness that surround the divine mysteries. This comes out in an interesting letter that he wrote to his friend, Everard Green, in October 1909:

> Thank you for Tyrrell's mortuary card. Poor Tyrrell. I sometimes am apt to think that he has not been 'well served'...in the house of, & by, 'friends'. Curious that I have never come across him, directly or indirectly, in any way, & have read none of his books but '*Mediaevalism*' —which was not *his* 'message' at all: not his own unprejudiced self. I say 'unprejudiced' in the sense of native originality and unfettered unconditioned expression of intimate souls—as I fancy *Nova et Vetera*, *Oil & Wine*, & books of that kind are...Nothing shall make me say that the 'dark' things *are* clear, & the 'hard' things are plain: I insist that they are what they are, 'dark' 'hard', & we must bear with them *as such*, as best we can...It is *here* you see that I put myself in direct opposition of mind & soul & heart to Tyrrell's contradictors.[3]

Two other passages in his letters to the same correspondent show what Bishop meant by the things that are 'dark' and 'hard'. One deals with the question of Christian origins:

> The Gospel documents, when tried by those strict tests [i.e. of the critical historian], afford *enough* evidence as to matter of fact to make it (*at the least*) unjustifiable in a believer to reject those primary articles of our Faith, the Incarnation and the Resurrection; but...the evidence for these events in the documents we possess is not sufficiently cogent to enable the Christian apologist to convince the unbeliever (who takes his stand on the ground of historical evidence) of these facts from the testimony of the documents themselves.[4]

The other passage refers to the inability of the theologians

---

[1] Bishop to M. D. Petre, 18 March 1914: BP.
[2] See Abercrombie, *op. cit.* pp. 383, 442 ff.; Bishop to M. D. Petre, 12 February 1913: BM, Add. MSS 45744.
[3] Bishop to Green, 24 October 1909: BP.
[4] 1904. Quoted by Abercrombie, *op. cit.* p. 300.

to meet the intellectual difficulties that are involved in belief:

All the papal artillery of the *Pascendi gregis* directed against 'sentiment' is to me so much *brutum fulmen*.—Catholicity is a great *religion*; it is the *only one* (sad as such a case may be) to which I own and can feel allegiance. But the Catholic 'Intellectual System of the Universe' —the great intellectual system elaborated by the theologians:—that is a different matter. All I can say is that (although such considerations were not absent, especially on the side of Holy Scripture) *I* never became a Catholic, 'embraced Catholicism', as *a solution of intellectual difficulties*. And the older I grow, and more I know, the less does it appear to me *to be so*. But just therein lies what I call 'the Venture of Faith'. Some people seem to me, whilst loudly talking (or writing) about that, to have no real intelligence of what that 'venture' really is— its nature.[1]

He had said much the same four years before to Cuthbert Butler, and I will conclude with this sentence which has the distinguishing flavour of Bishop's modernism:

To my notion so far from Catholicism being a solution of *intellectual* difficulties, on the main points the difficulties are as considerable for them as for Protestants, whilst Catholicism has in the light of new knowledge difficulties peculiar to itself. Its *strong* point (as Protestantism's weak point) is *religion*; but that is a different matter.[2]

---

[1] 1907. Quoted by Abercrombie, *op. cit.* p. 376.
[2] Bishop to Butler, 29 December 1903: BP.

Alfred Loisy

Henri Bremond

Monseigneur Mignot

His Holiness Pope Pius X

Baron Friedrich von Hügel, from the painting in the William
Rainey Harper Memorial Library of the University of Chicago

Alfred Leslie Lilley

Edmund Bishop

Marc Sangnier: pencil sketch by Henri de Nolhac

7

LESSER LIGHTS AND FELLOW TRAVELLERS

Alternative titles for this chapter could have been 'Odds and Ends' or 'Hints for Research Students'. During my burrowings, especially in the correspondence of the modernists, I have come across the mention of a considerable number of personalities about whom I should like to know more, but about whom I shall not be able to find out as much as I should like to know unless I defer the publication of this book till after I am dead. I have had to turn aside from many tempting inquiries that might, or might not, have proved fruitful for filling in the picture of the modernist movement, for understanding the influence that it had, and for tracing the sympathies and antipathies that it aroused. For instance, in the case of H. C. Corrance, about whom I am going to say something presently, I soon found that, in order to get to know all that I wanted to know about him, so much detective work would be necessary, including perhaps a visit to Australia, that I had to suspend my investigations.

At one time I thought of devoting a whole chapter to the fiction of the modernist movement, and someone else might well do that. It would need to be someone who was not only well acquainted with the history and background of the movement but who also had qualifications as a literary critic such as I cannot claim to possess. A comparative study of the variety of novels which the modernist movement prompted, inspired, or was attended by, would, I suspect, yield much illumination. From a literary point of view the most famous is no doubt one to which I alluded in connexion with Marcel Hébert,[1] namely Roger Martin du Gard's *Jean Barois* (1913). The novel that has the most assured place in the history of the movement is Antonio Fogazzaro's *Il Santo* (1905),[2] which in the winter of 1905–6 is

---

[1] See p. 70 above.
[2] E. T., *The Saint* (1906).

said, both on literary and religious grounds, to have been the event of the season in France as well as in Italy,[1] and which had the distinction of being placed on the Index on 5 April 1906.[2]

France as one would expect, was most productive in this field as in others. In addition to *Jean Barois*, there is Joseph Malègue's impressive *Augustin ou le Maître est là* (1933) of which 75,000 copies had been sold by 1953:[3] it is by way of being a Catholic rejoinder to *Jean Barois*. Then some of Paul Bourget's novels had the character of being an unsympathetic reaction to the modernist movement. Houtin observed to Loisy that *Le Démon de Midi* (1914) was 'a salad of modernism and of adultery' and that Bourget seemed to be more at home when studying the latter than the former sin.[4] Two other French novels, *La Lumière de la Maison* by Jean Nesmy (1909)[5] and *L'Anathème* by Albert Autin (1921),[6] which, I understand, are sympathetic to the movement, I have not yet been able to read. Some of George Fonsegrive's pseudonymous writings[7] also form part of the fiction of the movement.

So in England do novels by Mrs Wilfrid Ward and by Mrs Humphry Ward. Mrs Wilfrid Ward's *Out of due time* (1906) was taken by many to be directly concerned with modernism and Father C. C. Martindale supposed one of the characters in it to represent Baron von Hügel: it seems, however, that the book was mainly inspired by the story of Lamennais.[8] Mrs Humphry Ward's *The Case of Richard Meynell* (1911) is a modernist counterpart[9] to her better known, liberal protestant novel *Robert*

---

[1] See Raoul Gout, *L'Affaire Tyrrell*, p. 134.

[2] *Leila*, a further novel which Fogazzaro published shortly before his death in 1911 (E.T., 1911), was also placed on the Index. See *Index Librorum Prohibitorum* (1948), p. 176.

[3] See *Joseph Malègue* by Yvonne Malègue (1947).

[4] See *Mém.*, iii. 281. Bourget said Loisy was 'detestable'; see Frémont, ii. 563.

[5] See Richard Griffiths, *The Reactionary Revolution*, p. 282. 'Jean Nesmy' was the pseudonym of Henry Surchamp.

[6] See *ibid.* p. 20.

[7] Notably, *Le Fils de l'Esprit* (1905) by 'Yves le Querdec'.

[8] See Maisie Ward, *The Wilfrid Wards and the Transition* (1937), ii. ch. xiii; *Unfinished Business* (1964), p. 343.

[9] Mrs Ward's biographer said of her: 'Ever since the Loisy case she had been deeply possessed by the literature of Modernism, seeing in it the force which would, she believed, in the end regenerate the churches.' J. P. Trevelyan, *The Life of Mrs*

Elsmere (1888). The principal modernist in the U.S.A., William
L. Sullivan (1872–1935),[1] author of *Letters to His Holiness Pope
Pius X* (1910), also put his ideas into a novel that was entitled
The Priest: a tale of modernism in New England (1911). The most
surprising and not the least readable novel about a modernist
priest came from Ireland, namely *Father Ralph* by Gerald
O'Donovan (1914).

Although I think that the fiction of the modernist movement
would be a rewarding field of study, I must leave it on one side
and return to fact. I am going now to introduce a few minor
characters or lesser lights among the Roman Catholic modernists,
and then to take a look at some of the sympathizers, fellow-
travellers or interested parties who were outside the Roman
Catholic Church.

One of the things I have sought to bring out in this book is how
much those who have been lumped together as 'Catholic modernists' differed from one another, in kind as well as in degree.
Alfred Fawkes (1850–1930) differed from the others in kind, so
much so that, although he was certainly a participant in the
movement and one of its ablest publicists in England,[2] it might
be said that he was a modernist in appearance rather than in
reality, or a negative rather than a positive modernist. As Tyrrell
said, Fawkes 'never professed to believe in the *constructive* hopes
of Modernism'.[3]

Fawkes was educated at Eton and Balliol, and after a short
period as a high anglican curate became a Roman Catholic in
1875. He was ordained priest by Cardinal Manning in 1881.
When in 1903 von Hügel gave him a card of introduction to

[1] See *Under Orders: the autobiography of William Laurence Sullivan* (1944); John
Ratté, *Three Modernists* (1968), part iii.
[2] See his volume of collected articles and essays, *Studies in Modernism* (1913).
[3] See M. D. Petre, *Von Hügel and Tyrrell,* p. 172. Miss Petre herself was even more
definite: 'Alfred Fawkes was our firm friend throughout, though never a Catholic
Modernist': *My Way of Faith*, p. 250.

Humphry Ward (1923), p. 257. Mrs Ward had wanted Loisy to give the Jowett
Lectures in 1904: see Lilley to Loisy, 17 December 1903: BN, n.a.f. 15658. Of
Tyrrell she said: 'The greatest figure in the twenty years before the war seems to
me to have been George Tyrrell': see her *A Writer's Recollections* (1918), p. 366.

Loisy, he described him as 'a convert, an Oxford prizeman, a former member of the London Oratory, at present a secular priest at Brighton, a distinguished writer'.[1] At this time Fawkes appears to have had no parochial duties and to have been free to write and travel.[2] I presume that he had independent means.[3]

So far as I know, Fawkes is the only modernist who was a convert from anglicanism and who returned to the anglican ministry after the papal condemnation of the movement. What is more curious is that he is the only modernist who throughout the course of the movement was at bottom a Liberal Protestant. By this time his Catholicism was little more than a top dressing.

Among von Hügel's papers at St Andrews I came across a torn copy of a pamphlet by Fawkes entitled *Prophet and Priest*, printed at Brighton in 1898 'for private circulation'. Its thesis is plainly Liberal Protestant or Harnackian. Thus:

The distinctive note of Christ's personal teaching was inwardness. 'The Kingdom of God is within you', He said...He left us a religion, not a theology or a ritual; an example, not a law or a creed...Yet when we look on a generation or two at furthest all this is changed. Christianity is embodied as in our own time, in a visible Church; provided with a hierarchy, an external worship, strictly formulated codes dogmatic and ceremonial; the living waters flow, indeed, but they have been turned into fixed channels; their native freedom, their spontaneity is gone. How far are we here from Christ! how foreign are those things to His free Spirit! The Idea has materialized itself, and is scarcely to be recognised in its changed clothing.

At the same time, Fawkes asserts, what from then onwards was also a favourite theme of his, that the Church, though an evil, was a necessary evil.

This was a very different view from that which Loisy was to propound in *L'Evangile et l'Eglise*: indeed, it was the view he set out to controvert. It was not, therefore, to be expected that

---

[1] BN, n.a.f. 15653.

[2] See *Mém.*, ii. 418.

[3] H. D. A. Major's brief memoir of Fawkes, prefixed to his posthumously published book of sermons, *The Church a Necessary Evil* (1932), supplies hardly any information about his life as a Roman Catholic.

Fawkes would share the enthusiasm of his modernist friends, who already included Tyrrell and von Hügel, for Loisy's manifesto. Many years ago I picked up in a second-hand bookshop the copy of the first edition of *L'Evangile et L'Eglise* which was given to Fawkes by von Hügel, and on the title page Fawkes had written: '*Hic non ejicit daemones nisi in Beelzebub principe daemoniorum.*'[1] Von Hügel, who in the previous year had warmly praised an (anonymous) article that Fawkes had contributed to *The Pilot* attacking the Joint Pastoral of the English Roman Catholic bishops on Liberal Catholicism,[2] now told Tyrrell that he 'was a bit vexed to note how readily Fawkes discounted L[oisy]'s surely wonderful little book'. 'I see, of course, exactly *why* he does so', he wrote. 'He is busy with the abuses and blind alleys of our system; and he jibs at anything which brings, apparently, a fresh sanction to it.'[3]

Fawkes contributed a cool (unsigned) article on 'Recent Theories of Development in Theology' to the *Edinburgh Review* in July 1903, in which he said: 'It is possible to detach the kernel from the husk, the idea from its setting, the unchanging substance from its necessary changing forms. This is the real issue between Professor Harnack and M. Loisy; and Harnack is right and Loisy wrong. Ill would it be for us were it not so.'[4] And again: ' "L'Evangile et l'Eglise"...is an attempt on critical lines to defend an ecclesiastical position which, without greater modification than the author is willing—at least, explicitly—to concede, is defensible only at the expense both of critical and evangelical truth.'[5]

---

[1] Matt. xii. 24.
[2] See *The Pilot*, 2 February 1901, pp. 142 f.; and von Hügel to M. D. Petre, 26 March 1901: 'I have got and read K.'s admirable article...—quite unmistakably by my good friend, Fr Alfred Fawkes. I at once recognized in it books, combinations of ideas and phrases which I have watched him getting to know and developing.' BM, Add. MSS 45361.
[3] Von Hügel to Tyrrell, 28 November 1902: see M. D. Petre, *Von Hügel and Tyrrell*, p. 109. Tyrrell assured von Hügel that he was 'anti-Fawkes in regarding the "Catholicising" of Christianity as a *per se* result of the spirit of Christ and not as a perversion or accident'. See J. Lewis May, *Father Tyrrell and the Modernist Movement*, p. 184.
[4] *Op. cit.* p. 67.
[5] *Ibid.* p. 72. The more sympathetic essay on Loisy, which Fawkes reproduced in his

However, before the article appeared, Fawkes had paid his first visit to Loisy, which seems for the time being to have removed his misgivings. Tyrrell told Lilley that Fawkes's article would have been more favourable to Loisy if it had been written after, instead of before, this visit.[1] It was after the visit that Fawkes wrote to Loisy, somewhat apologetically, presumably alluding to their conversation: 'With regard to l'Evangile et l'Eglise... I admit that I am "somewhat tinged with harnackism"; and when I attempt to criticize this author I find myself almost like Balaam, who blessed Israel in spite of himself.'[2] Shortly afterwards, he wrote to thank Loisy for having sent him a copy of *Autour d'un petit livre* which he had read twice, though evidently he was not altogether satisfied with it.[3]

Loisy, for his part, did not consider that Fawkes understood his position at all,[4] and von Hügel's references to Fawkes became increasingly adverse. In 1902 he deplored Fawkes's intellectual impatience, anti-metaphysical bias and tendency to oversimplification.[5] In 1908 he wrote to Edmund Bishop: 'I have long had my doubts whether he ought ever to have joined the R. Catholic Church; his views, for the last ten years at least, have been more purely and pointedly individualist, than those of any of the non-Catholic German and English scholars and philosophers with whom I am intimate.'[6] In the following year he was wondering whether Fawkes 'has become as hopeless a special pleader as many of the men he, F., has got on the brain'.[7] By this time

[1] See Tyrrell to Lilley, 23 June 1903: LP. Fawkes seems to have been susceptible to the charms of Loisy's conversation, for the same thing happened in 1905, when he went to see Loisy 'in anything but a sympathetic mood, and all aglow with Harnack and Protestantism; but came away... quite satisfied that L. was of his mind'. Tyrrell to von Hügel, 25 January 1905: see J. Lewis May, *op. cit.* p. 190.

[2] Fawkes to Loisy, 25 September 1903: BN, n.a.f. 15653.

[3] See Fawkes to Loisy, 7 October 1903: *ibid.*

[4] See Loisy to von Hügel, 19 January 1905: BN, n.a.f. 15645.

[5] See von Hügel to M. D. Petre, 20 April 1902: Bedoyere, pp. 139 f.

[6] Von Hügel to E. Bishop, 16 June 1908: *Dublin Review*, 1953, p. 425. Tyrrell's view was that Fawkes had 'never been a Catholic since he outgrew his crabbed Oratorian Ultramontanism—which was surely a poorer thing than Protestantism'. See M. D. Petre, *Von Hügel and Tyrrell*, p. 172.

[7] Von Hügel to G. E. Newsom, 7 September 1909: *Selected Letters*, p. 167.

Studies in Modernism (pp. 48–78), appeared originally in the *Quarterly Review*, January 1904.

Fawkes had returned to the Church of England,[1] and von Hügel
had broken off relations with him.[2] Till the end of his life, however, Fawkes continued to correspond with Loisy, telling him at
length about political and ecclesiastical affairs in England, such as
the controversy about the Revised Prayer Book and the question
of disestablishment. He told Loisy that his were the only letters
that he kept.[3]

When Fawkes returned to the Church of England it was not
to anglo-catholicism that he reverted but to what he was fond of
calling 'the National Church of my country'. He was unusual in
being a self-confessed erastian. In 1904 he had written to Loisy:
'Pius X is said to be a saint: but, as a good erastian, I prefer the
government of sinners to that of saints.'[4] When Maude Petre
used sometimes to say to him, 'You *are* an erastian', he always
replied cheerfully, 'Yes, I am'.[5] Back in the Church of England,
he was able to give free rein to his Liberal Protestantism, as he
wrote to Loisy in 1911: 'I find myself more and more acquiescing
in Liberal Protestantism, and especially in the form in which we

[1] The occasion for his move was the withdrawal of his *celebret*. In June 1908 he saw
the Archbishop of Canterbury (R. T. Davidson), and at Easter 1909 the Bishop of
Hereford (J. Percival) gave him some clerical work in his diocese. Fawkes kept
Loisy informed about these developments, see his letters of 2 April 1908, 28 May
1908, 31 May 1908, 4 March 1909: BN, n.a.f. 15653. Fawkes might have made the
move sooner, had he not come under the influence of the wise and saintly abbé
Huvelin, to whom, by chance or providence, one day in 1905 in Paris, he made his
confession, not knowing whose confessional he had entered. See Fawkes to Loisy,
26 May 1907, 6 July 1927: *ibid.* Fawkes had the regrettable habit of not stating the
year when dating his letters, and many of his letters to Loisy in the Bibliothèque
Nationale are not in chronological order. I have given the probable dating.
[2] See M. D. Petre, *Von Hügel and Tyrrell*, pp. 171 f., where Tyrrell, on the other
hand, is quoted as saying: 'I shall make no difference whatever in my friendly
relation with A. F.' The last time Fawkes saw von Hügel was at Tyrrell's funeral:
see Fawkes to Loisy, 13 July 1927: BN, n.a.f. 15653. In 1917 von Hügel complained
to Dr James Hastings that the article on 'Papacy' in the *Encyclopedia of Religion
and Ethics* (ix. 620–8) had been entrusted to Fawkes. Hastings explained that it
was to have been written by H. M. Gwatkin who, some time before his death, had
asked that it be transferred to Fawkes. See Hastings to von Hügel, 7 September
1917: VHSA.
[3] Fawkes to Loisy, 8 May 1922: BN, n.a.f. 15653. Fawkes also corresponded with
Houtin till the time of his death in 1926, and he maintained his friendship with
Miss Petre who used to visit him in his vicarage at Ashby St Ledgers. See *The
Church a Necessary Evil*, p. 17.
[4] Fawkes to Loisy, 28 January 1904: BN, n.a.f. 15653.
[5] See *The Church a Necessary Evil*, p. 16.

have it in the English Church—where the historical element is more marked than in the more radically reformed Churches'.[1] But his enduring attachment to his modernist friends was shown finally in his decision to be buried alongside Father Tyrrell at Storrington, where Miss Petre was later to join them.

Another 'lesser light' was Henry Clemence Corrance, whom I have already mentioned. He was a friend of Fawkes and also lived at Brighton—or rather Hove—during the modernist movement, but unlike Fawkes he was an authentic modernist, a modernist of the deepest dye. I had come across Corrance's name and wondered a little about him, before I started work on this book. For instance, he is named once or twice (though wrongly initialled) in Bedoyere's life of von Hügel where he appears as one of the founder members of the London Society for the Study of Religion. An extract from von Hügel's diary for 25 October 1904 reads: 'Corrance arrived for night, at tea time. Talk with him. Drive with him in a cab to Caxton Hall, Westminster. 7.15 sharp. 1st formal meeting (Dinner) of London Society for Study of Religion.'[2] I knew also that Corrance had contributed modernist articles to one or two journals,[3] that he translated Bremond's book on Newman into English,[4] and that he is named by Houtin as a collaborator in the short-lived *Revue moderniste internationale*.[5]

What first made me want to find out more about him was the discovery, among the letters that G. W. Young gave me, of several from Corrance in which he explained his theological beliefs to Young. I therefore began to look for more information about him. I soon received the help of an exceedingly kind correspondent in Edinburgh[6] who became interested in the matter and,

[1] Fawkes to Loisy, 21 March 1911: BN, n.a.f. 15653.
[2] Bedoyere, p. 170. Cf. von Hügel to E. Bishop: *Dublin Review*, 1953, p. 75. There are also references to Corrance as a member of the Rota dining club in Abercrombie, *The Life and Work of Edmund Bishop*.
[3] E.g., on 'Progressive Catholicism and High Church Absolutism' in the *Hibbert Journal*, 1903-4, pp. 217-34; 'A Vindication of Modernism' in the *Nineteenth Century and After*, February 1908, pp. 311-26. Cf. Rivière, pp. 186, 397.
[4] *The Mystery of Newman* (1907).
[5] Houtin, *Histoire du modernisme catholique*, pp. 434 f.
[6] Mr A. W. Campbell.

among other things, procured for me a copy of Corrance's death certificate from New South Wales, and who in the end overwhelmed me with so many tracking suggestions that I had to desist from the chase. I had by this time got a copy of Corrance's will from Somerset House: it proved to be exceedingly long, and also curious and tantalizing in some of its provisions.

As a result of these inquiries, it is possible to give a summary, though incomplete, account of Corrance's career, which will show him to have had a character of his own among the modernists. He was born in 1858, the son of a Suffolk rector, whose family was of some standing in the county and continued to appear in Burke's *Landed Gentry* till 1925. Corrance went up to Christ Church, Oxford, in 1876, where Henry Scott Holland was his tutor for a time and where he took a second class degree in theology.[1] In the 1890s he was rector of West Bergholt, near Colchester. He married in 1892, but was judicially separated from his wife five years later, perhaps because of his decision to join the Roman Catholic Church, which he did in 1898. In the following decade he was much occupied with the modernist movement, as will appear later. It is probable that he came into money when his father died in 1896 and he no longer needed to work for his living. Incidentally, he was a Justice of the Peace.

It is odd that in 1904, when he was consorting with the English modernists, who were all highly respectable people, and while his wife was still alive (in fact she outlived him), he contracted an irregular union with a lady who appears already to have had two sons and by whom he had a daughter in 1906. During the first world war, in spite of his age, he served in the army and became a captain, and is thereafter described as Captain H. C. Corrance. He had been in Australia for over a year before his death in 1939. On his death certificate his profession was stated to be that of a soldier. Otherwise obscurity still hangs over what he was doing between the conclusion of the modernist movement and his death. I particularly wanted to find out what were his religious opinions during the latter part of his life. The only evidence that

[1] The Rev. Geoffrey Stephens has called my attention to the fact that Corrance wrote a letter to *The Church Review* of 4 July 1890, strongly defending *Lux Mundi*.

I have so far is that, when his body was cremated, the officiating minister was a clergyman of the Church of England, and I am told that 'in his latter years he was Church of England, although he didn't often attend a church'.[1] No clear inference can be drawn from the irregularity of his matrimonial arrangements. He does appear to have taken up spiritualism or psychical research, and in his will he bequeathed three sealed packets to the London Society for the Study of Religion or, if that had been dissolved, to Professor William McDougall, the well-known psychologist, or, failing him, to the London Society for Psychical Research. Unfortunately the papers in question appear to have been destroyed by enemy action during the second world war.[2]

Corrance's modernism had four distinctive notes. First, he became a modernist in the natural course of events, since he had abandoned High Anglicanism for Rome on the ground that Roman Catholicism was more broadly based, more liberal, less narrow and absolute in its appeal to history. In one of his early letters to G. W. Young he drew with some pungency the contrast that had moved him:

Gore is quite right. Loisy's position is quite impossible from any Anglican standpoint whatever...Lilley I look upon as a complete exception. His views really stand outside Anglicanism. He is too broad for any of them.

I can remember, as an Anglican, looking upon poor old Gore as very liberal, though I never could swallow his primitive-Churchism. A scientific theologian of any kind—Protestant, Jew, Turk, infidel or Buddhist, who had learnt the difficult lesson of regarding the phenomena of religion apart from its essence and not confusing the two—such a man could always appreciate Loisy's position. But the Anglicans have not a single such man in their ranks—except Lilley—even among their so-called Broad Churchmen. They are all committed, from Wace[3] downwards, to the logical absurdity of a Primitive Church whose development was infallible up to a certain point and no further. The first six centuries seem to be now the popular limit (why

[1] Mrs L. Ritherdon (Corrance's daughter-in-law) to A. R. V., 21 January 1969. She describes him as 'a wonderful man with high ideals'.
[2] Trower, Still and Keeling to A.R.V., 31 January 1969.
[3] Henry Wace (1836–1924), Dean of Canterbury 1903–24.

first six?). To those who show their minds so impervious to science and philosophy as thus to absolutise a certain period, and who imagine that faith is wedded to a certain particular view of history, Loisy's position must indeed seem impossible.[1]

The second note of Corrance's modernism is already apparent, namely his firm subscription to what he called 'Loisy's position'. By that he meant in the main Loisy's distinction between science and faith. In two letters to *The Pilot*, early in 1904, he took up the cudgels in behalf of this position:

There cannot be. . .'Catholic history' v. 'Protestant ditto', any more than there can be 'High Church geology' or 'Nonconformist mineralogy'.

Unfortunately, in the past, the *a priori* standpoint has been allowed too much to obscure or distort the facts of history and of Biblical criticism. . .

What he [Loisy] stands for is not particular views, but a principle, that of the application of the scientific method to Scripture and history.[2]

And in a subsequent letter he wrote:

The only solid ground upon which to rest is the principle that Catholics must accept the faith of the Church but must not be required to believe that dead members of the Church, at any period of her history, held a particular form of faith, for this is a matter which comes within the province of the critical historian. . .

I cannot agree that [Mignot's] position is historical and objective in attempting to read into the Synoptics the faith of Nicea. In this point it seems to me that M. Loisy, in common with the best German critics, stands on solid ground.[3]

But, thirdly, Corrance was addicted to forms of philosophical or metaphysical speculation which Loisy eschewed. In two long

[1] Corrance to Young, 29 November 1904: YP. Corrance made the same point more temperately in an article on 'L'Eglise d'Angleterre et le modernisme' in the *Revue moderniste internationale*, 1910, pp. 211–18.
[2] *The Pilot*, 16 January 1904, p. 63. See also Corrance's article in the *Nineteenth Century and After*, 1908, pp. 311–26, where he insists that in historical and textual criticism all theological prepossessions must be set aside, but at the same time allows that there is necessarily an '*à priori* element in criticism' which is in no way peculiar to theology.
[3] *The Pilot*, 13 February 1904, p. 160.

letters to Young he sought to distinguish his position from that of philosophical idealism and from the Liberal Protestantism of Harnack and Fawkes.

I dissociate myself [he wrote] from that standpoint because it seems to me to take away all metaphysical reality from the Christian system, by reducing it to a mere system of ideas which begin and end in the human mind, and whose sole reality is their moral implications...

Broad Protestantism, of Prof. [T. H.] Green's kind, is unable to do without a metaphysical basis to its moral ideal and seems to find this in the Idea of God alone. From the point of view of pure idealism, no doubt, the idea of God is arrived at in a manner which does not necessitate its further implications. And so, all the rest of the creed may be mythical except in its relation to this one idea. This is the raison d'être of all the rest: all doctrines, forms of worship etc. in short all the phenomena of religion are simply like a painted window breaking up the white light of the Absolute. 'The One remains, the many change and pass',[1] as Fawkes is so fond of quoting. I suppose this is what he means. It is not my creed: it is another form of Unitarianism ... it rests and must rest simply on an Idealist position and I am not an Idealist in the particular sense of that word.'[2]

And again:

I believe... in a spiritual reality external to myself, just as I believe in a phenomenal world external to myself. But, of course, in both cases I reject the attitude of crude realism which is worked out philosophically in scholasticism. But I believe the phenomenal world is symbolic of a reality behind, with which my mind is brought into contact through these symbols.[3]

Fourthly, Corrance did not drop his modernist beliefs and hopes as soon as Pius X dealt them a death-blow. In 1910 he became the English correspondent of the *Revue moderniste internationale*, which represented an attempt to continue the movement on a wider platform. Hoping to interest G. W. Young in the *Revue*, he wrote: 'It will be quite independent of the Church and

---

[1] Shelley, *Adonais*, LII.
[2] Corrance to Young, 30 January 1905: YP.
[3] *Ibid.* 27 January 1905.

will seek its support from Modernists of all religions.'[1] By that
time, Corrance's own attitude seems to have broadened so much
as to be doubtfully Catholic or Christian. Soon after Tyrrell's
death, in a letter to *The Nation*, he had written:

The particular contribution of Father Tyrrell to the religion of
humanity is that he illustrates, in a very special manner, the effort of
the religious sense to free itself from the trammels of a dead theology.
It is a movement which is common to many sections of Christianity
and to other religions at the present time.

To those who believe that the religious sense is as real and universal
as the mechanical reason, it will seem impossible to attach too great
significance to Father Tyrrell's attitude (not 'position', which implies
fixity) of mind.[2]

In 1911 we find von Hügel writing to Lilley as though he
considered that Corrance, like Loisy, was finally settling into
'pure immanentism'.[3] It may be that von Hügel's fears were
more justified in Corrance's case than in Loisy's. But, as I have
said, I am still in the dark about Corrance's religious beliefs and
practices during the rest of his life. If his religious interests
turned in the direction of psychical research and/or spiritualism,
this will not have been an altogether fresh development, for in his
earlier letters to Young he had written appreciatively of F. W. H.
Myers's posthumous book, *Human Personality and its survival of
bodily death*, and of 'the many strange facts observed in the course
of their investigations' by Sir Oliver Lodge and Professor
William James.[4]

Two other 'lesser lights', whose part in the modernist movement

---

[1] Corrance to Young, 1 January 1910: YP.
[2] *The Nation*, 21 August 1909.
[3] Von Hügel to Lilley, 13 April 1911: LP. Reviewing *Christianity at the Cross Roads*.
   Corrance had criticized Tyrrell for being unfair to Liberal Protestantism, of which
   he himself now seemed to take a more favourable view (*Revue moderniste internationale* 1910, pp. 35–8), and in an article entitled 'Une nouvelle Christologie,
   est-il possible?' he rejected any idea of a metaphysical or ontological Christology,
   'La seule base réelle pour croire à la divinité de Jésus est d'ordre moral et pratique.'
   See *ibid*. pp. 135–9.
[4] Corrance to Young, 27 and 30 January 1905.

would be worth investigating, are the journalists Emile Joseph Dillon (1854–1933) and Robert Dell (1865–1940). Dillon was an Irishman who tested his vocation in two religious communities, studied oriental languages in seven European universities and theology at the seminary of Saint Sulpice, and was a professor of comparative philology in the University of Kharkov, before settling at the age of thirty-three on journalism as his career. From 1887 to 1914 he was correspondent of the *Daily Telegraph* in Russia and so was not normally on the spot during the modernist movement. But he was a constant traveller and Loisy, who for forty years looked upon him as a devoted friend, said of him: 'He is a man who has closely observed all the events of our time and has known all its notable political personalities.'[1] Dillon was also a friend of Mgr Mignot.[2]

His numerous letters to Loisy are now in the Bibliothèque Nationale. Many of them are concerned with matters of recondite scholarship. I can best indicate Dillon's modernist enthusiasm by making four brief quotations from those that are of more general interest.

3 February 1903: 'An abyss separates modern catholicism from the modern world and you have managed to throw a golden bridge over it. I should rather say an ethereal bridge, for it is only by spiritualising those grosser conceptions which suited a ruder age than the present, that one can render the dogmas of the Church credible today...Reform can only come from inside the Church.'

20 December 1903: 'I am inclined and so I am sure are many thousands of others to regard your Apology for Catholicism as the most genial work of any Catholic for several hundred years.'

25 February 1908: 'I may tell you at once unreservedly that your view of the life of Jesus...is the view which I have taken ever since that day when I called on Mgr d'Hulst and expressed my surprise that he should have done nothing to shield you from the blame which you had incurred through his articles—not yours.'[3]

21 July 1930: 'Although I see you so seldom, I have always kept in close touch with your work which today interests me as intensely as a

---

[1] *Mém.*, i. 337.
[2] See BLE, 1966, p. 13.
[3] This refers to the events of 1892–3: see MMRC, pp. 81–6.

quarter of a century ago. Wherever I go I always take one of your books with me.'[1]

Robert Dell was a 'lesser light' of lighter weight, if I may mix a metaphor, but when he died in 1940 *The Times* newspaper described him as 'one of the most familiar figures in international journalism in Paris and Geneva during the last 30 years'.[2] He was in Paris during the crisis of the modernist movement and put so much journalistic ardour into his espousal of the cause that the more moderate modernists regarded him as an indiscreet and dangerous associate.[3] Like Paul Sabatier, whose book *À propos de la Séparation des Églises et de l'État* he translated into English,[4] he was something of a busybody. He was always for aggressive action. It will suffice to quote from one of his letters to A. L. Lilley, written just after he had heard that Tyrrell had been deprived of the sacraments because of his letters to *The Times* in which he had criticized the *Pascendi*.

I had a postcard from Tyrrell last night [Dell wrote] telling me the news and asking me to let Houtin know, which I did at once...

I agree with you entirely as to the desirability of a public protest, but whether it is possible to make an effective one is another matter. You know what miserable cowards most of our people are; Laberthonnière's conduct[5] is deplorable but not exceptional...It would be far better to stop publication like 'Demain'; that is cowardly but it is at least honest and Laberthonnière's conduct is not. Personally I lose all respect for people who act in such a way; it is one of the few offences that is unforgivable. If is it [*sic*] the salvation of their miserable souls that they are thinking about, that makes the matter worse; it is that perpetual pre-occupation that I cannot stand in Newman; after all we have high authority for believing that those who are willing to lose their souls in the cause of truth are those who will find them. I really think it is less culpable, because more human, to submit from worldly considerations...

What is wanted, as you say, is a manifesto involving excommunica-

[1] For Dillon's letters to Loisy, see BN, n.a.f. 15652.
[2] *The Times*, 22 July 1940.
[3] See von Hügel's letters to E. Bishop in the *Dublin Review*, 1953, pp. 286 f., 291 f.
[4] *Disestablishment in France* (1906).
[5] See p. 115 above.

tion for all who sign it; if there are to be excommunications, the more the better; I have always thought that.[1]

It is not altogether surprising that Dell subsequently became a convinced agnostic.

The last of my 'lesser lights' is one that, after being extinguished for about 30 years, shone to some effect during the second world war. In 1965 there was published that singular and strangely moving book by Antonia White, entitled *The Hound and the Falcon* and sub-titled *The Story of a Reconversion to the Catholic Faith*. It told how, after having been received into the Church as a child, she had lapsed as a young woman, and then after 15 years had been reconverted in consequence of an extraordinary correspondence with a man whom she addressed as 'P.T.' or 'Peter', which was not his real name, and who had returned to the Church after a lapse of 30 years.

Her book *The Hound and the Falcon* consisted mainly of the letters that she had written to him during 1940–1 when he was living in North Wales and she was working for the B.B.C. in London and enduring the blitz.[2] 'Peter's' side of the correspondence had disappeared. He had started it after reading Antonia White's first novel, *Frost in May*, which was based on her experience of a convent school. He had wanted to know what was her contemporary attitude to the Church. Although they had never met, and in fact did not meet for quite a long time, the correspondence very quickly took the form of long love letters which were most concerned with questions about Catholic faith and practice.

What especially interested me was that 'Peter' urged Miss White to read von Hügel and Tyrrell, and that her reconversion was largely due to the impact that these modernists made upon her. Two quotations from her book will show that Tyrrell's influence was more decisive than von Hügel's:

I suppose for some time I had been realising that I definitely needed

[1] Dell to Lilley, 25 October 1907: LP.
[2] She gives her *curriculum vitae* in *op. cit.* pp. 52 ff.

the external practice of a religion. I am, I think, incurably religious by temperament. I wanted to be *pratiquant*; what I found exceedingly difficult was to be *croyant*.[1]

It would not, for me and for many other people, in any way affect the value of the Catholic faith if the whole of Catholic theology turned out to be a symbolic rendering of spiritual truths. The oldest of all philosophical errors is the confusion of the *expression of a thing* with the thing itself. And I am convinced that the sphere of religion is something fundamentally apart from philosophy, science, ethics and sociology though it has relations with them all.[2]

Naturally, I wanted to know who 'Peter' was. His name was carefully concealed, but I found that there was an incidental allusion to a book that he had written, and this enabled me to identify him. He was Joseph P. Thorp who, I discovered, had published an autobiography in 1931. From that I learned that for many years he had been the dramatic critic of *Punch* where he had used the *nom de plume* 'T.' which he had also used for his autobiography. It was more to the point that as a young man he had been a Jesuit novice and a close friend of Tyrrell with whom he had kept in touch till his death.

My wife and I [he wrote] like to think of Tyrrell, most lovable man, as we last saw him in our modest flat in Battersea whither he often came in his last dark days...

I asked him only a few weeks before his death: 'Tell me something, sincerely. You've travelled a long way from your old beliefs. So have I. What have you got left?' He said, after a few moments' thought: 'Nearly all the detail's gone. But every day it becomes more clear that the only thing that matters at all is—to find God and Truth.'[3]

When recording how much he 'owed to that great-souled, witty, difficult, affectionate, brilliant Irishman, Father George Tyrrell', Thorp said that he had kept many of Tyrrell's letters.[4] I therefore wrote to Antonia White in the hope of being able to trace their whereabouts. She kindly gave me the address of

[1] *Ibid.* p. 160.
[2] *Ibid.* p. 99.
[3] 'T.' (=J. P. Thorp), *Friends and Adventures*, pp. 40 f.
[4] See *ibid.* p. 37.

Thorp's widow who was still alive at a very advanced age. So I
wrote to *her*, but alas! in a spirited reply she told me regretfully
that 'an *enemy*' had long ago destroyed Tyrrell's letters.

Thorp was evidently a gifted man, an artist rather than a
thinker—Tyrrell called him 'mercurial'. The only mention of
him that I have come across in the correspondence of the
modernists is von Hügel's naming him to Mgr Mignot as one of
the people that the archbishop had met during his visit to England
in 1904.[1] I shall have more to say about that occasion in a moment:
it leads me expeditiously from 'lesser lights' to 'fellow travellers'.

I intend 'fellow travellers' to be a rough and ready term for those
who were not Roman Catholics and who exhibited some degree
of sympathetic interest in, or fellow feeling for, the modernist
movement. W. R. Inge is therefore excluded since, although he
was certainly interested, his interest was consistently hostile.[2] In
my previous book on the modernist movement I had a chapter[3]
on those outside the Roman Catholic Church who were influenced
by the movement, and I might have entitled that 'fellow travellers',
but I was not then acquainted with the term. I am not going to
repeat what I said there, but I have now a good many more
pieces of information about English sympathizers with the movement, which I have derived mainly from unpublished correspondence, and which may be of interest in themselves and useful
to any who are pursuing the subject further. A few of the following notes will be about lesser lights. I should say that the very
best examples of fellow travellers are G. W. Young, of whom I

[1] Von Hügel to Mignot, 4 August 1904: VHSA.
[2] Von Hügel, who approved of some of Inge's writings, said of him: 'He loves the
Modernists far too little, to be able really to understand them.' To A. L. Lilley,
8 December 1909: LP. And again: 'What a curious incapacity he seems to have
ever to get beyond a grudging, sulky recognition of any good at all in Liberal
"Romanists" of any kind!' To G. W. Young, 6 January 1910: YP. The late Sir
John Sheppard told me that, when he was Provost of King's College, Cambridge,
he had Inge and Alexander Nairne to dinner in the Lodge one evening, and this
conversation took place: Nairne: 'I should like to know what you think of Abbé
Loisy.' Inge tartly: 'A man with no religious feeling whatever.' Nairne: 'I'm told
that he is deeply attached to his mother and his church.' Inge: 'I don't know about
his affection for his mother, but he certainly has none now for his church.'
[3] MMRC, pp. 234–69.

have already spoken,[1] and James A. Walker, who became Miss Petre's literary executor.[2] Shortly after Father Tyrrell's death Walker wrote to von Hügel:

Though I call myself a non-Catholic I ought to explain that if Father Tyrrell's conception of Church authority had been tolerated by the authorities, I should now be a Roman Catholic... I cannot conceal my profound disappointment that I should have been led to the threshold of that Church, only to find that the cause to which Tyrrell and many another saint and martyr have dedicated their lives has fallen a prey to the worst type of priestcraft.[3]

Some years later, Miss Petre described him to Loisy in these terms: '...still quite a young man, a Liberal journalist, very intelligent, passionately interested in religious questions. He is anglican. He was attracted at one time towards the Roman Church, but still more attracted by Tyrrell's ideas. He is a fine soul, frank and sincere.'[4]

A good way of sampling some groups or collections of fellow travellers is to look at the list of persons in London, Oxford, Cambridge and Eton, who met Mgr Mignot when he visited England in July 1904. I have no intention of commenting on, or even of seeking further to identify, them all, though I have a few notes to make on some of them, and on some who would no doubt have also met the archbishop, if his visit had not taken place during the Long Vacation or as early as in 1904. A few of those named, as will appear, were Roman Catholics, and as regards all or any of them there can seldom be much assurance about the exact extent of their fellow travelling. After the visit, von Hügel, with characteristic thoroughness, sent Mignot the list which I am now going to reproduce.[5] He explained that those whose names he had underlined (here italicized) had rendered exceptional services, and to those doubly-underlined (here in capital letters)

---

[1] See pp. 8 f. above.
[2] See his article in the *Hibbert Journal*, July 1943, and his introduction to M. D. Petre, *Alfred Loisy* (1944).
[3] Walker to von Hügel, 1 August 1909: VHSA. Walker compiled a book of selections from Tyrrell's writings which was published under the title *The Way of Truth*.
[4] M. D. Petre to Loisy, 10 May 1917: BN, n.a.f. 15660.
[5] Von Hügel to Mignot, 4 August 1904: VHSA.

he hoped that the archbishop might be willing to send one of his publications as a token of esteem or gratitude.

I. LONDON

1. The *Revd Dr Arthur Headlam*, King's College, London W.C.
2. Robert Dell, Esq., Colaba Cottage, Stock, Ingatestone, Essex.
3. The Revd Prof. Charles Dessoulavy, St John's Seminary, Wonersh, Guildford.
4. Hubert Bland, Esq., Well Hall, Eltham, Kent.
5. G. B. M. Coore, Esq., 47 Egerton Gardens, London S.W.
6. Joseph Thorpe, Esq., 28 Ashley Place, Westminster, London S.W.
7. The *Very Reverend Armitage Robinson*, The Deanery, Westminster, London S.W.
8. *His Grace Monsignor Francis Bourne*, Archbishop of Westminster, Archbishop's House, Westminster, London S.W.
9. *James F. Hope. Esq. M.P.*, Norfolk House, St James's Square, London S.W.
10. Professor Sir Richard Jebb, M.P., Cambridge.
11. The Right Honourable George Wyndham, M.P., House of Commons, Westminster, London S.W.
12. Lord Hugh Cecil, M.P., ditto.
13. Wilfrid Ward, Esq., Lotus, Dorking, Surrey.
14. The Hon. William Gibson, Moorhurst, Holmwood, Surrey.
15. The Revd Dr Manuel Bidwell, St Mary's, Cadogan Street, Chelsea, London S.W.
16. The Revd B. Maturin, 27 Warwick Square, London S.W.
17. The Revd Dr C. van den Biesen, St Joseph's College, Mill Hill, Hendon, London N.W.
18. THE REVD A. L. LILLEY, St Mary's Vicarage, Paddington Green, London W.
19. Miss Maude Petre, 26 Victoria Road, Richmond, Yorkshire.
20. The Revd Lionel Goodrich, Catholic Church, Harrow-on-the Hill...
21. *Dr Wallis Budge*, Oriental Department, British Museum, London W.C.
22. *Le jeune conservateur* qui nous a montré les collections, — je ne connais son nom.
23. The Revd T. Lacey, Highgate, London N.

24. The Revd C. J. Sharp, Christ Church Vicarage, Crouch End, London N.
25. The Revd Conrad Noel, 15 Paddington Green, London W.
26. The Revd Mr Shaw-Stewart, St Mary's Vicarage, Paddington Green, London W. *Please forward.*
27. H. C. Corrance, Esq., 30 Wilbury Gardens, Hove, Sussex.
28. —Scott Stokes, Esq.

II. OXFORD

29. J. A. SMITH ESQ., Balliol College, Oxford.
30. GEORGE W. YOUNG, ESQ., 33 Beaumont Street, Oxford.
31. *The Revd O'Fallon Pope*, Pope's Hall, Oxford.
32. *The Revd Arthur Day*, St Aloysius, Oxford.
33. The Revd Vincent Hornyold,   "   "
34. *Dr Edward Caird*, Master of Balliol College, Oxford.
35. The Revd Prof. Dr S. R. Driver, Christ Church, Oxford.
36. — Strachan Davidson, Esq., Balliol College, Oxford.
37. — *Fisher, Esq.*, Fellow of New College, Oxford.
38. *The Revd Dr Hastings Rashdall*, New College, Oxford.
39. *Dr Spooner*, Warden of New College, Oxford.
40. Mrs Spooner
41. Mrs Temple, c/o Dr Hastings Rashdall...
42. Mrs Fisher (comme pour son mari).
43. Mrs Reginald Poole, c/o Dr Hastings Rashdall...
44. *Clement Webb*, *Esq.*, Magdalen College, Oxford.
45. The Revd Prof. Dr Charles, 47 Broadmore Road, Oxford.
46. The Revd Dr Brightman, Magdalen College, Oxford.
47. A. Cowley, Esq., Reader in Rabbinical Literature, Oxford.
47b. The Very Reverend T. B. Strong, Dean of Christ Church, Oxford.

III. CAMBRIDGE ET ELY

48. BARON ANATOLE VON HÜGEL
49. BARONNE   "   "   "   Croft Cottage, Barton Road, Cambridge.
50. *S. E. Madame la Baronne de Hügel*, Wayside, Barton Road, Cambridge.
51. *Monsignor Christopher Scott*, D.D., V.G., The Presbytery, Cambridge.

52. The Revd Richard Barnes, Llandaff House, Regent's Street, Cambridge.
53. The Revd Dr Stanton, Ely Professor of Divinity, Cambridge.
54. *F. C. Burkitt, Esq.*, Trinity College, Cambridge (et Mrs Burkitt).
55. W. Hurrell Mallock, Esq., Croft Cottage, Barton Road, Cambridge.
56. Dr W. W. Wingate, 60 St Andrew's Street, Cambridge.
57. *The Right Reverend Lord Alwyn Compton*, Bishop of Ely, The Palace, Ely.
58. Lady Alwyn Compton, ibidem.
59. DOM E. CUTHBERT BUTLER, O.S.B., St Gregory's Abbey, Downside, Bath.
60. The Revd Dr Kennett, Regius Professor of Hebrew, Cambridge.
61. Professor A. A. Bevan, Trinity College, Cambridge.
62. The Revd Professor Dr W. E. Barnes, Theological Schools, Cambridge.
63. The Revd C. H. W. Johns, Reader in Assyriology, Cambridge.
64. The Revd J. F. Bethune-Baker, Pembroke College, Cambridge.
65. N. McLean, Esq., Reader in the Septuagint, Cambridge.
66. Israel Abrahams, Esq., Reader in Rabbinical Literature, Cambridge.
67. The Revd Edward Conybeare, Cambridge.
68. The Revd Professor Dr Skinner, Westminster College, Cambridge.
69. *The Revd H. F. Stewart*, The Malting House, Cambridge.
70. Mrs Stewart, ibidem.
71. Revd Dr St John Parry, Trinity College, Cambridge.
72. Miss Parry (sous couverture au même).
73. Professor Sedley Taylor, Trinity College, Cambridge.
74. — Prior, Esq., Trinity College, Cambridge.
75. *Monsignor Edmund Nolan*, M.A., St Edmund's House, Cambridge.
76. — Wyatt-Davies, Esq., Trinity College, Cambridge.

IV. ETON

77. H. E. LUXMOORE, ESQ., 'Westons', Eton, Windsor.

Now for a few notes on some of those who are named.

A. C. Headlam (1826–1947), who in 1904 was Principal of King's College, London, had visited Loisy about 1896. W. Sanday reported to von Hügel: 'My friend and fellow-worker A. C.

Headlam has just come back from Paris where he was greatly delighted and encouraged by his intercourse with Abbé Loisy, M. Batiffol and others.'[1] In January 1904 von Hügel told Mignot that Headlam was one of those who had 'pronounced for Loisy'.[2] Headlam did indeed contribute three articles to *The Times Literary Supplement* in support of Loisy.[3] Before long, however, Headlam took his stand with the much more cautious Batiffol. In 1908 we find G. C. Rawlinson writing to von Hügel: 'I was, like you, very sorry to see the Times review on Loisy. I suppose it was Headlam. Well, people like Sanday and Headlam are the last who ought to blame anyone else for philosophical presuppositions.'[4] In 1920 Loisy told von Hügel that he presumed that it was Headlam who had proposed Batiffol for an honorary degree at Oxford, since 'he had always been on good terms with him'.[5]

Charles L. Dessoulavy (1875–1944) was one of the priests who ministered to George Tyrrell on his deathbed.[6] In October 1904 von Hügel told Mignot that Dessoulavy, who had so much enjoyed seeing him during his visit to England, had lost his professorship of philosophy at the Southwark diocesan seminary 'as the first act of Mgr Amigo' (the new bishop).[7] Dessoulavy was a school chaplain from 1907 to 1922, but though allowed to hear confessions he was not allowed to preach. He was not allowed to do either when he was subsequently chaplain to a convent of the Little Sisters of the Poor.[8]

Joseph Armitage Robinson (1858–1933) visited Mgr Mignot at Albi in April 1907. In September 1904 Loisy wrote to Houtin: 'I don't know the work of Hens. Henson.[9] I only know from

---

[1] Sanday to von Hügel, 13 February 1896(?): VHSA.
[2] Von Hügel to Mignot, 20 January 1904: VHSA.
[3] See Ronald Jasper, *Arthur Cayley Headlam* (1960), pp. 107, 364.
[4] Rawlinson to Von Hügel, 16 May 1908: VHSA. Later he told von Hügel that he had got to review Batiffol's *Credibility of the Gospel* 'which I don't find satisfying'. 8 March 1912 (?): *ibid.*
[5] *Mém.*, iii. 394. 575. The presumption was correct: see Jasper, *op. cit.* pp. 131, 360.
[6] See M. D. Petre, *Autobiography and Life of G. Tyrrell*, ii. 429.
[7] Von Hügel to Mignot, 28 October 1904: VHSA.
[8] I owe this information to a letter that I received in 1945 from Peter Thornton-Pett who had been a pupil at the school of which Dr Dessoulavy had been chaplain.
[9] Herbert Hensley Henson who was then a canon of Westminster.

M. de Hügel's last letter that this person's biblical statements are causing a lot of stir in the anglican world and that they are giving much anxiety to the dean of Westminster, Armitage Robinson.'[1] In the following year, after von Hügel had visited Lord Halifax and tried 'to inject a little more light into his mind with regard to the reality, the importance, the urgency and the nature of *la question biblique*', Halifax sent him a copy of *The Study of the Gospels* by Armitage Robinson, asking him to read the two lectures on the Johannine problem. Von Hügel's comment to Mignot was as follows: 'I read them attentively and in fact I thus learned, once more, that the most effective way of realizing the feebleness of an indefensible position is to study a defence of it by a loyal and superior mind.'[2] This is only one instance among many of the way in which anglican theologians were regarded by the modernists.[3]

Francis Bourne (1861–1934), from 1911 Cardinal Bourne, had come under the influence of J. B. Hogan at the seminary of Saint Sulpice.[4] He was much less unsympathetic to the modernists than some other prelates.[5] He spoke French fluently and appears to have got on well with Mignot.[6] In 1909 Dessoulavy wrote to von Hügel about Tyrrell's funeral: 'With your surmise regarding Bourne, I quite agree...had he had the business in his own hands he would have found a way of satisfying both parties. I well remember, some years ago, how angry he was at cardinal Vaughan's action in the case of Mivart.'[7]

The Hon. William Gibson (1868–1942), from 1913 Lord

---

[1] Loisy to Houtin, 19 September 1904: BN, papiers Houtin XXXI.

[2] Von Hügel to Mignot, 30 November 1905: VHSA. Mignot, on the other hand, thought highly of Armitage Robinson's lectures: see G. C. Rawlinson to von Hügel, 13 August 1908: *ibid.*

[3] E.g., Tyrrell to Lilley, 22 November 1906: LP. 'One feels that [Gore] shrinks from the flux of the full dynamic interpretation of Christianity and hugs certain mid-channel rocks lest he shd be swept away by the stream that rushes past them. I can certainly understand and sympathise though I cannot agree, nor comfort myself with self-imposed assurances.' Cf. *Mém.*, ii. 154, 409 (on Armitage Robinson).

[4] See *Mém.* ii. 263. Cf. p. 65 above.

[5] See *ibid.* ii. 154, 247, 273, 409; iii. 137; Bedoyere, pp. 117, 152, 275, 349: Heaney, p. 282; W. S. Blunt, *My Diaries*, ii. 266 f.   [6] See Bedoyere, p. 171.

[7] Dessoulavy to von Hügel, 30 July 1909: VHSA. On the Mivart case, see J. W. Gruber, *A Conscience in Conflict* (1960).

Ashbourne, had visited Loisy in 1898, who had sent this report to von Hügel:

I saw the other day a Mr William Gibson...He has written a life of Lamennais[1] which he presented to me and which I find interesting. He is a philosopher and a man of letters rather than a critic, but he is very broad-minded and gets on well with Abbé Marcel Hébert. These gentlemen claim to be Christian positivists. I see nothing against their doing so.[2]

Gibson, though an eccentric Irishman,[3] was rightly looked upon by the modernists as one of themselves. In November 1907 Tyrrell wanted him to write an article for *The Times* newspaper in support of the view that Newman had in effect been condemned by the *Pascendi*.

I know [Tyrrell wrote to Lilley] that the *Times* would have taken a *signed* article by me on the subject. And that lunatic of a Gibson who *could* have done it wouldn't because it was against his Sinn Fein principles to acknowledge the existence of the Times...
P.S. Gibson *did* write a letter at my suggestion *to a paper called* 'The Peasant'. It may be translated into Earse.[4]

In 1910 Gibson described himself as 'a former "modernist" ',[5] but he never became a pillar of orthodoxy.

T. A. Lacey (1835–1931) was chaplain of the London Diocesan Penitentiary at Highgate in 1904. I have, in earlier books,[6] illustrated his sympathy with the modernist movement which was chiefly expressed in his contributions to the *Church Times*[7]

---

[1] *The Abbé de Lamennais and the Liberal Catholic Movement in France* (1896).
[2] Loisy to von Hügel, 27 March 1898: BN, n.a.f. 15644.
[3] According to *The Times* (26 January 1942) he was 'a prominent and picturesque figure' in the 'Irish-Ireland' movement, in which his chief part was the revival of the ancient Irish costume—coat and kilt of saffron, a cloak of the same colour fastened at the shoulder by a magnificent tara broach, and a cap also of saffron'. When he made his only speech in the House of Lords, it was the first time that Gaelic had been heard there.
[4] Tyrrell to Lilley, 12 November 1907: LP.
[5] In a letter to *Droits de l'homme*, 27 November 1910: 'en ma qualité d'ancien "moderniste" (je dis ancien, car le mouvement n'existe plus).' Cf. Hyacinthe Loyson to M. D. Petre, 10 May 1910: BM, Add. MSS, 45744.
[6] See W. L. Knox and A. R. Vidler, *The Development of Modern Catholicism*, pp. 194–8; MMRC, pp. 251 ff.
[7] Lacey's article in the *Church Times* (15 January 1904) 'On the Case of the Abbé Loisy' was republished posthumously in his *Wayfarer's Essays* (1934), pp. 141–5.

and in his booklet *Harnack and Loisy* (1904). When Tyrrell received that, he wrote to Lilley: 'Lacey's "Harnack and Loisy" looks, at first glance, more liberal and sympathetic than I had expected from one whom I associated with dreary controversies about "orders".'[1]

Conrad Noel (1869–1942), who became famous as vicar of Thaxted, was in 1904 curate to A. L. Lilley at St Mary's, Paddington Green, and so will have heard plenty about the modernists. His own modernist sympathies have recently been brought out in an essay about him by Robert Woodifield.[2]

Before leaving the London fellow travellers I should mention that there was one notable absentee from von Hügel's list, namely *G. C. Rawlinson* (1868–1922). He may have been away on holiday, or perhaps he was not known to von Hügel in 1904, for I take the following note of June 1905 from von Hügel (to G. W. Young) to imply that they were not yet personally acquainted. 'You should read the review of Père Billot's book "de Sacra Traditione" in the "Church Times"...by a Revd Mr Rawlinson: it is capital! Fancy the "C.T." writing like *that*!'[3]

I have written about Rawlinson elsewhere,[4] but since, after A. L. Lilley, he was the anglican priest who was most attached to the modernists,[5] I give some additional information about him here, and first I may recall that shortly before his death in 1922 I attended a retreat which he conducted. It was an unforgettable experience. Rawlinson was the nearest counterpart in the Church of England to Abbé Huvelin[6] in France. Like Huvelin, he was content to remain an assistant curate in the metropolis till the end of his life. He was a man of profound spiritual insight, large

---

[1] Tyrrell to Lilley, 15 January 1904: LP. Lacey was joint author of *De Hierarchia Anglicana* (1895).
[2] See *For Christ and the People*, edited by M. B. Reckitt (1968), pp. 137, 154 f., 161.
[3] Von Hügel to Young, 27 June 1905: YP.
[4] See W. L. Knox and A. R. Vidler, *The Development of Modern Catholicism*, pp. 191 ff.; MMRC, pp. 251 f.
[5] Cf. the letter of 3 December 1908 from von Hügel to Tyrrell, quoted in M. D. Petre, *Von Hügel and Tyrrell*, pp. 177 f.
[6] See *Un prêtre: l'abbé Huvelin 1838–1910* by M. Th. Louis-Lefebvre (1958), which is, however, an unsatisfactory book: cf. the review of the Eng. trans. in *The Tablet*, 18 May 1968. See preferably *Mém.*, i. 287 f.

culture and liberal outlook, whose sanctity was enhanced by the way in which he too surmounted ill health and physical handicaps.

Secondly, in France Rawlinson was specially attached to Loisy, Mignot, Laberthonnière and Le Roy, all of whom he visited,[1] and to Loisy above all. After his excommunication, Rawlinson wrote to him:

Allow me to say, now that you are treated as a heretic and an infidel, and greeted with so many insults, how much personally I owe to you. If one speaks...of troubled souls, ah well! I have known this trouble myself, and it is from your books that I have been able to find, or so I think, a way of accepting the Christian experience without the melancholy necessity of declaring war on all modern science. I am sincerely grateful.[2]

In England Rawlinson was most attached to von Hügel, who in introducing him to Henri Bremond in 1910 wrote:

Pray allow me to present to you my good friend the Revd G. C. Rawlinson, a member of the Church of England of London, a strong High Churchman, with much knowledge of and sympathy with critical work. He has long had a warm admiration for your books, and can give very useful effect to his views in his articles in the 'Church Times',—about the best that appear in that paper which is largely still far from very perceptive in such matters...He is a very loyal, tactful and discreet man, and can be trusted without any fear of his making mischief.[3]

His connexion with the *Church Times*, the weekly organ of anglo-catholicism, is the third point about Rawlinson. It was because of his and Lacey's contributions to that paper, but of his more than of Lacey's, that it appeared for several years to be remarkably sympathetic to the modernist cause. Even so, Rawlinson could not speak out his whole mind there as he explained to Loisy in February 1908: 'I have to be prudent, since most of the readers of the *Church Times* are pious and timid people who are pretty ignorant. I should like to be able to be more useful to you, and I hope that my little efforts are not

---

[1] See Rawlinson to von Hügel, 26 October 1906, 13 August 1908, and 25 October 1912 (?): VHSA.
[2] Rawlinson to Loisy, 3 April 1908: BN, n.a.f. 15660.
[3] Von Hügel to Bremond, 14 October 1910: VHSA.

entirely fruitless.'[1] Later in the same year the prospects of being useful through the *Church Times* seemed even less bright. Von Hügel wrote to Lilley: 'Rawlinson explained and proved to me, the other day, how fully and deliberately the Halifax–Lacey— "Church Union", "Church Times" group have now dropped and turned their backs upon all modernism.'[2] However, shortly afterwards, the outlook seemed less dark. Referring to a review by Rawlinson of Paul Sabatier's *Modernism*, von Hügel conjectured: 'I expect the Editor [of the *Church Times*] is much like Cox [i.e. J. G. Snead-Cox, editor] of the "Tablet"—drawn hither and then thither according as his contributors and advisers are, at any particular moment, this man or that.'[3]

I turn now to the list of those in Oxford who met Mgr Mignot in July 1904. There are only two names on the list about which I have some further notes to offer, but there were also some absentees who deserve mention.

S. R. Driver (1846–1914), the Regius Professor of Hebrew, was the chief anglican authority on the Old Testament at the time. In the first letter that von Hügel wrote to Loisy (in 1893), he urged him to come to England as soon as possible so that he could meet 'Robertson Smith,[4] Claude Montefiore,[5] Driver, etc.'[6] In 1896 Driver was gratified by an article that Loisy wrote about his commentary on Deuteronomy,[7] and von Hügel observed to Loisy that they could well learn something from Driver and Sanday 'without believing in their orders'.[8] Mignot, we know, was already an admirer of Driver's work,[9] so that it is no surprise to learn that at a dinner in Balliol College, during Mignot's visit

---

[1] Rawlinson to Loisy, 17 February 1908: BN, n.a.f. 15660.
[2] Von Hügel to Lilley, 10 December 1908: LP.
[3] Von Hügel to Lilley, 17 February 1909: LP.
[4] William Robertson Smith, the Scottish O.T. authority, died in 1894.
[5] Montefiore, the Jewish biblical scholar, was a warm admirer of Loisy: there are many letters from him to von Hügel among the latter's papers at St Andrews.
[6] See *Mém.*, i. 288.
[7] See *ibid.* i. 404.
[8] *Ibid.* i. 424. A controversy about the validity of anglican orders was raging at that time.
[9] See Mignot to Loisy, 13 September 1896: BN, n.a.f. 15659.

to Oxford in 1904, the archbishop and the regius professor paid 'very sincere and agreable compliments' to one another.[1] Before securing the collaboration of C. A. Briggs in 1906, von Hügel had unsuccessfully approached Driver to join with him in his criticism of the Pontifical Biblical Commission's decree on the Pentateuch.[2] In 1904 von Hügel had told Mignot of Driver's dissatisfaction with the series of Westminster Commentaries (which were originally called Oxford Commentaries).

As regards the question of the 'Westminster Commentaries', I find that the good Driver himself has declared that he was deceived by false representations about the character of this series which is really so little scientific, if not even anti-critical. There is a 'Job' by a Mr Gibson, a man who is practically unknown, and volumes on the N. T.—not at all up to their great subjects.'[3]

Hastings Rashdall (1858–1924) was in 1904 a Fellow of New College. He became a prominent representative of anglican 'modern churchmanship'.[4] The sympathetic interest that he took in the modernist movement is shown in the papers about it which he published.[5] In 1905, with reference to a scheme that was being canvassed for a series of tracts or small books in the interests of liberal churchmanship, he wrote to Lilley:

I do not think it would be wise to give any special prominence to the Liberal Roman Catholics. A few of them might with great advantage be asked to write...But any attempt to emphasise the idea of a Liberal *Catholic* movement (whether Roman or Anglo-Catholic) would be misunderstood by the great majority of those who would be attracted by the Liberal side of the movement. I have a strong personal sympathy with liberal Roman Catholics: their work is valuable both in influencing members of their own communion and as showing that Liberalism does not mean bare negation. But the use of the word 'Catholic' in connexion with a movement or a party or a publication or a series

---

[1] *Mém.*, ii. 409.
[2] See *The Papal Commission and the Pentateuch*; and *Mém.*, ii. 496.
[3] Von Hügel to Mignot, 28 October 1904; VHSA. The reference is to *The Book of Job* by E. C. S. Gibson, who was then vicar of Leeds and later bishop of Gloucester.
[4] See my *20th Century Defenders of the Faith*, pp. 123 f.
[5] 'Harnack and Loisy' (1904), republished in *Principles and Precepts* (1927); 'George Tyrrell' (1913) and 'Modernism' (1918), republished in *Ideas and Ideals* (1928).

would infallibly suggest ideas about sacraments & apostolic succession which are the negation of Liberalism, and which are not really held by the Liberal Romans, though they are held by the people who are commonly called Liberal High-churchmen. Any title with the word Catholic in it would be thought to mean simply Gore and the persecutionists over again.'[1]

After Rashdall died in 1924, von Hügel said:

I dare say that, had I known him when I was quite young and if he had been my senior, I should have felt only his ethical greatness and not his—surely—strangely great lack of the specifically religious sense—or, at the very least, of the mystical element of religion. He has established himself permanently in my mind as a living example of how greatly ethical a soul can be with little of the specifically religious sense.[2]

A notable absentee when Mignot visited Oxford was the Oriel Professor of the Interpretation of Scripture, *T. K. Cheyne* (1841–1915). In January 1904, when he was going to be in Paris, he had asked A. L. Lilley for an introduction to Loisy.

I do feel drawn to him [he wrote] because he has not only learning but character, and his union of keen criticism with devout churchmanship is something which I have long been looking for in vain in my own country...

I do not however desire to become a 'Roman', as H. C. Corrance in the Hibbert for January wd evidently tell me I ought, if I wish for this union.[3]

During the next six months Cheyne sent long and frequent letters to Lilley not only about Loisy but about von Hügel and Tyrrell, to whose writings Lilley had introduced him, and kindred subjects. The most interesting is that which reports on his visit to Loisy:

Passing through Paris, I called on Loisy. It was a grey day, and as I left his house, the snow fell. It was an off-day for him; he had lectured the day before, and as usual was tired. But he was pleased to see me,

[1] Rashdall to Lilley, 18 June 1905: LP.
[2] Von Hügel to C. C. J. Webb, 15 February 1924: quoted in Bedoyere, p. 311.
[3] Cheyne to Lilley, 6 January 1904: LP. See also Cheyne to Loisy, 9 January 1904: BN, n.a.f. 15650. For Corrance, see p. 160 above.

and we had an hour's chat about his position, the prospects of progress, the state of things in England, Lagrange as an Old Testament scholar &c.

What charmed me was his sense of humour; he was perpetually bursting into a good-natured laugh. Not only no bitterness, but perfect serenity. Yet I could not help wanting something—& that was the trace of a hobby. I do not know more than he told me or than I could see in his face & bearing. But I longed to see some evidence of a recreation—some task or predilection outside his work. No picture on the wall indicated a love of art. Yet, in his French prose, there is, surely, a natural art. At any rate, he has been taught, or has taught himself, to write.

He has good hopes for the future, & thinks warmly of his English friends & sympathizers, & specially of you.[1]

Cheyne did not lose interest in Loisy. In August 1913 he sent him a photograph about which Loisy consulted von Hügel, since he was not sure whether it had come from Cheyne himself or from someone else.

Perhaps you can save me from a slight embarrassment. The other day I received in an open envelope, which looked like a prospectus, a post card on the back of which was a portrait with the signature T. K. Cheyne. It is the portrait of an old man in a little carriage such as those in which invalids go out. Will it be *le brave Cheyne* who has sent me this souvenir? I don't know what to think of it, nor whether to risk writing to him.[2]

Another absentee was *William Sanday* (1843–1920), the Lady Margaret Professor of Divinity. In the previous January, he had contributed 'An Anglican View of M. Loisy' to *The Pilot*[3] which was friendly but much too sanguine. It opened thus: 'Many of us in the Church of England have been following with deep interest and sympathy the fortunes of M. Loisy. Neither the interest nor the sympathy have been wholly personal. Of course, I need not say that the Abbé Loisy himself is an attractive figure and even more than attractive figure.' He then said that the Church of

---

[1] Cheyne to Lilley, 21 February 1904: LP.
[2] Loisy to von Hügel, 9 August 1913: BN, n.a.f. 15645.
[3] 23 January 1904, pp. 84 f.

England had been, and was still, passing through a crisis that had culminated much more rapidly in the Church of Rome.

In this one decade, and largely through the work of this one man, the Church of Rome seems to have caught and even in some ways passed us. For I look upon it that in his main object M. Loisy has practically succeeded. The cause of freedom, within limits, is substantially won. It is not likely that the shadow on the dial will ever go seriously backward.

Later in the article Sanday expressed his agreement with Loisy about the 'relativity of Christian doctrine', but dissented from his view of the Fourth Gospel.[1] In the following issue of *The Pilot*[2] there appeared a letter from A. L. Lilley in defence of Loisy's radicalism as a critic. 'M. Loisy', he wrote, 'is a radical historical critic, but he can afford to be one because of the wide sweep and the boldness of his theological outlook, because of the freedom of his faith from dependence upon past habits of thought.' When Loisy received a copy of this letter, he wrote to Lilley: 'Your reply to the Rev. Sanday's article is excellent. I do not see how these half-critical conservatives can maintain their position. It seems to me that they adopt a lofty tone, which does not remedy the fragility of their arguments.'[3]

Mgr Mignot, whose critical views were and remained nearer to what Sanday's were in 1904 than to Loisy's, seems to have been distressed when, in the last year of his life, he heard rumours of Sanday's change of front. He wrote to von Hügel: 'Has Sanday written a life of Our Lord? I have been told that he no longer believes in Our Lord's divinity?'[4]

Before leaving Oxford for Cambridge, I would make mention of three younger men who afterwards became well known but who were too young to meet Mgr Mignot in 1904. For a time at least, they were fellow travellers after the manner of young men. In November 1904 M. Jacques Chevalier, who was an associate of the modernists and a friend of A. L. Lilley and G. W. Young,

---

[1] Later on, Sanday was to change his mind about this: see p. 117 above.
[2] 30 January 1904, pp. 116 f.
[3] Loisy to Lilley, 14 February 1904: LP.
[4] Mignot to von Hügel, 8 January 1917: VHSA.

wrote to Loisy about a young cousin of Lord Salisbury who would be enchanted if Loisy would allow him to visit him at Garnay. This was

Mr Algernon Cecil, who has just finished his studies at Oxford and is going to spend some months in Paris. I got to know him quite recently at Pusey House...
This young Oxford man struck me as very distinguished and very intelligent; he is as Catholic as it is possible for an anglican to be, and his catholicism would, I think, please you, since it is hardly at all scholastic and hardly at all puseyite, but his religion is open-minded, sensitive to the future as well as to the past...He has written some pages about *L'Evangile et l'Eglise* in an issue of the Oxford Magazine for May 1904.[1]

Two still younger men, Scholars of New College and Balliol respectively, were A. G. Hebert (1887–1963) and D. L. Murray (1888–1962). In June 1908 G. W. Young wrote to Lilley:

I have this term made the acquaintance of a couple of young Oxford Scholars who are deeply interested in the Modernist movement, & who after reading your book on Modernism are most anxious to have the privilege of meeting you, & of talking over certain difficulties in connection with their position as High Churchmen who wish to take Orders in the Church of England.
I have ventured to suggest that they should *not* break with the High Church party, to which they seem to me to be deeply attached, but should endeavour to combine their Liberalism with their Catholicism.
But both men seem anxious to consult you about the matter...I may add that they are keen students of M. Loisy's works, & I think both are likely to prove men of mark.[2]

This anticipation was justified. Hebert, who became a member of the Society of the Sacred Mission at Kelham, was one of the most influential anglican theologians of his generation. In 1957 he expressed the opinion that the 'Liberal Theology', whether of liberal protestantism or of catholic modernism, had completely

---

[1] Chevalier to Loisy, 6 November 1904: BN, n.a.f. 15650. The review in question, entitled 'The Gospel and the Church', appeared in *The Oxford Magazine: Literary Supplement*, 25 May 1904, pp. 3 ff.
[2] Young to Lilley, 15 June 1908: LP.

collapsed since the advent of the 'Biblical Theology' of which Sir Edwyn Hoskyns was 'the great protagonist' in England.[1] D. L. Murray did not take holy orders, but became a well-known man of letters and edited *The Times Literary Supplement* from 1938 to 1944. He published a small book on *Pragmatism* in 1912, which was warmly commended by F. C. S. Schiller. He appears to have maintained an interest in religious questions since he wrote a booklet on *Reservation, its purpose and method* for the Alcuin Club in 1923, but I infer from a remark in his book *Scenes and Silhouettes* (1926, p. 295) that his sympathy with the modernists waned.

I come at last to Cambridge and to the last of the fellow travellers about whom I have something to say. In 1904 Friedrich von Hügel's mother, his brother Anatole and his sister-in-law were living in Cambridge, and Dom Cuthbert Butler was at Benet House, so that the modernists were not without contacts. It was Dom Butler who made arrangements for a gathering to meet Mgr Mignot.

F. C. Burkitt (1864–1935) had an enduring sympathy with Loisy, as two of his letters will show. At the time of Loisy's excommunication, he wrote to him:

I feel I can delay no longer in writing to you to express my very sincere sympathy with you...and to express...the sense of personal fellowship that many Liberal Christians feel with you.

I know perfectly well that both as an English Churchman and as a Historical Critic my inherited and personal views are different in many ways from yours; but, for all that, you are fighting for us the great battle. You and I do from our hearts believe in the reality and the irrevocability of history, of the *fait historique*, a thing which no decree on earth or in heaven can define or change.[2]

Then in 1934, the year before his death, Burkitt wrote to Loisy in terms that suggested an even closer affinity:

---

[1] See Gabriel Hebert, *Fundamentalism and the Church of God* (1957), pp. 21 f. On Hebert's theological evolution, see an article by George Every in the *S.S.M. Quarterly*, September 1963, pp. 60 ff.

[2] Burkitt to Loisy, 17 March 1908: BN, n.a.f. 15650. See also *Mém.*, ii. 413.

In England, as in France, there are too many people who do not at all understand the position of the 'Modernist', of him who is dissatisfied with the traditional form of the Christian ethic...of the 'imperialist' organization—I thank you for this adjective—of the society of Christians, but who does not want to stand aside altogether from the Christian effort and who recognizes that there is an ideal expressed imperfectly by this tradition which he wants to express more in accordance with modern conditions.[1]

J. F. Bethune-Baker's (1861–1951) interest in, and appreciation of, the modernists is revealed in a paper on 'The Way of Modernism' which he read in 1924[2] and in which he treated the teaching of Le Roy, Loisy and Tyrrell as specially instructive. Indeed, he said that, in his own book *The Faith of the Apostles' Creed* (1918), he had tried to expound Le Roy's view of dogma.[3] His review of Rivière's *Le modernisme dans l'Eglise* and of Loisy's *Mémoires*[4] was a further indication of where his sympathies lay.

The seven young Cambridge divines[5] who sent an address of gratitude and sympathy to Father Tyrrell in 1907 either had not come to years of theological discretion in 1904 or were too junior to be invited to meet Mgr Mignot. They constituted a group that met regularly for fellowship, worship and discussion. The diary of one of them has been entrusted to my keeping. On 14 November 1907 it contains this entry: 'The Brethren met as usual...and decided to send a letter to Fr Tyrrell expressing sympathy.'[6]

If E. C. Hoskyns (1884–1937) had been in Cambridge at this time, he might have been one of the signatories of the letter. Anyhow, according to one of his pupils, he used after the first world war to 'expound the New Testament largely in terms of Catholic

---

[1] Burkitt to Loisy, 23 October 1934: BN, n.a.f. 15650.
[2] Published in his book *The Way of Modernism* (1927), pp. 1–18.
[3] His appreciation of Le Roy is also shown in *The New View of Christianity* (n.d.), pp. 132 f.
[4] *Journal of Theological Studies*, July 1931, pp. 442 ff.
[5] H. Leonard Pass, Will Spens, E. Gordon Selwyn, G. H. Clayton, W. L. Mackennal, S. C. Carpenter and J. C. H. How. See Petre, *Autobiography and Life of Tyrrell*, ii. 371.
[6] Diary of J. C. H. How.

Modernism' and his teaching betrayed the influence of Loisy.[1] But by 1930 he had reacted violently from Liberalism in all its forms and had become what Father Hebert called the great protagonist of Biblical Theology. An interchange of letters that I had with him in 1934 will illustrate this mutation and will, I hope, be a not uninteresting way of concluding this chapter.

In my book *The Modernist Movement in the Roman Church* I had said that in England Loisy's part in establishing the eschatological interpretation of the original gospel was sometimes overlooked, and I had added this footnote:

E.g. by Sir E. C. Hoskyns (*Essays Catholic and critical*, p. 155n.), who in this connexion appears to give all the credit to J. Weiss and Schweitzer and to ignore Loisy entirely. The same writer, when referring to Catholic modernism in general and to *L'Evangile et l'Eglise* in particular, likewise overlooks the importance of Loisy's work as an historical criticism of liberal Protestantism (see *ibid*. pp. 158 f.).[2]

When he had read my book, Hoskyns wrote to me as follows:

I have just finished 'The Modernist Movement in the Roman Church'; and, of course, noticed your rebuke to me. As a result, I re-read the essay in Essays Catholic & Critical, which I had not read for some years.

On the whole, I think your rebuke unnecessarily hard. I was not concerned with the history of the recognition of eschatology in the Gospels, or with giving 'credit'; but simply with the fact that it was Weiss and Schweitzer who introduced the tension of eschatology into technical N. T. work for most of us. We ought perhaps to have got it from Loisy, but we did not.

My memory of the importance of the publication of L'Evangile et l'Eglise when it first appeared was that, for those of us who combined catholic faith with critical work upon the N. T., for the time being at least, it removed the acute pain of our technical work. There was less tension. That is what I tried to say in Essays Catholic and Critical. I did not mean that Loisy and Harnack agreed about the historical picture of Primitive Christianity or even of Jesus, and differed about

[1] See E. C. Hoskyns, *Cambridge Sermons* (1938), pp. xvi f.
[2] MMRC, p. 124.

the deductions which should be drawn, but that Loisy belonged critically within the orbit of liberal–radical N. T. criticism, and then, as a catholic, sat lightly to its results, because the Church was an altogether bigger thing than the particular beliefs and practices of Primitive Christianity. No doubt, as you say in your book, Loisy still held the Jesus of history to be important, but in such a manner as to relieve us of the sense for His ultimate authority.

That is what I intended to convey in Essays Catholic and Critical. I have personally travelled a long way from the situation as it appeared in the years immediately following the publication of L'Evangile et l'Eglise. The whole N. T. situation looks different, and we seem to have to face up once again to the authority of the N. T. Of that I was aware when I wrote the essay in E.C. & C. Hence, the rather aloof attitude to technical Catholic Modernism.

By the authority of the N. T. I mean, of course, much more than 'Hebrew monotheism' and a certain 'quality of ethics' and more even than the 'worship of Jesus Christ'. This is, however, a further question. I could have wished that, in your last chapter, you had dealt more with the influence of Roman Catholic Modernism upon English Biblical Studies, which you rightly say was the fundamental issue, and that you had said something about the temporary character of that influence. Some of us were held by it during a very difficult period, but it raised more problems than it solved—I mean in technical N. T. work—and I now find Loisy's commentary on the 4th gospel not adequately described as a work of 'pure scholarship': it was very much a livre d'occasion, in which most of the real problems of the 4th gospel were roughly—though in very fluent French—disregarded.

I enjoyed your book very much, but could not help feeling that it was not written by a man who has felt where the shoe is actually pinching in N. T. work, or indeed where it has pinched in these long years since the publication of Das Wesen des Christentums.

I replied as follows:

Many thanks for your letter. I am sorry that you think my note with reference to your essay in Essays Cath. & Crit. was hardly justified. The fact that for you it was Weiss and Schweitzer and not Loisy who introduced the tension of eschatology into technical N. T. work may explain your omission of any reference to Loisy in this connexion, but, since for many it was Loisy who did this, I think that in a volume of Essays *Catholic and critical* it was reasonable to look for a reference to him. But the other point is more important. I still think that to treat the aspect of Catholic Modernism with which you were concerned as simply a reflection of the Liberal Protestant reconstruction of Christian origins involves a serious depreciation of the position of Loisy, as also of Tyrrell and Heiler,—and that in the very limited space at your disposal it would have been possible to give a juster account of the difference between the Liberal Protestant and Catholic Modernist reconstructions.

The attitude to eschatology is one point of difference: more fundamental was the determined refusal to let theological or anti-theological presuppositions condition the reconstruction of history. I do not suppose you regard this as a merit, and in any case you do not appear to consider that the modernists were more successful than the liberal protestants in resisting the tendency to interpret primitive Christianity 'in terms of modern thought'. It is probably because I think they *were* far more successful, and regard this as a considerable merit, that I find what you say unsatisfactory and depreciative.

Thus, as you suggest in your letter, the difference between your view of the matter and mine may be due to a difference of attitude towards N. T. criticism and the problem of Christian origins. My experience is of course much shorter and more limited than yours, but I have always been pretty acutely conscious that the shoe pinches. I may not feel that it pinches just as you feel it to do. I can see the attractiveness of taking 'the last step in the historical reconstruction of the origin of the Christian religion' which you say in your essay is 'almost inevitable'. But I am not convinced that one can take that last step in the way you wish; nor do I think it desirable that the religious and intellectual challenge of Catholic theology should be bound up with, and made to depend upon, one particular reconstruction of the history of Christian origins...[1]

---

[1] I have reproduced this letter from a pencilled draft. I note now that in 1932 Paul Elmer More wrote: 'I had supposed that the "*liberalische Theologie*" had received its death-wound from Loisy and its *coup de grâce* from Schweitzer.' See A. H. Dakin, *Paul Elmer More* (1960), p. 322.

8

MARC SANGNIER AND THE SILLON

This chapter is about a manifestation of social or sociological, as distinguished from doctrinal or ecclesiastical, modernism. It is arguable whether the terms 'modernism' and 'modernist' should be applied to the proponents of ideas other than those which the papacy condemned, or intended to condemn, in the *Lamentabili* and the *Pascendi*. Jean Rivière, for example, the author of *Le modernisme dans l'Eglise*, objected to this extended use of the terms, which he described as a 'polemical exploitation' of them.[1] But Albert Houtin included a consideration of the Christian democrats and of sociological modernism in his *Histoire du modernisme catholique*. He was certainly justified in doing so, if we take the word 'modernist' to be applicable to all those Catholics who at the beginning of this century sought to adapt the teaching and practice of the Church to what they regarded as the requirements of contemporary culture in ways that incurred their condemnation by the papacy. There is no doubt whatever about the condemnation of the Sillon: it was condemned all by itself in a long papal brief of 25 August 1910. Already there had been one or two passages in the *Pascendi* which could be used, and were used, by the opponents of the Sillon to associate it with doctrinal modernism.[2] In any case, Pius X himself authorized an extended use of the terms in a papal brief that he issued shortly after the condemnation of the Sillon.[3] Here, if nowhere else, one can say: *Roma locuta est; causa finita est.*

On the other hand, while social modernism was contemporaneous with doctrinal modernism and was condemned with equal severity, they should by no means be confused. A man could be a doctrinal modernist without being anything of a social modernist

---

[1] See *op. cit.* Part VI, ch. iii.
[2] See Caron, pp. 641 ff.
[3] To G. Decurtins, 15 September 1910: *Acta Apostolicae Sedis*, 10 October 1910, pp. 738 ff. Cf. *Mém.*, ii. 582 f. and p. 103 above.

and *vice versa*. Marc Sangnier and the sillonists, in particular, prided themselves upon their doctrinal orthodoxy and upon their docility to the Vicar of Christ in the field of faith and morals. 'We are not theologians', wrote Sangnier in 1899. 'Each man has his own task; we have not received a mission to form part of the teaching Church; we are not charged to fabricate the catechism, but only to learn it.'[1] This was one of their constant themes. So in 1907 we find Sangnier saying in an interview: 'We do not involve ourselves in theology. The Sillon is a lay movement. We do not concern ourselves at all with Abbé Loisy and new methods of exegesis, of the existence of which most of our comrades are totally ignorant.'[2]

The sillonists differed from the doctrinal modernists in other important respects. Whereas the latter were mostly men of mature years and of protracted experience, the Sillon started as a youth movement: M. Dansette has described it as 'the finest religious movement among youth that France has ever known'.[3] Then, what is more important, the Sillon possessed a coherence and a unified leadership, a singleness of purpose and an agreed aim, such as the doctrinal modernists never had. While, as I shall explain, it would be misleading to call the Sillon an 'organization', it was surely an organism, with organs expressive of its corporate life and sense of mission. Its other distinguishing features will become clear as we proceed.

But, before I proceed, I should explain that, whereas in previous chapters I have made large use of unpublished sources, I have not attempted to do so in this case. For one thing, a long and comprehensive work on the subject, that was based on an extensive research in official and private archives and on the recollections of still surviving participants in the movement, was recently published: I refer to *Le Sillon et la démocratie chrétienne 1894–1910* by Jeanne Caron. It was a doctoral thesis in the Sorbonne, and by chance I was in Paris when its oral examination

---

[1] *Le Sillon*, 1899: I. 547.
[2] *Ibid.* 1907: I. 312. Cf. *ibid.* 1903: II. 127; 1904: I. 241; Louis Cousin, *Le Sillon et les Catholiques* (1909), pp. 73–6.
[3] A. Dansette, *Religious History of Modern France*, ii. 288.

took place in April 1967. I was able to be present at a proceeding which, I may say, was both longer and more formidable than any that I have experienced on a similar occasion in this country. Dr Caron's is the most authoritative book on the Sillon that has so far been produced and I have depended much upon it.[1] But I have had other sources at my disposal. For instance, I am the fortunate possessor of a complete set of the fortnightly journal, *Le Sillon*, from 1899 to 1909: the perusal of those volumes has given me the feel of the whole Sillon movement more than anything else I have read.

I propose first to say something about the origins of the movement and then about its characteristics and evolution, and finally to examine its relations with the ecclesiastical authorities and the crisis that led to its suppression. The movement originated in 1894 among a group of pupils and ex-pupils of the Collège Stanislas in Paris. This was a Catholic school—what in Britain would be called a public school—conducted by the Marianists, a religious society that had both clerical and lay members. In the early 1890s both Paul Desjardins, who was known as a neo-Christian,[2] and Maurice Blondel were on the staff of the school and exercised a stimulating influence.

What developed into the movement known as the Sillon had a twofold beginning, though the promoters of both enterprises were closely associated. On the one hand, there was the review founded in January 1894 by Paul Renaudin and Augustin Leger, which they entitled *Le Sillon*. They had both been pupils of Blondel at the Collège Stanislas. On the other hand, there was the group of friends, in which Marc Sangnier was from the start the moving spirit, who were allowed to hold meetings out of school hours in a basement room, called the Crypt, at the Collège Stanislas. They were all fervent young Catholics who were eager to devote their lives to the service of Christ and of his Church. A year or two before, Sangnier, when he was only nineteen, had in

---

[1] Except where otherwise stated, it is the principal source of my information. *Le Sillon de Marc Sangnier* by Jean de Fabrègues (1964) is a more popular work.

[2] Desjardins (1859–1940) sympathized with all forms of liberal catholicism and he founded more than one organization to bring together religious seekers and inquirers. For many years his associates met at the Abbey of Pontigny which he bought.

a prize essay on 'The evolution of the idea of the fatherland'[1] adumbrated ideas about the nature and needs of a democratic society that were to be worked out as the movement developed.

It is to be borne in mind that France was at this turn of the century a deeply divided country as indeed it had been for a long time. The anti-clerical policies of the Third Republic were gathering momentum. The Catholics, despite the new leads that Leo XIII had recently given them, were still for the most part anti-republican, royalist, and politically and socially conservative. The Dreyfus affair, which began in this very year 1894, was to be a sorry revelation of the passions and tempers of the time. Intelligent, imaginative and idealistic young Catholics had every motive to make them want to contribute to some kind of a breakthrough. Leo XIII, in his encyclical *Rerum novarum* (1891) and in his letter *Au milieu des sollicitudes* (1892) to the Catholics of France, urging them to rally to the republican régime, had pointed to the directions in which they might look for a brighter future both for their church and for their country.

Marc Sangnier (1873–1950) was splendidly endowed for the part he was to play. He was the grandson of Charles Lachaud (1818–82), an eminent lawyer of the Second Empire, renowned for his eloquence, a gift that Marc inherited. Marc's physical appearance does not seem to have been seductive except for his luminous eyes and a great charm of manner and gesture.[2] 'Marc Sangnier', said a bishop who was criticizing him, 'is a charmer, he is greatly gifted and he has a heart of gold.'[3] He also inherited a large fortune which he was at liberty to use in the service of any cause that he adopted. Through the influence of his grandmother and mother a high standard of Catholic piety had become habitual in the family. The bonapartist tradition of his family was also an advantage to Marc since it meant that he was free from any of that attachment to the Bourbon dynasty which still had so baneful a hold on French catholicism. There was nothing to inhibit him from embracing wholeheartedly the policy of rallying

[1] See Caron, pp. 37 ff.
[2] See H. Rollet, *L'action sociale des catholiques en France* ii. 19 f.
[3] See Caron, p. 619.

to the Republic, and I may add that the Marianists, who were responsible for the Collège Stanislas, had been won to this policy well before 1892. Finally, it was fortunate for Sangnier, as well as for his friends, that they had not experienced and could not remember the damping effects that the *Syllabus errorum* of 1864 had had on all liberal or progressive Catholic enterprises.

Sangnier himself was never a pupil of Blondel nor was he philosophically minded, but the presentation of Christian thought that derived from the 'philosophy of action' and the 'method of immanence' was certainly congenial to him, with its preference for dynamic to static concepts and its emphasis on experience as against speculation.[1] Laberthonnière was to be a friend of the Sillon and a contributor to its journal.[2] I should like to find a parallel to Sangnier's relation to the movement but there is none that is altogether close. 'Le nouveau Montalembert'[3] perhaps comes as near as any: Montalembert was the young Prince Charming of the Avenir movement with which the Sillon had many affinities, but Sangnier's role was more like that of Lamennais. The British, or at any rate the Scots, could learn something about Sangnier's leadership of the Sillon by comparing it with George Macleod's leadership of the Iona Community.

The group of fifty or so young men, mostly from the Ecole polytechnique, who in the early years met in the Crypt, received its impetus from Sangnier though he could not always be with them since he had to do his military service during this period. It was not until 1898 that he was free to give his whole time to the cause. The atmosphere of the meetings in the Crypt, of the intense friendship that sprang up there and the sense of missionary vocation, comes across in these sentences which were written in 1897:

We felt a great need to talk to one another about all these ardent

---

[1] Cf. Sangnier's letter (quoted by C. Maurras, *Le dilemme de Marc Sangnier*, p. 26) in which he says that he distrusted 'la vanité séduisante des somptueux édifices intellectuels' and preferred 'se laisser faire par la vérité et par la vie'.

[2] See Caron, pp. 65, 82 f., 106, 108, 357; and *Le Sillon*, 1903: II. 98, 218 f., 427–30; 1904: I. 129–34. Le Roy was also associated with the Sillon in its early days: see Caron, pp. 65, 152.

[3] See J. Brugerette, *Le prêtre français et la société contemporaine*, iii. 227.

desires that were burning in our hearts...to form and maintain among ourselves a sort of common soul...to prepare ourselves for the great battles ahead by a sort of fraternal vigil of arms... We talked about everything and nothing, with inexperience and presumptuousness perhaps, but with the conviction that we must do something...

in this small room... mysteriously hidden underground, into which the crowd of us used to dash jostling one another, with this thrilling sensation of a great task to be undertaken for which one was preparing in the half-light.[1]

Out of the preliminary confusion of their talk certain definite needs became clear and urgent—the need to reconcile the Church and the Republic, and the Church and the people, and to tackle the pressing social problems to which the socialists were directing attention. Very soon these young men perceived that they must begin to act as well as to talk. So we find them going out to meet young workers in the church clubs and elsewhere, not with a view to doing them good or to entertaining them, but in order to get to know them and to encourage them to act on their own behalf. By 1898-9 Marc Sangnier was founding the study circles for young workers which became a cardinal feature of the strategy of the Sillon.

The Crypt was by this time producing its own Bulletin, and meanwhile the monthly review, *Le Sillon*, was making its modest way. In this, its first, phase it was a literary journal which discussed and criticized contemporary trends of thought and art, particularly those that made for scepticism or dilettantism. To begin with, it was reticent on the subject of religion, but by 1896 it was affirming its definite allegiance to the Catholic faith. At the end of 1898 the Bulletin of the Crypt was incorporated in *Le Sillon* and Sangnier took over the editorship. It soon abandoned its literary interests and firmly eschewed purely theological questions. Henceforth it was primarily a journal of social action, and it appeared fortnightly. Two years later the Sillon became the name of the movement as well as the title of the journal.

[1] See Caron, pp. 55 f.

It is not certain whether the title 'Sillon' was first thought of by Sangnier or Renaudin. Renaudin, in the first issue, had indicated why the title appealed to them. 'Let us young people, leaving behind all sterile agitation, collect our thoughts, modestly and resolutely, humbly and confidently like the grain that in winter keeps vigil beneath the furrow and silently matures the coming summer's harvest. Our day will not be long in coming; it may be quite near; we must be ready.'[1] This sense of expectancy, of small beginnings and great ends, and of dedication to a cause, was always characteristic of the Sillon.

From its small beginnings the Sillon did indeed spread and expand with striking speed. I have so far mentioned only the study circles for young workers. Twenty of these had been formed by the middle of 1900 in Paris and its suburbs, and by the beginning of 1904 this number had risen to fifty.[2] The idea of Catholics organizing groups of young workers for purposes of instruction, recreation and Christian fellowship was not of course new.[3] What was new about the Sillon's study circles[4] was their avoidance of paternalism. Although most of the circles had a chaplain, the president was a young working man, and the members themselves were responsible for all that was done. They were expected to study hard and to tackle a large variety of social problems. In order to assist them in doing their home-work and in preparing for the meetings, the Sillon opened reading rooms (*salles de travail*) furnished with books and journals, where expert advisers were present on certain nights in the week.[5] The study circles both in Paris and in the provinces were the spearhead of the whole movement, and reunions and congresses for the members which were regularly held fostered not only the

---

[1] See Caron, p. 78.

[2] For some information about the number of *cercles d'étude* in the provinces, see Sangnier, *Discours*, i. 275 f.

[3] E.g. see Charles Maignen, *Maurice Maignen et les origines du mouvement social catholique en France*, esp. Book I, ch. ix and Book II, ch. i.

[4] On the *cercles d'étude*, see G. Hoog, *Histoire du catholicisme social du France 1871–1931*, pp. 130–3.

[5] On the *salles de travail* see *Le Sillon*, 1900: I. 430–2; II. 126–32, 369–74; 1901: I. 349–52.

enthusiasm of the movement but also its coherence and aware-ness of its aims.

Exacting demands were necessarily made on the members of the study circles. In order to reach out more widely and to provide easier opportunities for what would now be called further or adult education, the Sillon arranged for public lectures, which soon became part of the activity of what were known as the People's Institutes (*instituts populaires*)[1] which organized courses of professional and cultural instruction. The People's Institutes were a counterpart to the People's Universities (*universités populaires*)[2] which were being sponsored at this time by other agencies and which despite their profession of religious neutrality were mostly anti-clerical. The Sillon stood not for neutrality, but for pluralism, i.e. for encouraging the free expression of different opinions on moral and religious subjects.[3]

The Sillon welcomed opportunities of public debate, and Sangnier insisted that his audiences, even when predominantly Catholic or sympathetic, should give a fair hearing to speakers who wanted to controvert him. In 1903, for example, when the ex-priest Victor Charbonnel, who had become ferociously anti-clerical, and his followers were interrupting church services,[4] Sangnier called a meeting in Paris to defend liberty of worship. There was an audience of three thousand. After he had spoken, he secured silence for Charbonnel and another anti-clerical speaker to address the meeting. Meanwhile there was a rowdy mob outside the hall and when at the end the sillonists left for their headquarters in order to hold a private meeting they were set upon by a crowd of anti-clerical hooligans. Many were injured and blood was shed, before at last the police restored order. This came to be known as 'the Bloody Meeting'.[5]

The disorder and damage might have been greater if it had not

---

[1] On the *instituts populaires* see *Le Sillon*, 1900: II. 72–7; 101–4; 1901: I. 65–76, 80–9; Hoog, *op. cit.* pp. 136–41.
[2] On the *universités populaires* see *Le Sillon*, 1900: I. 91–108, 277; II. 92–5; 1902: I. 8–16.
[3] See Caron, p. 157; cf. *ibid.* pp. 468 f.
[4] See *Le Sillon*, 1903: I. 394 ff.
[5] See *ibid.* 1903: I. 401–21.

been for the presence of the Young Guard (*La Jeune Garde*).[1]
This was another constituent section of the Sillon, a kind of
cadet corps that was recruited mostly from young workers aged
16 to 25. They had to be prepared for a high standard of both
religious and military devotion and discipline. The Young Guard
was founded in 1902 and in its first years its chief function was to
provide stewards and to maintain order at public meetings and
other gatherings arranged by the Sillon. By all accounts this
was done with efficiency and courtesy and without any resort to
rough methods.

From 1905 onwards the Young Guard was responsible for
selling on the streets the popular paper that was launched by the
Sillon in October of that year. It was entitled the *Eveil démocratique* and was an instant success. Within a year it attained a
circulation of 60,000. It was an instrument of propaganda and the
task of selling it gave young sillonists a very practical way of
participating in the movement. By this time the movement had
spread in all directions and there were many Sillons in the
provinces and even in rural areas. Some of the local Sillons
issued their own paper which they could now combine with the
Eveil démocratique.

Before coming to the ideas or the ideology that were propa-
gated, I must say something about how the movement was
organized, or rather about how it managed without having the
kind of organization that most movements develop. The Sillon
began and continued as a group of friends, of young people who
shared a common faith and found that they had what they called
a 'common soul' (*âme commune*). They insisted that the Sillon
was not an institution, a party or a sect: it was a life, a leaven, a
way of thinking and acting and growing together, a fellowship
not of the letter but of the spirit. The members addressed one
another as 'comrade' and they referred to one another as 'our
friend(s)'. Whenever Sangnier is mentioned it is as 'our friend'
or 'our friend Marc Sangnier'.

Even when the movement had acquired national proportions,

---

[1] On *La Jeune Garde*, see Caron, pp. 158–65.

Sangnier was determined that it should, so far as possible, retain this informal, spontaneous character. The Sillon had no formal membership, no rules for admission or resignation. 'We leave individuals and groups', wrote Sangnier in 1904, 'to come to us quietly and to leave us as and when they will.'[1] And again in 1905: 'The Sillon has neither a rigid constitution, nor statutes, nor contracts to be entered into, nor admissions, nor dismissal of members.'[2] A leading article of 1908 in *Le Sillon* reiterated the point: 'The Sillon has no written constitution whatever, no charter printed on parchment or engraven on stone. It is quite simply the mutual agreement of souls who share the same ideal and want to realise it by working together as brothers. The Sillon is an immaterial bond between friends...a group constituted on the principle of a maximum of moral cohesion and a minimum of external discipline.'[3] As Dr Caron says, when you tried to penetrate to the administrative arrangements of the Sillon, what you found at once was 'a network of personal relationships'.[4]

There had, of course, to be some organization and allocation of responsibilities. Notably, there was the Central Sillon in Paris, which served the whole movement, and there was Marc Sangnier as 'President' at *its* centre. To its members was assigned responsibility for one or other of the Sillon's principal activities—the study circles, the reading rooms, the People's Institutes, the Young Guard, etc., etc., and there was a secretary-general. But there was considerable fluidity in the membership of the Central Sillon and much coming and going. The members were not elected. It was a favourite maxim of the Sillon that selection was to be preferred to election.[5] Élites selected themselves. It seems clear that the Sillon depended for its harmony, above all, on the personal prestige and influence of Sangnier.

It is remarkable that these informal methods, which permeated the whole movement, worked as well as they did. Naturally there

---

[1] *Le Sillon*, 1904: I. 81.
[2] *Ibid.* 1905: II. 42.
[3] *Ibid.* 1908: II. 241, 246.
[4] Caron, p. 234.
[5] E.g., see *Le Sillon*, 1904: II. 10–14, 369–72; 1905: I. 218 f.

was friction at times, and there were at least two major crises. In 1905 a very efficient secretary-general, Charles d'Hellencourt, was in effect driven from office by Sangnier who considered that he was introducing elements of order and organization which were inconsistent with the spirit of the Sillon.[1] Undoubtedly, a clash of temperament as well as of principle was involved. Sangnier's magnetic charm and lofty idealism were compounded with a certain imperiousness and impetuosity. This was the cause of the other serious crisis which resulted in the loss to the Sillon in 1907 of Abbé Jean Desgranges (1874–1958) who had been leader of the Sillon at Limoges and one of the movement's most vigorous personalities and orators.[2] He claimed that, so far as he was concerned, Sangnier's methods had become intolerably dictatorial.

But it is time to turn to the ideology of the movement, though 'ideology' is too grand or sophisticated a term for the ideas or aims that animated the Sillon during its brief existence. This was not a doctrinaire movement. Its ideas were generated by its experience, and it was experience that led the sillonists apparently to change their course after a time.

As we have seen, the movement began with a group of young middle-class Catholics who wanted to make their faith a reality and to commend it to others in all walks of life. That is to say, in its first phase it was a religious movement with a missionary and social concern. It is true that the sillonists always accepted Leo XIII's policy of rallying to the Republic and of seeking to christianize the democracy, but they disclaimed political intentions or ambitions. In any case, they were modest enough to recognize that they were too young to exercise any direct political influence. Their task was to train themselves and to help others to qualify as an élite for action in the future.

In 1902, when Sangnier had been urged to stand as a candidate in the parliamentary elections of that year, *Le Sillon* explained why he had not done so: 'We well know that the elections will not be able to assure the success of the ideas in which we have faith

---

[1] See Caron, pp. 354 ff.
[2] See the introduction by Denise Aimé-Azam to Abbé Desgranges, *Carnets intimes.*

and that next Sunday's voting will not diffuse that free and fraternal Christian life that alone is capable of animating our democracy. That doesn't really come into the question.'[1] And in the following year, in a speech on 'The Future of Democracy', we find him saying:

To make the Republic a reality by allowing the national energies to develop and bear their fruit, isn't this the political task that is actually laid upon us? But, for that, we must first renounce all politics, or at least acknowledge that what has to be done is not simply to demand the liberties of which they want to deprive us. The work that must be undertaken goes deeper: it consists in developing men's powers of comprehension and awareness, in changing public opinion in France by enlightening it, by directing it, or rather by allowing it to direct itself towards social justice and the flowering of the energies of France.[2]

What was needed was a campaign of moral and religious education and of training in responsibility.

Until this time, the Sillon was so manifestly a religious, and not a political, movement that even the extreme right-wing papers, which subsequently were to attack it relentlessly, were so far favourable to it. They were misled by its patriotic ardour and by its defence of the Church; for what most attracted attention in this period was the Sillon's opposition to anti-clericalism and to the government's assaults on liberty of education, on the religious orders, etc.

Various factors converged to push the Sillon inexorably towards political engagement.

First, the large expansion of the movement,[3] the enthusiasm that was thereby generated, and the fact that the early members were no longer youths but were now ripe for participation in

---

[1] *Le Sillon*, 1902: I. 281 f.

[2] M. Sangnier, *Discours 1891–1906*, pp. 119 f. Cf. *Le Sillon*, 1903: I. 405: 'Au Sillon nous ne faisons pas de politique.'

[3] Since there was no formal admission or resignation of members, there is no record of the total number of sillonists at any period. But an indication of the movement's growth may be seen in the fact that the number of subscribers to its journal, *Le Sillon*, which was 400 in 1902, had risen to 4,000 in 1906. See Caron, p. 400. I have already noted that the circulation of the Sillon's paper, *Eveil démocratique*, was 60,000 in 1906: see p. 199 above.

public affairs:[1] these circumstances all fostered a desire for more effective social action which would evidently have to include political action.

Secondly, it became increasingly clear that the sillonists would not be able to support either of the existing political *blocs*. The Right was clerical,[2] conservative and monarchist. The Left was fanatically anti-clerical and intolerant. The Sillon was always opposed to the formation of a Catholic party,[3] since that would involve confounding the things of God with the things of Caesar and would imply that all Catholics should have the same political opinions. Moreover, in his encyclical *Graves de communi* of 18 January 1901, Leo XIII had forbidden Catholics to form or join a Christian democrat party.[4] It was natural, therefore, that the Sillon should come to favour the formation of a political party in which it could be at home. It would have to be republican and democratic, non-confessional and pluralist, with a programme of radical social reform.

Thirdly, the sillonists' conception of democracy which, as Sangnier himself confessed, had been 'at first only a vague and indefinite dream',[5] had been steadily acquiring substance and precision and was now distinctive. When one considers how many people use the term 'democracy' without ever attempting to define it, it must be reckoned to the credit of Sangnier and his colleagues that they never tired of repeating and enlarging upon[6] their own definition which was that 'democracy is the social organization that tends to raise the civic conscience and responsibility of everyone to the maximum'. They contrasted what they meant by democracy with the republican régime that actually existed in France with its *étatisme* and its intolerant anti-clericalism. The kind of democracy that was advocated by the orators of the Sillon was much like what has since been advocated under such captions as 'The Responsible Society' and 'The Open

[1] See Hoog, *op. cit.*, p. 181.
[2] On the meaning of the terms 'clerical' and 'anti-clerical', see Caron, pp. 441–6.
[3] See Sangnier, *Discours*, i. p. 313; Caron, 455 f.
[4] See p. 209 below.
[5] Sangnier, *op. cit.*, I. 309.
[6] E.g. see Sangnier, *L'Esprit démocratique* (1905).

Society'. It reminds me much of John Middleton Murry's pleading in his book *The Defence of Democracy* (1939). The sillonists acknowledged that their ideal could never be perfectly realized in history,[1] but it pointed to the direction in which society should be moving. In France as it was in the opening decade of this century, riddled with fanatical feuds, it must have been extremely refreshing and exhilarating to contemplate the ideal order that Sangnier knew how to paint in glowing colours. Professor Michael Fogarty, while recognizing the far-reaching and salutary influence of the Sillon, has said that 'its doctrine was often gaseous and sentimental, with an absence of hard edges'.[2] That may not be denied, but it could be said of nearly all political idealists before they have had to shoulder the recalcitrant tasks of government.

Fourthly, the Sillon's interest in, and involvement with, the trade union movement increased as time went on, and by 1906 had become one of its principal spheres of activity.[3] As between the so-called Yellow and Red unions the Sillon preferred the latter since they stood unequivocally for the interests of the workers. The Yellow unions were sponsored by the employers. Sillonists were encouraged to join the unions affiliated to the Confédération Générale du Travail (C.G.T.) except where Catholics were excluded by religious intolerance. Often sillonists were elected to office in the unions, particularly as treasurers of local branches because dependence could be placed upon their honesty. While the sillonists looked forward to the end of the capitalist system,[4] they would not go along with those who wanted to overthrow it by violence: hence they became wary of talk about 'revolution' which otherwise would have been congenial to them. They were however broadly in sympathy with the socialism that was professed in the C.G.T. This then was another factor that pushed the movement in a political direction, and

---

[1] See *Le Sillon*, 1905: I. 442. It was not, however, a mere ideal, since it already existed in the kingdom of God. Here there was a resemblance between Sangnier's teaching and that of F. D. Maurice: see Sangnier, *Discours*, i. 278; Vidler, *F. D. Maurice and Company*, p. 274.
[2] Michael P. Fogarty, *Christian Democracy in Western Europe 1820–1953*, p. 266.
[3] See Caron, pp. 477–507.
[4] See Sangnier, *Discours*, i. 338.

similar was the effect of the considerable sillonist participation in the cooperative movement.[1]

Fifthly, the need for a republican democratic party as an alternative to the *blocs* of the Right and Left was borne in upon the Sillon by particular experiences, notably its campaign about the so-called *Taupe*,[2] in which it received more support from the Left than from the Right, from atheists than from Catholics.

All these factors served to turn the Sillon from what at first had been regarded as a religious movement into a political movement. That is what it appeared mainly to be from 1906 to 1910. It was still indeed *une œuvre de catholiques*, but no longer *une œuvre catholique*.[3] It was still, that is to say, *une œuvre de catholiques*, but not of Catholics only, for it now welcomed the collaboration of non-Catholics who shared its social and political aims. This is what Sangnier called *le plus grand Sillon*.[4] Another sign of this evolution was the change of *Le Sillon's* sub-title, at the beginning of 1905, from *Revue catholique d'action sociale* to *Revue d'action démocratique*. This development into a political party for all who wanted a pluralist, tolerant democracy and a comprehensive program of social reform was never completed, but it went steadily forward. Protestants and other sympathetic non-Catholics associated with the movement. Then, in order to test the ground, Sangnier stood as a candidate for parliament, first at a bye-election early in 1909 and again at the general election in the spring of 1910, and although in neither case was he elected the result of the experiment was sufficiently encouraging.

It had already been realized that in order to launch a political party it would be essential to have a daily newspaper as its organ. A large capital sum of money was raised for this purpose by remarkable sacrifice on the part of sillonists, and those who

[1] See Caron, pp. 507–23.

[2] The *Taupe* was a more or less secret organization which took in hand the preparation of boys who were about to enter the Ecole polytechnique and to which at this time serious moral objections could be taken. See *Le Sillon*, 1905: II. 361–7, 371–83; Caron, pp. 403–6, 413; Charles Maurras, *Le dilemme de Marc Sangnier*, pp. 226–40.

[3] See Albert Lamy on 'Notre œuvre civique' in *Le Sillon*, 1906: II. 81 ff.

[4] See *Le Sillon*, 1907: II. 231–3.

possessed the necessary skills gave voluntary service to the paper when it was started.[1] Its title was *La Démocratie* and the first number appeared on 17 August 1910, just twelve days before Pius X dissolved the Sillon.

The question whether or not, when it grew into a non-confessional political movement, it fundamentally changed its character was of course arguable. It must be borne in mind that under the new conditions the Catholic core of sillonists not only preserved its identity as *le plus intime Sillon*, but they maintained their high standard of religious discipline and devotion. It was because of their social and political activities, in which they took part with others as citizens and not as churchmen, and so claimed therein to be free from ecclesiastical control, that the movement was alleged to have fundamentally changed its character. Undoubtedly, its appearance or its public image had changed, but Sangnier and his colleagues asserted that this was a development that had been intended from the beginning and one that involved no inconsistency.

Thus Louis Cousin, writing in 1909,[2] said that 'the entry of the Sillon into the political field properly so-called is not...a revolution...but a normal evolution that was foreseen from the outset', and he was able to quote statements that had been made by Sangnier and others which justified this contention. It would have been premature, they said, to have embarked on a political movement before they had prepared an élite for the undertaking. Their strategy all along had been to educate an élite drawn from all social ranks that would take the lead in the full responsibilities of citizenship. If they really meant business they were bound sooner or later to engage in politics. This was surely the natural evolution of the movement.

What however is arguable is whether they were not in too much of a hurry to move on to the creation of a political party and whether it would not have been wiser to have prepared the ground more thoroughly. But they had a reason for hurrying. The gathering hostility of a majority of the French bishops and

---

[1] See Hoog, *op. cit.* p. 164.
[2] L. Cousin, *Le Sillon et les Catholiques*, p. 30.

the menacing rumours that came from Rome made it seem urgent to secure a basis for future operations that would not be subject to the control of the ecclesiastical authorities. Thus there was a weighty motive for pressing on with the formation of a non-confessional political party as quickly as possible.[1] But this brings us at last to a consideration of the Sillon's relations with the Church.

In its early days the Sillon received much benevolence and encouragement from the church authorities who could hardly fail to smile upon a group of lively and intelligent young men who were ardent in their practice of the faith and eager to win others to it both in the scholastic world and among young workers. The sillonists, for their part, were keen to receive approval for their plans, which differed from those of existing church organizations for youth. They could reasonably depend upon the goodwill of Pope Leo XIII in view of their support of his policy of *le ralliement* and of his encyclical *Rerum novarum*. When he was succeeded by Pius X in 1903, they were no less confident of receiving papal approval. They at once organized a public meeting that was addressed by Abbé Naudet[2] on 'Un pape démocrate'.[3] An Italian friend of the Sillon wrote to assure them that the new pope, when Patriarch of Venice, had taken an active part in the Christian democratic movement in the north of Italy. Pius X could be relied on to follow the directives of Leo XIII.[4]

This was in August 1903. In order to make sure of the state of play, in the following month Sangnier took a party of about twenty sillonists on a pilgrimage to Rome[5] that was arranged by Léon Harmel, a leading social catholic of an older generation.[6] The object of the sillonists was to secure the favour of the new

---

[1] See Caron, p. 580.
[2] Paul Naudet (1859–1929), one of the most prominent of the *abbés démocrates*: see Robert Cornilleau, *L'Abbé Naudet* (1933).
[3] See *Le Sillon*, 1903: II. 119.
[4] See *ibid.* 1903: II. 129.
[5] See *ibid.* 1903: II. 121 f., 241 ff.
[6] See my *A Century of Social Catholicism*, pp. 123 ff. Harmel organized such pilgrimages annually.

pope and his advisers, and they had a very heartening reception in the Eternal City.[1] Mgr della Chiesa (the future Benedict XV) said of Sangnier that he had hardly ever come across in a layman 'so sure and precise a knowledge of the most delicate points of theology'.[2] The pilgrims were received in audience by Pius X and Sangnier was given the opportunity to explain to him at length their designs and their hopes.

Next year, that is, in September 1904, the sillonists organized their own pilgrimage to Rome.[3] They formed a party of six hundred including a detachment of the Young Guard which, when the Sillon was given its main papal audience, was allowed to take over the duties of the Swiss Guard in the Vatican—an unprecedented privilege. To the address that Sangnier read to him the pope could hardly have replied more warmly and he kissed the flag of the French Republic which was offered to him. Still further countenance seemed to be given to the Sillon, and especially to its leader, when later in the same year he was invited to address the World Marial Congress in Rome that was held to celebrate the fiftieth anniversary of the promulgation of the dogma of the Immaculate Conception.[4]

By this time the Sillon needed such encouragements for criticism of, and hostility to, its activities had been mounting over the years. As early as in 1899 when Leo XIII condemned 'Americanism'[5]—the so-called 'phantom heresy'[6] of which no one ever discovered an avowed supporter either in the old world or in the new—the opponents of Christian democracy gloated as though all its manifestations were, or were going to be, condemned.[7] Writers in *Le Sillon* needed and attempted to show that they were not affected.[8]

---

[1] See *Le Sillon*, 1903: II. 281–92.
[2] See *ibid.* 1903: II. 287.
[3] See *ibid.* 1904: II. 201–23.
[4] For the text of his discourse, see *Le Sillon*, 1904: II. 401–6; Sangnier, *Discours*, i. 291–7.
[5] See Houtin, *L'Americanisme* (1904), which provides (pp. 325–50) a French translation of *Testem benevolentiae*, the letter which Leo XIII addressed to Cardinal Gibbons on 22 January 1899. See also *Lettres apostoliques de S.S. Léon XIII*, v. 182–201.
[6] See *Mém.*, ii. 253.

This was the time when those who surrounded the aged pope seemed to be succeeding in persuading him to go back on some of his bolder advances. In 1897 Mignot had written to Loisy: 'Abbé Duchesne told me that the wind was blowing towards reaction in the entourage of the pope.'[1] And in 1899 Mignot wrote to von Hügel: 'Like you I am sorry to note that reaction is becoming more and more powerful in the entourage of the sovereign pontiff.'[2] The papal encyclical on 'Christian Democracy' (*Graves de communi*, 18 January 1901[3]) was to some extent a sign of this reaction though it was intended to be a sequel to *Rerum novarum*. It said that Catholics could be Christian Democrats only in a social sense, not in a political sense. They must not suppose that a democratic form of government is always to be preferred to a monarchical or aristocratic form. They must not slight the upper classes. There must be no 'Christian Democrat' political party. Christian democracy is in future to mean for Catholics only devotion to the social, moral and religious welfare of the poorest classes. This encyclical was aimed at the *abbés démocrates* and all who made a profession of Christian Democracy, rather than at the Sillon. It did not directly hit the sillonists since, although they were on friendly and collaborating terms with the Christian Democrats[4] and were liable to be confused with them, they had not adopted this appellation for themselves and were at pains, before as well as after the appearance of the encyclical,[5] to maintain their independence of all other movements. In the words of Marc Sangnier: 'As young French democrats of the XXth century we have a quite distinct conception of republican

---

[1] Mignot to Loisy, 11 Feburary 1897: BN, n.a.f. 15659.

[2] Mignot to von Hügel, 28 January 1899: VHSA. See also René Rémond, *Les deux congrès ecclésiastiques de Reims et de Bourges 1896–1900* (1964), p. 125; Frémont, ii. 194.

[3] See *Lettres apostoliques de S.S. Léon XIII*, VI. 178–207. See also Hoog, *op. cit.* pp. 119–23.

[4] See Caron, pp. 327 ff.   [5] See *ibid.*, pp. 331 f.

---

[7] See Houtin, *op. cit.*, p. 405.

[8] See *Le Sillon*, 1899: I. 262 ff., 346 ff. Likewise, when shortly afterwards a French nun was censured in Rome for having publicly advocated a modernization of the teaching methods of the religious orders, a writer in *Le Sillon* sought to explain away the *prima facie* effect of the censure: *ibid.* pp. 301–4.

democracy, and we want to work for the ideal which we have conceived in our independence as citizens.'[1]

It was in 1903 that the Catholic press of the Right, and especially the Action Française,[2] began relentlessly to attack the Sillon and Marc Sangnier. The only bishop who so far was conspicuously hostile was Mgr Turinaz of Nancy. On 27 June 1903 in his diocesan paper he urged his priests and the faithful to keep out of the way of the Sillon.[3] The sillonists responded by circulating a letter of encouragement that they had received from Cardinal Rampolla on behalf of Leo XIII.[4] Mgr Turinaz renewed his attack on Christian Democrats in general as well as on the Sillon in a brochure that he brought out in July 1904.[5]

Before this, Pius X had issued a *Motu proprio*[6] on 18 December 1903 which was, for the most part, a repetition of propositions from Leo XIII's encyclicals but also contained further instructions that were designed to prevent any participation of Christian Democrats in politics. The *Motu proprio* was directed primarily to the Italian Christian Democrats who were going through a crisis at this time.[7] But it also applied to Catholics generally, and was calculated to cause some embarrassment to the Sillon. Sangnier's embarrassment is shown by the fact that he asked Cardinal Richard, the archbishop of Paris, whether he need publish the *Motu proprio* in *Le Sillon*. The Cardinal, who was still very well disposed,[8] appears to have told him that he need not do so since it 'did not have an official character'.[9] However, Sangnier did eventually publish it, but not till 10 May 1904, and then in connexion with a reassertion that the sillonists in their

---

[1] Sangnier, *Discours*, i. 349. Cf. Sangnier's article on 'Christianisme et démocratie' in *Le Sillon*, 1904: I. 201–5.

[2] See Caron, pp. 186 f., 277. Henri le Floch (1862–1950), who like Louis Billot was a prominent clerical supporter of the Action Française, said of the sillonists: 'They had to be condemned. They would have made Breton priests accept the Republic.' See Weber, *Action Française*, p. 66.

[3] See Caron, p. 222.

[4] See *ibid.* p. 264; *Le Sillon*, 1903: I. 52 f.

[5] See Caron, p. 287.

[6] See *Le Sillon*, 1904: I. 334–7.

[7] See my *A Century of Social Catholicism*, pp. 157 ff.

[8] See *ibid.* p. 135.

[9] See Caron, p. 274.

entire liberty as citizens had the right to work for the democratic Republic that was their ideal.[1]

Sangnier took the view that the papal definition of Christian Democracy as 'charitable action on behalf of the people, based on natural law and the precepts of the Gospel', was now so broad as to denote a universal Christian duty. It might have been said that 'we are all Christian Democrats now'. But then he had to get round the papal requirement that Christian Democrats must be entirely submissive to ecclesiastical authority and, in particular, must submit all writings that concerned Christian morality and natural ethics for censorship before publication. While he wanted to maintain that the work of the Sillon was of service to the Church, he could still hold that, since the democracy they aimed at was distinct from what the pope meant by Christian Democracy, the instructions in the *Motu proprio* did not concern the sillonists as such. The favourable reception that they were given in Rome during their pilgrimage in September 1904 seemed to imply that the foregoing interpretation was tolerated. But there was still cause for apprehension, especially when the sillonists moved more into political action. The Sillon's contention was, and continued to be, that the papacy recognized that lay Catholics, provided that their obedience to the Church and its authorities was irreproachable in regard to religious faith and practice, were free to act in the political sphere on their own responsibility and without committing the Church. Dr Caron remarks that this claim, 'which could seem exorbitant in the opening years of the XXth century, is much less so today'.[2] Even then, however, it was not as novel ('absolument inusité')[3] as she suggests. It was what Lamennais had claimed in the period between the promulgation of the encyclicals *Mirari vos* and *Singulari nos*, and in its last years the Sillon implicitly acknowledged its affinities with the *Avenir* movement.[4]

The Sillon's relations with the ecclesiastical authorities

[1] See *Le Sillon*, 1904: I. 328. Cf. Caron, p. 292.
[2] Caron, p. 636.
[3] *Ibid.* p. 593.
[4] See *Le Sillon*, 1908: II. 6–14, 457–65; 1909: I. 27–37.

deteriorated sharply from 1906 onwards. A growing number of bishops took steps to withdraw their priests from ministering to sillonist groups. In May 1907 Sangnier went to Rome to seek a clarification of the situation, and afterwards he reported in *Le Sillon*[1] that there was no need to worry since the Vatican recognized that, while priests should not normally act as propagandists of the Sillon, they should certainly as priests be at the service of sillonists as of 'all those who have recourse to their ministry'. Nevertheless, between 1906 and 1910 about forty bishops dissociated themselves from the Sillon, some further than others.[2] They considered that the sillonists did not show enough deference and docility to episcopal authority, and they preferred the Association Catholique de la Jeunesse Française (A.C.J.F.) which was free from that objection and to which the Sillon was a disturbing rival.

Until 1907 the objections to the Sillon that were publicly expressed were on the ground of discipline, not of orthodoxy. But after the promulgation of the *Pascendi* and with the increasing virulence of the campaign of the integrists against every form of liberal catholicism, the orthodoxy of the sillonists began to be suspected. Indeed, when the notorious Montagnini papers[3] were published in 1907, it was found that Sangnier was among the many personalities whom Montagnini had been maliciously calumniating in his communications to Merry del Val, the Cardinal Secretary of State in Rome. For instance, in 1904 he had told Merry del Val that Sangnier was not only an ambitious vulgarian who got recruits for the Sillon by bribery, but was theologically unsound and did not believe in hell.[4] The Montagnini papers also revealed that behind the scenes Merry del Val[5]

[1] 1907: I. 361–4.
[2] See Caron, pp. 636 f., 680.
[3] Carlo Montagnini (1863–1913) was an Italian prelate who, after France broke off diplomatic relations with the Holy See in 1904, was put in charge of the Paris nunciature. On the ground that he was involved in irregular proceedings, the French government seized his papers in December 1906 and they were released for publication in the press at the end of March 1907. See *Les fiches pontificales de Monsignor Montagnini* (1908).
[4] See *ibid.* pp. 201–7.
[5] *Ibid.* On Sangnier's relations with Merry del Val, see Caron, pp. 654, 693.

and Pius X had been adversely judging Sangnier, and so were another motive for his supposedly clarifying visit to Rome.

In the spring of 1908 Abbé Emmanuel Barbier (1851–1925), the most vociferous of the integrists—whom Henri Bremond called 'the terrorist'[1]—who scented heresy everywhere and whose denunciations made the bishops tremble, went to Rome and submitted a memorandum to Pius X which was certainly hostile to the Sillon and which probably served its purpose.[2] It was soon afterwards that the bishop of Bayonne (Mgr Gieure) let it be known that, on a recent visit to Rome, Pius X had told him how disquieted he was about the Sillon, and had said: 'These young people are following a ruinous course: *Viam sequuntur damnosam.*'[3] The integrists had already acquired great strength in the Vatican and would go on acquiring more till the death of Pius X in 1914.

In France the sillonists were accused of wanting to democratize the Church, of weakening the spirit of absolute submission to the hierarchy, and of flirting with Protestantism; other vague charges too were laid against them.[4] There were cases of priests refusing to give communion to sillonists unless they recanted, and of seminarists being forbidden to read the *Eveil démocratique* and having their ordination deferred.[5]

On the other hand, the Sillon still had its friends and defenders among the French bishops. Mgr Chapon of Nice, who had once been secretary to Mgr Dupanloup, took an initiative by writing a confidential letter to a number of archbishops and bishops in which he said that he was gravely troubled by the episcopal condemnations to which the Sillon was being subjected. He considered that the Action Française was the chief prosecutor and hoped to profit from the Sillon's condemnation. Its detractors

---

[1] Bremond to Loisy, 21 April 1925: BN, n.a.f. 15650. On Barbier, see also A. Blanchet, *Histoire d'une mise à l'index*, pp. 82 ff.; Frémont, ii. 679.

[2] See the letter which, on his return to Paris, Barbier wrote to Mgr Turinaz, quoted in Caron, p. 645. Turinaz certainly encouraged, and may well have helped, Barbier in his undertaking.

[3] See Caron, p. 658.

[4] See *ibid.* pp. 660 f., 672, 677 f.

[5] See *Ibid.* pp. 680 ff., 694.

made imprecise accusations, supported with citations torn from their contexts. For his part, Mgr Chapon said, he had never come across any saying of Sangnier's that 'could not be explained in an orthodox sense and was contrary to the teaching of the Church'. The bishop justified the Sillon's claim to be free from episcopal control in its political and social enterprises. It was doing an invaluable work and was reaching professional and intellectual circles that had hitherto been impenetrable: it was a work that the A.C.J.F. was incapable of doing. 'In a word, the Sillon is our *avant-garde*, a bit venturesome, but so valiant...For goodness' sake, do not let us shoot it down beneath the eyes and to the applause of the enemy, for that would really be to fire on our own troops.'[1] While some other bishops had since 1906 expressed favourable judgments on the Sillon, none, as Dr Caron says, had so well understood Sangnier's position.[2]

Towards the end of 1909 a journalist approached all the bishops in an attempt to ascertain their attitude to the Sillon.[3] Most of the replies that he received were too indefinite or non-committal to be significant. Of the eleven replies that were quite definite, nine were unfavourable, and two favourable. The episcopate was probably divided rather more evenly than those figures suggest. Anyhow by this time there was so much confusion about the Sillon's position that an intervention from Rome was almost inevitable.

Ominous signs began to appear of the likely nature of that intervention. Early in January 1910 an article that was a violent attack on the Sillon, such as only an integrist could have written, appeared in the official part of the *Osservatore Romano*, the Vatican newspaper. It moved Archbishop Mignot to try to rally episcopal opinion in France that was favourable to the Sillon and anxious to prevent its condemnation in Rome. While some bishops responded warmly to his lead, its outcome was on the whole disappointing, and when it became known its effect was to provoke more attacks. Now that the division among the bishops

[1] See Caron, pp. 666–70.
[2] See *ibid*. p. 670.
[3] See *ibid*. pp. 673–80.

was being publicized, Merry del Val wrote a stiff letter to Cardinal Coullié, archbishop of Lyon, saying that the Holy Father desired the episcopal polemics about the Sillon to stop at once and asking that the archbishop of Albi (Mignot), in particular, should be informed of this desire. Henceforth the bishops had to keep quiet, but the controversy continued in the press.[1]

The blow, which could have been anticipated but which apparently came as a devastating shock to the sillonists, fell at the end of August. One of them many years later recalled their sensations at the time.

That sad date...Monday 29 August 1910. It was on this day that, towards the end of the morning, the rumour of the condemnation of the Sillon by Pope Pius X began to spread through Paris. I was editorial secretary of the review *Le Sillon*, and I remember my emotion and that of my comrades...The Sillon condemned! Our first impression was as of a clap of thunder that shattered and destroyed our whole dream. Our whole youth seemed to collapse in a moment. What consternation there was in our faces on which, in many cases, tears were flowing! The Sillon condemned! Was it possible?[2]

The Letter—'Notre charge apostolique'[3]—that the pope addressed to the archbishops and bishops of France on 25 August 1910 is a long document: the English translation occupied nearly six pages of *The Tablet*.[4] While we cannot be absolutely sure, until the Vatican Archives are opened, how the Letter was composed, Dr Caron shows that the extensive writings of Emmanuel Barbier about the Sillon were undoubtedly utilized and also a series of hostile articles that had recently appeared in *La Croix*. How far *L'Action française* was utilized is less certain. Dr Caron also gives reasons for thinking that the Letter was drafted by Mgr Sevin, bishop of Châlons,[5] who had been one of the most forward advocates of a condemnation of the Sillon.[6]

---

[1] See *ibid.* pp. 683–92.
[2] Georges Hoog, *Histoire du catholicisme sociale en France 1871–1931*, pp. 179 f.
[3] See *Acta Apostolicae Sedis*, 31 August 1910, pp. 697–33.
[4] 10 September 1910.
[5] H. I. Sevin (1852–1916). Cf. Poulat, *Intégrisme et catholicisme intégral*, p. 368. He became archbishop of Lyon in 1912.
[6] See Caron, pp. 665, 707–11.

The opening paragraph of the Letter gives a clue to its presuppositions which are those of the theory of the Counter-Revolution[1] that stemmed from the thought of Joseph de Maistre and had been cultivated ever since by ultramontane, intransigent and integrist Catholics. Thus the pope refers at once to 'the doctrines of the pretended philosophers of the eighteenth century, those of the Revolution and of the Liberalism which has so many times been condemned', and says that the theories of the Sillon were of this sort. Before this theme is developed, a nostalgic tribute is paid to the early or 'palmy' days of the Sillon when it was marked only by youthful devotion and apostolic zeal and so received encouragement and approbation from the episcopate and the Holy See. 'This religious fervour was able to veil the true character of the sillonist movement.'

Its true character was revealed in its claim to evade ecclesiastical authority in the temporal field and to improve upon the traditional and fixed principles of Catholicism about the social order. Echoing de Maistre, the pope declares:

No, Venerable Brethren, —We must again emphatically declare in these days of social and intellectual anarchy when everyone poses as a teacher and legislator—the State is not to be built otherwise than as God has built it; society will not be built up unless the Church lay the foundations and direct the works; no, civilisation is not now to be invented nor the new State to be established in the clouds. It has long existed, it exists still; it is Christian civilisation, the Catholic State.

It was of course true that the Sillon had abandoned the theory of the Catholic or confessional State, and had adopted the pluralist theory, that is, of a democratic republic in which there would be religious freedom and toleration. After looking at the social doctrines of the Sillon concerning liberty, fraternity and equality, the Letter says: 'The breath of the Revolution has passed this way, and we may conclude that if the social doctrines of the Sillon are erroneous, its spirit is dangerous, and its education disastrous.'

[1] See my *A Century of Social Catholicism*, pp. 70–6, 112, 116, 121, 123.

Its political pluralism is condemned in these terms:

There was a time when the Sillon, as such, was formally Catholic. It recognised but one moral force, that of Catholicism, and it went about proclaiming that democracy would either be Catholic or would not be at all. Then the time came when it changed its mind. It left each person his own religion or philosophy. It gave up calling itself Catholic, and for the formula 'democracy will be Catholic', it substituted this other— 'democracy will not be anti-Catholic', any more than anti-Jewish or anti-Buddhist. All working men, no matter what their religion or their sect, were called upon to take part in the building up of the State of the future. They were only asked to accept the same social ideal, to show respect to all beliefs, and to carry a certain equipment of moral forces.

Of the wider basis on which the Sillon had deliberately come to stand, the pope says: 'What is to be thought of the promiscuity in which young Catholics will find themselves in company with the unorthodox and unbelievers of all sorts in a work of this character?'

The theoretical part of the Letter ends with this eloquent peroration:

Let them remember that the social question and social science were not born yesterday; that at all times the Church and the State, happily working together, have established...organisations that have proved fruitful; that the Church which has never betrayed the happiness of the people by compromising alliances, has not to sever herself from the past, and that she has only to take up again, with the assistance of the true workers of the social restoration, the organisms destroyed by the Revolution, and, in the same Christian spirit which inspired them, to adapt them to the new situation created by the material development of contemporary society: for the true friends of the people are neither revolutionaries nor innovators, but traditionalists.

In a brief final section, the pope gives his practical rulings and expresses his confidence that they will be obeyed. The Sillon as it at present exists must be dissolved, but the members are to be encouraged to range themselves by dioceses in 'Catholic Sillons', 'to work under the direction of their respective bishops for the Christian and Catholic regeneration of the people'. These Catholic Sillons were to be independent of each other. Thus the Sillon as as a united and coordinated movement under lay leadership was to be destroyed.

The hold that the integrists had got at that time on the policy of the papacy suffices to explain the condemnation of the Sillon. Rome was not yet ready to change its traditional social doctrines or to replace static by dynamic conceptions.

Sangnier, like Lamennais nearly eighty years before in similar circumstances,[1] at once made his submission. He had no mind to break with the Church whatever it demanded of him. In a statement to *Le Temps* newspaper he said that in the whole of his public life he would carefully avoid everything which might appear to be contrary to the teachings of the Church, and he continued as follows:

I know that my attitude will disappoint certain anti-Clericals, and especially, perhaps, certain reactionary Roman Catholics who counted upon my not submitting. But I do not regret having to suffer for my faith, and I hope that God will accept the offering of my grief, since I shall be happy if by this sacrifice I may still serve the cause to which I have devoted my life, and help to give to the Republic a moral inspiration and to the democracy a Christian spirit. Since I am, and intend to remain, above all a Roman Catholic, the question does not even arise whether I shall or shall not submit to the discipline of the Church.

He added that he intended to labour for the good of his country so long as he had the means.[2]

He could no longer do so through the Sillon. He did continue to champion the democratic cause, but henceforth on exclusively political grounds, and never again with the same effect. Pope Benedict XV is said to have acquitted him of the errors that Pius X had condemned.[3] The other sillonists followed his example, and it is to be remarked that, just as many of the disciples of Lamennais in the days of the *Avenir* were active subsequently in

---

[1] See my *Prophecy and Papacy*, p. 215.

[2] Sangnier's statement to *Le Temps* is quoted by M. D. Petre, *Modernism*, pp. 239 f.

[3] See Dansette, *Religious History of Modern France*, ii. 287 f., where Sangnier's subsequent career is summarized.

some of the liveliest movements in the French Church of the nineteenth century, so it was to be with Sangnier's disciples. Of them it has been said:

One finds them at the origin of one movement after another. The Scouts...the Y.C.W. [Young Christian Workers] and specialised Catholic Action...of Christian trade unionism...of the pacifist movement...at the beginnings of the Youth Hostel movement...of the renewal of parish life. One finds them in publishing...in journalism...in literature...in philosophy...in economic and social thought ...in social action.[1]

It might be argued that, though this was not exactly his intention, Pius X served the cause of French Catholicism well by dispersing the sillonists in so many directions.

As regards the fate of the Sillon itself, and indeed as regards the whole course of events on which this book has touched, I cannot do better than conclude with an extract from what Mgr Mignot wrote to Loisy after his reception of Pius X's Letter of 25 August 1910:

Assuredly I am distressed by what has happened to us in the case of the Sillon...What saddens me most is the calm way in which the execution has been carried out! It seems to me that the associates of His Holiness ought to have remembered that those whom they are striking are the best among the good. I have seen close at hand a certain number of sillonists and I have always admired their simple faith, their generosity, their devotion, their piety which is infinitely superior to that of *la jeunesse catholique*...

But is it only the Sillon that they have wanted to get at? It seems to me that they have aimed higher and that they have very skilfully grouped together errors which M. Sangnier never professed. They have proceeded in the same way as with Modernism. The Letter has been very skilfully drafted. It attributes to the sillonists, as previously to the

---

[1] Jospeh Folliet in *Chronique Sociale de France*, March–April 1950, pp. 127 f.; quoted by M. P. Fogarty, *Christian Democracy in Western Europe 1820–1953*, p. 267. Cf. J. de Fabrègues, *Le Sillon de Marc Sangnier*, pp. 9 f.

modernists, a fully worked out system which has never been theirs. . .
It is the triumph of *l'Action française.*[1]

[1] Mignot to Loisy, 3 September 1910: BN, n.a.f. 15659. Cf. *Mém.*, iii. 196 ff., where Loisy comments: 'La jeunesse catholique dont parle Mgr Mignot. . .est la jeunesse formée sous l'influence des jésuites, non démocratique, comme était *le Sillon.* Et ce qui a contribué à la perte du *Sillon*, c'est qu'il était né au collège Stanislas, qu'il avait grandi en dehors de la sphère où la puissante Compagnie exerçait son crédit.' On the Action Française, see Eugen Weber, *Action Française: royalism and reaction in twentieth-century France* (1962).

BIBLIOGRAPHY

This bibliography includes only sources that have been used in the preparation of the present work. For further bibliographical information, see Poulat in *Vie de Loisy*, pp. 303–409; *Histoire, dogme et critique*, pp. 33–42, 648–77; Rivière, pp. xiii–xxix; R. Aubert in *Concilium*, September 1966, pp. 47–55; MMRC, pp. 274–9.

UNPUBLISHED SOURCES

Bibliothèque Nationale: Papers of A. Houtin, L. Lacroix, and A. Loisy.
British Museum: Papers of M. D. Petre.
Downside Abbey: Papers of Edmund Bishop.
Private Archives: Papers of A. L. Lilley, A. R. Vidler and G. W. Young.[1]
St Andrews University Library: Papers of F. von Hügel.

BOOKS

Abercrombie, Nigel, *The Life and Work of Edmund Bishop* (1959).
Alfaric, Prosper, *De la foi à la raison* (1955).
Altholz, Josef L., *The Liberal Catholic Movement in England: the 'Rambler' and its contributors 1848–1864* (1962).
Bampton, J. M., *Modernism and modern thought* (1913).
Barbier, Emmanuel, *Histoire du catholicisme libéral...en France*, 5 vols (1924).
Bedoyere, Michael de la, *The Life of Baron von Hügel* (1951).
Bethune-Baker, J. F., *The Faith of the Apostles' Creed* (1918).
—— *The Way of Modernism* (1927).
Blanchet, André, *Histoire d'une mise à l'index: la 'Sainte Chantal' de l'Abbé Bremond* (1967).
Blondel, Maurice, *L'Action* (1893).
—— *Correspondence* (with Auguste Valensin), 3 vols (1957–65).
—— *Correspondence philosophique* (with Lucien Laberthonnière) (1961).
—— *Letter on Apologetics and History of Dogma*, edited by A. Dru and I. Trethowan (1964).
—— *Lettres philosophiques* (1961).
Bourdon, Hilaire, see Tyrrell.
Bourget, Paul, *Le démon de midi* (1914).
Bourne, Vincent, *La queste de vérité d'Irénée Winnaert* (1966).
Boyer de Sainte Suzanne, R. de, *Alfred Loisy entre la foi et l'incroyance* (1968).
Braun, F. M., *L'œuvre du Père Lagrange* (1943).
Bremond, Henri, see Leblanc.

[1] The papers of Lilley and Young have now been presented to St Andrews University Library.

Catholic Modernists

Brugerette, J., *Le prêtre français et la société contemporaine*, 3 vols (1933–8).
Butler, Cuthbert, *Religions of Authority and the Religion of the Spirit* (1930).
Caron, Jeanne, *Le Sillon et la démocratie chrétienne 1894–1910* (1967).
Cock, Albert A., *A Critical Examination of von Hügel's Philosophy of Religion* (n.d.).
Collins, L. John, *Faith under Fire* (1966).
Congrès d'histoire du christianisme : jubilé Alfred Loisy, 3 vols (1928).
Cornilleau, Robert, *L'Abbé Naudet* (1933).
Cousin, Louis, *Le Sillon et les Catholiques* (1909).
Crehan, Joseph, *Father Thurston* (1952).
Dagens, J., and Nédoncelle, M., *Entretiens sur Henri Bremond* (1967).
Dakin, A. H., *Von Hügel and the Supernatural* (1934).
Daniel-Rops, H., *Edouard Le Roy et son fauteuil* (1956).
Dansette, Adrien, *Religious History of Modern France*, 2 vols (1961).
Davies, D. R., *On to Orthodoxy* (1939).
Delafosse, Henri (= J. Turmel), *Le Quatrième Evangile* (1925).
Dell' Isola, Maria, *Alfred Loisy* (1957).
Desgranges, Jean, *Carnets intimes : journal d'un conférencier populaire* (1960).
Détrez, Alfred, *L'Abbé Loisy* (1909).
d'Hendecourt, M. M., *Essai sur la philosophie du Père Laberthonnière* (1947).
Eastwood, D. M., *The Revival of Pascal: a study of his relation to modern French thought* (1936).
Fabrègues, Jean de, *Le Sillon de Marc Sangnier* (1964).
Falconi, Carlo, *The Popes in the Twentieth Century* (1967).
Fawkes, Alfred, *The Church a Necessary Evil* (1932).
—— *Prophet and Priest* (1898).
—— *Studies in Modernism* (1913).
Fogarty, Michael P., *Christian Democracy in Western Europe 1820–1953* (1957).
Fogazzaro, Antonio, *The Saint* (1906).
Fonsegrive, George L., *Le catholicisme et la vie de l'esprit* (1899).
Gibson, William, *The Abbé de Lamennais and the Liberal Catholic Movement in France* (1896).
Gout, Raoul, *L'affaire Tyrrell* (1910).
Green, Martin, *Yeats's Blessings on von Hügel* (1967).
Griffiths, Richard, *The Reactionary Revolution* (1966).
Grüber, Jacob W., *A Conscience in Conflict: the life of St George Jackson Mivart* (1960).
Harnack, Adolf, *What is Christianity?* (1901).
Hayen, André, *Bibliographie blondélienne 1888–1951* (1953).
Heaney, J. J., *The Modernist Crisis: von Hügel* (1969).
Hébert, Marcel, *Plato and Darwin: a philosophic dialogue* (1899).
—— *Souvenirs d'Assise* (1899).
Heiler, Friedrich, *Alfred Loisy: der Vater des katholischen Modernismus* (1947).
—— *Der Katholizismus: seine Idee und seine Erscheinung* (1923).
Hogan, J. B., *Clerical Studies* (1898).
Hoog, Georges, *Histoire du catholicisme social en France 1871–1931* (1946).

Bibliography

Hoskyns, Sir E. C., *Cambridge Sermons* (1938).
—— (with F. N. Davey), *The Riddle of the New Testament* (1931).
Houtin, Albert (with F. Sartiaux), *Alfred Loisy: sa vie, son œuvre.* Ed. by E. Poulat (1960).
—— *Une vie de prêtre 1867–1912* (1928).
—— *L'Américanisme* (1904).
—— *La controverse de l'apostolicité des églises de France au xixe siècle*[3] (1903).
—— *Histoire du modernisme catholique* (1913).
—— *Ma vie laïque 1912–1926* (1928).
—— *Les origines de l'église d'Angers: la légende de saint René* (1901).
—— *Le Père Hyacinthe*, 3 vols (1920–4).
—— *Un prêtre symboliste: Marcel Hébert 1851–1916* (1925).
—— *La question biblique chez les catholiques de France au xixe siècle*[2] (1902).
—— *La question biblique au xxe siècle*[2] (1906).
Hügel, Friedrich von, *Du Christ éternel et de nos christologies successives* (1904).
—— *La méthode historique en son application à l'étude des documents de l'Hexateuque* (1898).
—— *Essays and Addresses on the Philosophy of Religion*, 2 vols (1921–28).
—— (with C. A. Briggs) *The Papal Commission and the Pentateuch* (1906).
—— *Selected Letters 1896–1924* (1927). Ed. by B. Holland.
Index librorum prohibitorum (1948).
Jasper, Ronald, *Arthur Cayley Headlam* (1960).
Jordan, L. H., *Modernism in Italy* (1909).
Klein, Félix, *La route du petit Morvandiau*, 6 vols (1946–50).
Knox, W. L., and Vidler, A. R., *The Development of Modern Catholicism* (1933).
Laberthonnière, Lucien, *Critique du laïcisme ou comment se pose le problème de Dieu.* Ed. by L. Canet (1948).
—— *Esquisse d'une philosophie personnaliste* (1942).
—— *Essais de philosophie religieuses* (1903).
—— *Les fruits de l'esprit* Ed. by M. M. d'Hendecourt (1961).
—— *La notion chrétienne de l'autorité.* Ed. by L. Canet (1955).
—— *Pangermanisme et christianisme.* Ed. by L. Canet (1945).
—— *Le réalisme chrétien et l'idéalisme grec* (1904).
—— *Théorie de l'éducation*[10] (1935).
Lacger, Louis de, *Monseigneur Mignot* (1933).
Lagrange, M. J., *M. Loisy et le modernisme* (1932).
—— *Le Père Lagrange au service de la Bible: souvenirs personnels* (1967).
Leblanc, Sylvain (= H. Bremond), *Un clerc qui n'a pas trahi: Alfred Loisy d'après ses Mémoires* (1931).
Lebreton, Jules, *Le Père Léonce de Grandmaison* (1932).
Lecanuet, E., *La vie de l'Eglise sous Léon XIII* (1930).
Le Roy, Edouard, *Dogme et critique*[5] (1907).
—— *Introduction à l'étude du problème religieux* (1944).
—— *Le problème de Dieu*[5] (1929).
Lester-Garland, L. V., *The Religious Philosophy of Baron F. von Hügel* (1933).

Catholic Modernists

Levie, Jean, *Sous les yeux de l'incroyant*[2] (1946).
Lilley, A. L., *Modernism: a record and a review* (1908).
—— *The Nation in Judgment* (1911).
—— *Nature and Supernature* (1911).
—— *The Religion of Life* (1910).
—— *The Soul of St Paul* (1909).
Loisy, Alfred, *Autour d'un petit livre* (1903).
—— *Choses passées* (1912–13). E.T. *My Duel with the Vatican* (1924).
—— *La crise morale du temps présent et l'éducation humaine* (1937).
—— *L'Eglise et la France* (1925).
—— *L'Evangile et l'Eglise* (1902). E.T. *The Gospel and the Church* (1908).
—— *Les Evangiles synoptiques*, 2 vols (1908).
—— *George Tyrrell et Henri Bremond* (1936).
—— *Histoire et mythe à propos de Jésus-Christ* (1938).
—— *Mémoires pour servir à l'histoire religieuse de notre temps*, 3 vols (1930–1).
—— *La morale humaine*[2] (1928).
—— *Un mythe apologétique* (1939).
—— *La naissance du christianisme* (1933). E.T. *The Birth of the Christian Religion* (1948).
—— *Le Quatrième Evangile* (1903).
—— *Quelques lettres sur des questions actuelles et sur des évènements récents* (1908).
—— *La religion*[2] (1924).
—— *Religion et humanité* (1926).
—— *Simples réflexions*[2] (1908).
Lubac, Henri de, *Blondel et Teilhard de Chardin: correspondance commentée* (1965).
Maignen, Charles, *Maurice Maignen et les origines du mouvement social catholique en France*, 2 vols (1927).
Malègue, J., *Augustin ou le Maître est là* (1933).
Maritain, Jacques, *The Peasant of the Garonne* (1968).
Marlé, René, *Au cœur de la crise moderniste: le dossier inédit d'une controverse* (1960).
Martin du Gard, Maurice, *De Sainte-Beuve à Fénelon: Henri Bremond* (1927).
Martin du Gard, Roger, *Jean Barois* (1913).
Maurras, Charles, *Le dilemme de Marc Sangnier* (1907).
May, J. Lewis, *Father Tyrrell and the Modernist Movement* (1932).
Mignot, E. I., *L'Eglise et la critique*[2] (1910).
—— *Lettres sur les études ecclésiastiques*[2] (1908).
Montagnini, Carlo, *Les fiches pontificales* (1908).
Nédoncelle, Maurice, *La pensée religieuse de Friedrich von Hügel* (1935). E.T. *Baron von Hügel* (1937).
O'Donovan, Gerald, *Father Ralph* (1914).
Petre, M. D., *Alfred Loisy: his religious significance* (1944).
—— *Autobiography and Life of George Tyrrell*, 2 vols (1912).
—— *Modernism: its failure and its fruits* (1918).
—— *My Way of Faith* (1937).

Bibliography

Petre, M. D., *Von Hügel and Tyrrell* (1937).
Poulat, Emile, *Histoire, dogme et critique dans la crise moderniste* (1962).
—— *Intégrisme et catholicisme intégral* (1969).
Practical Questions: lectures on modern difficulties in church life (1905).
Rashdall, Hastings, *Ideas and Ideals* (1928).
—— *Principles and Precepts* (1927).
Ratté, John, *Three Modernists* (1968).
Rawlinson, A. E. J., *Dogma, Fact and Experience* (1915).
Rivière Jean, *Bibliographie et souvenirs* (1952).
—— *Le modernisme dans l'Eglise* (1929).
—— *Monseigneur Batiffol* (1929).
Robidoux, Réjean, *Roger Martin du Gard et la religion* (1964).
Rollet, Henri, *L'action sociale des catholiques en France 1871–1914*, vol. ii (1958).
Sabatier, Paul, *Disestablishment in France* (1906).
—— *France To-day ; its religious orientation* (1913).
—— *Modernism* (1908).
Sangnier, Marc, *Discours*, 2 vols (1910).
—— *L'Esprit démocratique*[3] (1905).
Sartiaux, Félix, *Joseph Turmel; prêtre, historien des dogmes* (1931).
Scoppola, Pietro, *Crisi modernista e rinnovamento cattolico in Italia* (1961).
Selwyn, E. G. (Ed.), *Essays Catholic and Critical* (1926).
Sforza, Carlo, *Makers of Modern Europe* (1930).
Siegfried, Agnès, *L'Abbé Frémont*, 2 vols (1932).
Speaight, Robert, *Teilhard de Chardin* (1967).
Stebbing, L. Susan, *Pragmatism and French Voluntarism* (1914).
Steinmann, Jean, *Friedrich von Hügel* (1962).
Sullivan, William L., *Letters to His Holiness Pope Pius X* (1910).
—— *Under Orders* (1944).
Thorp, J. P., *Friends and Adventures* (1931).
Tresmontant, Claude, *Introduction à la métaphysique de Maurice Blondel* (1963).
Trevelyan, J. P., *The Life of Mrs Humphry Ward* (1923).
Turmel, Joseph, *Comment j'ai donné congé aux dogmes* (1935).
—— *Comment l'Eglise romaine m'a donné congé* (n.d.).
Tyrrell, George, *Christianity at the Cross Roads* (Ed. by A. R. Vidler, 1963).
—— *The Church and the future* (1910). 1st edition by 'Hilaire Bourdon' (1903).
—— *Medievalism*[4] (1909)
Vidler, A. R., *A Century of Social Catholicism* (1964).
—— *Essays in Liberality* (1957).
—— *The Modernist Movement in the Roman Church* (1934).
—— *Prophecy and Papacy : a study of Lamennais, the Church and the Revolution* (1954).
—— *Twentieth Century Defenders of the Faith* (1965).
Ward, Mrs Humphry, *The Case of Richard Meynell* (1911).
Ward, Maisie, *The Wilfrid Wards and the Transition*, 2 vols (1934–7).
Ward, Mrs Wilfrid, *Out of Due Time* (1906).
Weber, Eugen, *Action Française: royalism and reaction in twentieth century France* (1962).
White, Antonia, *The Hound and the Falcon* (1965).

Catholic Modernists

PERIODICALS

Acta Apostolicae Sedis, Annales de philosophie chrétienne, Bulletin critique, Bulletin de littérature ecclésiastique (Toulouse), *Cambridge Journal, Cambridge Review, Catholic Book Notes, Catholic Times, Church Times, Commonwealth, Concilium, Contemporary Review, Correspondant, Demain, Downside Review, Droits de l'homme, Dublin Review, Edinburgh Review, Etudes, Faith in Wales, Guardian, Heythrop Journal, Hibbert Journal, Journal of Theological Studies, Modern Churchman, Month, Nation, Nineteenth Century and After, Peasant, Pilot, Quarterly Review, Quinzaine, Revue archéologique, Revue d'histoire ecclésiastique, Revue d'histoire et de littérature religieuses, Revue d'histoire et de philosophie religieuses, Revue de l'histoire des religions, Revue historique, Revue moderniste internationale, Revue de Paris, Revue des sciences religieuses, Sillon, Studies, Tablet, Theology, The Times, Times Literary Supplement.*

INDEX

Index

Index

Index

Index

Pascal, B., 80, 83
Pascendi, 6 f., 15–8, 81, 84, 87, 92, 101 f., 106, 108, 115, 124, 135, 142, 167, 177, 191, 212
paternalism, 197
peasant popes, 49
Peasant, The, 177
pentateuch, 50, 57 f., 76, 96, 107, 118, 181
Percival, J., 159
Petre, M. D., 2 f., 10 ff., 22, 31, 44, 46, 52 f., 55, 86, 102, 109 ff., 113, 115 f., 120, 123, 125, 127, 129–32, 134, 136, 139, 141, 146, 150 f., 155, 157–60, 171 f., 177, 218, 224 f.
Pfleiderer, O., 129
Philips, G., 56
philosophy of action, 80 f., 83, 119, 195
Pilot, The, 157, 163, 183 f.
Pius IX, 48
Pius X, 1, 7, 16, 18, 20, 30, 47–50, 54, 84, 89 f., 101–6, 124, 138, 142, 150, 159, 164, 191, 206 ff., 210, 212, 215–9
Pius XI, 48
Plato, 66 f.
pluralism, 198, 203, 205, 216 f.
positivism, 32, 140 f., 177
Poulat, E., 13, 16, 20, 22 f., 40, 42, 47, 49, 51, 55 f., 63 f., 81, 90, 99 ff., 116, 118, 215, 225
pragmatism, 17 f., 54, 90, 186
protestantism, 127, 152, 158, 164, 205, 213
pseudonyms, 41, 59 ff., 150
psychical research, 162, 165
Punch, 169
Pusey, E. B., 111

Quarterly Review, 158
Quinzaine, La, 118, 120

ralliement, 194 f., 201, 207
Rambler, 135
Rampolla, M., 210
Ramsey, I. T., 41
Rashdall, H., 9, 173, 181 f., 225
Ratté, J., 44, 155, 225
Rawlinson, A. E. J., 2, 225
Rawlinson, G. C., 136, 175 f., 178 ff.
Reinach, S., 75, 77
religion of humanity, 53, 165
religious experience, 89, 120, 122, 126

Rémond, R., 209
Renan, E., 51
Renatus, St, 25
Renaudin, P., 193, 197
Rerum novarum, 194, 207, 209
resurrection narratives, 66, 68, 71 f., 100, 133, 151
Revue archéologique, 27
Revue du clergé français, 6
Revue de l'histoire ecclésiastique, 42
Revue de l'histoire et de littérature religieuses, 21, 59 ff.
Revue de l'histoire et de philosophie religieuses, 42
Revue de l'histoire des religions, 60
Revue historique, 16, 33, 73
Revue moderniste internationale, 160, 163 ff.
Revue de Paris, 94
Revue des sciences religieuses, 42, 45
Richard, F. M. B., 47, 72 f., 101, 107, 210
Richardson, A., 118
Rinnovamento, 116
Ritschlians, 129
Rivière, J., 5, 16 f., 42, 56, 63 f., 75, 134, 191, 225
Robidoux, R., 70, 225
Robinson, J. A., 172, 175 f.
Rollet, H., 194, 225
Rota dining club, 137, 142
Rouquette, R., 44

Sabatier, A., 67
Sabatier, P., 15, 20, 57, 91, 108, 110, 167, 180, 225
Saint Sulpice, 64, 76, 94, 166, 176
salles de travail, 197, 200
Saltet, L., 59
Sampson, A., 11
Sanday, W., 9, 94, 117, 174 f., 180, 183 f.
Sangnier, M., 19, 191–220, 225
Sanson, P., 88
Sartiaux, F., 17, 22, 26–9, 32 f., 55–61, 223, 225
Schiller, F. C. S., 186
scholastic philosophy and theology, 19, 36, 40 f., 54, 78, 80 ff., 98, 116 f., 140, 145, 164, 185
Schweitzer, A., 188, 190
Scoppola, P., 15, 225
Selwyn, E. G., 187, 225
Sevin, H. I., 215

231

Index